A Harmony of Interests

Books by Manfred Weidhorn

Dreams in Seventeenth-Century English Literature (1970)

Richard Lovelace (1970)

Sword and Pen: A Survey of the Writings of Sir Winston Churchill (1974)

Turn Your Life Around (with Stanley Nass) (1978)

Sir Winston Churchill (1979)

Napoleon (1986)

Churchill's Rhetoric and Political Discourse (1987)

Robert E. Lee (1988)

A Harmony of Interests: Explorations in the Mind of Sir Winston Churchill (1992)

Jackie Robinson (forthcoming)

A Harmony of Interests

Explorations in the Mind of Sir Winston Churchill

Manfred Weidhorn

Rutherford • Madison • Teaneck
Fairleigh Dickinson University Press
London and Toronto: Associated University Presses

© 1992 by Associated University Presses, Inc.

All rights reserved. Authorization to photocopy items for internal or personal use, or the internal or personal use of specific clients, is granted by the copyright owner, provided that a base fee of $10.00, plus eight cents per page, per copy is paid directly to the Copyright Clearance Center, 27 Congress Street, Salem, Massachusetts 01970. [0-8386-3466-4/92 $10.00+8¢ pp, pc.]

Associated University Presses
440 Forsgate Drive
Cranbury, NJ 08512

Associated University Presses
25 Sicilian Avenue
London WC1A 2QH, England

Associated University Presses
P.O. Box 39, Clarkson Pstl. Stn.
Mississauga, Ontario,
L5J 3X9 Canada

The paper used in this publication meets the requirements
of the American National Standard for Permanence of Paper
for Printed Library Materials Z39.48-1984.

Library of Congress Cataloging-in-Publication Data

Weidhorn, Manfred, 1931–
   A harmony of interests : explorations in the mind of Sir Winston Churchill / Manfred Weidhorn.
     p. cm.
   Includes bibliographical references and index.
   ISBN 0-8386-3466-4
   1. Churchill, Winston, Sir, 1874–1965—Political and social views.
2. Churchill, Winston, Sir, 1874–1965—Views on international relations.   3. Churchill, Winston, Sir, 1874–1965—Views on war.
I. Title.
DA566.9.C5W365   1992
941.084'092—dc20   91-58591
                                                                     CIP

PRINTED IN THE UNITED STATES OF AMERICA

to
Phyllis

who patiently watched and waited
while the "little book"
on Churchill grew
(during the 1960s, 1970s, 1980s, 1990s)
into a tetralogy

Into those 14 years you have compressed unique experiences in war by sea and land, in diplomacy, in House of Commons' work, and in constructive legislation. . . . Five volumes of immortal history is a wonderful addition to this great period of administrative activity.
—A. J. Balfour to Churchill, 1929

There is no-one alive engaged on history work with your experience of politics, government, and war.
—Lewis Namier to Churchill, 1934

Contents

Preface	9
Acknowledgments	13
1. The Polemist	17
2. The Conservative	45
3. The Warhorse	59
4. The Dreamer	77
5. The Semi-American	110
6. The "Great Man"?	142
Notes	167
Bibliography	184
Index	189

Preface

THERE is no end to the writing of books about Sir Winston Churchill. The potential reader of a new tome on the subject has every right to ask what could possibly be said that is new. The man led, to be sure, an extremely long, varied, and exciting life; he amassed as many experiences and achievements as it would take a dozen merely talented individuals to do. Still, the number of volumes about him has been proportionally high.

What may justify this book is that it does not fit into any of the categories to which the other works of Churchilliana belong. It is not a biography, a chronological survey of his plans and deeds. It is not a book of memoirs or a collection of reports from individuals who either knew him intimately or whom he brushed by on his numerous rendezvous with history. It is not a monograph on one facet of his personality, such as his relations with the Irish or the Jews, or on his performance at the Admiralty in World War I or at the helm in World War II. It is not a study of his writings—neither a chronological one which records the changes in his outlook during various personal and historical phases, nor a synoptic one which collates his abiding themes, regardless of the niceties of chronology.

It is, rather, a study of his sensibility, an attempt to portray the ineffable mental processes at the border of thought and feeling, through a scrutiny of Churchill's written and spoken words, as well as of the inferences drawn by acquaintances, critics, and historians. The operations of a unified imagination are traced in his ideas about politics, war-making, international relations.

One cannot pretend that some of the topics have not already been subjected to searching scrutiny, and by personages of the stature of Isaiah Berlin, A. L. Rowse, Malcolm Muggeridge, H. S. Commager, J. H. Plumb, A. J. P. Taylor, Martin Gilbert, Kenneth Thompson, and R. R. James. What I do claim is to have brought a greater comprehensiveness to the subject, mainly as a result of the wealth of material that has been published in the past decades.

Since Churchill was as much a professional writer with awesome accomplishments in print as he was a perdurable politician and statesman, I begin at the juncture of literature and politics. His writing and speaking careers, his sensitivity to the resonance of names, words, and phrases, his proficiency in the forging of powerful sentences, images, witticisms, and his production of a large number of multivolumed works placed him in the company of literary artists, literally as well as figuratively. The subject of his relations with the literary eminences of his age—and his age stretches from late Victorian to neo-Elizabethan, encompassing some two or three generations—has been scarcely broached. What did the literary set think of him, and he of them? Was he (to paraphrase Falstaff) not only the source of literature in himself but the cause that literature is in other men—does he, in short, appear in literary works? How did his political interests, his frequent oscillations between right and left on various issues and at various junctures, affect his responses to the literati? Of special interest are his relations with the literary quartet—Arnold Bennett, John Galsworthy, H. G. Wells, George Bernard Shaw—that dominated British letters in the first decades of the century.

Since the discussion of his literary tastes inevitably touches on his politics, the second chapter examines Churchill's conservatism, a topic which is, unlike that of the first chapter, all too familiar. My aim is to show that by ignoring chronology and by making distinctions among different fields of interest, one comes up with something other than the conventional answers.

No delineation of Churchill's political sensibility and of the vagaries of his putative conservatism can avoid becoming bogged down in the quagmire of his apparent love of war. Everyone has noticed that there was something curious in his attitude to combat, and nearly everyone, depending on his own disposition and ideology, has praised or blamed him accordingly. No one has, however, tried to bring together virtually all the relevant facts and anomalies lying about in the historical and biographical records. The subject requires such treatment because on it turns nothing less than one's reading of human nature and one's definition of civilization.

Churchill's obsession with war and war-making crystallized in his lifelong interest in his ancestor, the first Duke of Marlborough. Though he had had, after all, more peaceable ancestors, he was fascinated by John Churchill because he was fascinated by war, and vice versa. That that interest should tie the biography he wrote about Marlborough to his own world war memoirs, written both before and after the biography; that the eighteenth century career should in some way be—or seem to be—duplicated in the twentieth century; that pipe dreaming should become indistinguishable from prophecy; that history writing should look forward as well as back, in a personal fashion—all these notions are touched on by the *obiter dicta* of students of his career, but no one has until now worked out the eerie parallels in chapter and verse and their psychological ramifications. At issue here are the inmost stirrings of the soul. Although the man himself was probably only half aware of these, the parallels are none the less real. That Churchill was destined to be a Marlborough—or doomed to try in vain to emulate the Duke—was something that haunted his imagination; it also sometimes inspired, and more often irritated, his contemporaries.

If Churchill was highly conscious of being the descendant of Marlborough, he was hardly any less aware of being the son of an American mother and of having a mother's land as well as a fatherland. No exploration of his psyche can be complete that does not include his thoughts about America and about the Anglo-American mystique and that does not see these as being as important as his ventures into the literary forum, his ambiguous conservatism, his ambivalence toward war, and his Marlborough connection. The large subject of Churchill and America is in fact the subject of two books, but one is an anthology of quotations and the other is an ancedotal chronicle. This is the first systematic attempt to define his ideas and to place them in the historical context.

The sense of uniqueness which comes from being, as few Englishmen are, a descendant of Marlborough and a semi-American, as well as from being the son of Lord Randolph and someone who seemed called upon to play a special role on the stage of history abetted those archaic tendencies in Churchill which were inclined to see history as shaped by Great Men. Yet his thoughts on the subject were buffeted by the winds of experience, and a survey of Churchill's changes of mind on this problem in the philosophy of history makes for an interesting study of the interplay of theory and experience and traces the impact of twentieth-century events on one sensibility.

My limiting the study of substantive issues to six is not arbitrary. Churchill had firm and well known positions on numerous other topics, but they were not as central to his personality as this sextet was. These topics or interests are determined in good part by the circumstances of his life. While everyone's fate is, of course, partly so influenced, Churchill had rather unusual circumstances to contend with and was blessed, or cursed, with a reverence for origins, tradition, and history. Some of the circumstances—the existential roots of his interests—were *données* at birth: his being half-American, a Marlborough scion, a member of the aristocracy. Others grew out of his childhood experiences—his pugnacity, his love of toy soldiers, his ineptness at classics, his starting out as a cadet and officer. Still other circumstances came much later: his being prime minister at the time of the Anglo-American alliance and of the displacement of Britain by America as a world power.

These circumstances and influences interweave. Because of his ineptness at classics, he was made to learn English instead, gaining along the way a mastery of his native tongue and a love of its literary heritage. His enjoyment of toy soldiers and his mediocre school record closed off all careers for someone of his circle except the military one. His proficiency in writing now fused with his prowess as a soldier and brought him fame as warrior and writer. This success in turn combined with his aristocratic origins to ease the entry into politics, and those origins kept the ship of his political thought tilting to the right even when veering to the left during the most radical storms. The coming of large wars meshed with his Marlborough roots and his perennial interest in combat. The informal British alliance with America in two world wars endowed the son of a Brooklyn-born woman with a sense of special mission and a personal pride. And through it all, the writer produced a stream of essays and books, making literature, studying it (albeit fitfully and selectively), and pronouncing on it, at least when it touched on politics and history. Literature, conservatism, war, Marlborough, America, the Great Man—he who undertook to know Churchill and who knew his thoughts on only these topics will have encompassed most of his project. For this "harmony of interests" (Churchill's phrase) formed his own peculiar song, or set of songs.

Acknowledgments

MR. Richard M. Langworth, founder and president of the International Churchill Society and nerve center of worldwide activities devoted to the study of Sir Winston Churchill, was kind enough to go through my manuscript with a fine-tooth comb. His alertness, erudition, and concentration saved me from perpetrating errors of fact, judgment, and overstatement. I am deeply indebted to him.

Many thanks are also due to Ms. Harriet Nachmann of the office of the executive vice president of Yeshiva University. She struggled heroically to put a sometimes illegible manuscript through the word processor.

Chapter 1 originally appeared in a different version in *Shaw: The Annual of Bernard Shaw Studies*. Chapter 2 originally appeared in *Southern Humanities Review*. Chapter 4 originally appeared in a slightly different version in *Thought* and is reprinted by permission of the publisher; copyright © 1975 by Fordham University Press. Chapter 6 originally appeared in *Connecticut Review*.

Quotations are from:
- *The Gathering Storm*, Volume I, by Winston S. Churchill, copyright 1948 by Houghton Mifflin Co., renewed © 1976 by Lady Spencer Churchill, the Honorable Lady Sarah Audley, and the Honourable Lady Soames. Reprinted by permission of Houghton Mifflin Co.
- From *Their Finest Hour*, Volume II, by Winston S. Churchill. Copyright 1949 by Houghton Mifflin Co., renewed © 1976 by Lady Spencer Churchill, the Honourable Lady Sarah Audley, and the Honourable Lady Soames. Reprinted by permission of Houghton Mifflin Co.
- From *The Grand Alliance*, Volume III, by Winston S. Churchill. Copyright 1950 by Houghton Mifflin Co. Copyright © renewed 1977 by Lady Spencer Churchill, the Honourable Lady Sarah Audley, and the Honourable Lady Soames. Reprinted by permission of Houghton Mifflin Co.
- From *The Hinge of Fate*, Volume IV, by Winston S. Churchill.

Copyright 1950 by Houghton Mifflin Co. Copyright © renewed 1978 by Lady Spencer Churchill, the Honourable Lady Sarah Audley, and the Honourable Lady Soames. Reprinted by permission of Houghton Mifflin Co.

• From *Closing the Ring*, Volume V, by Winston S. Churchill. Copyright 1951 by Houghton Mifflin Co. Copyright © renewed 1979 by the Honourable Lady Sarah Audley and the Honourable Lady Soames. Reprinted by permission of Houghton Mifflin Co.

• From *Triumph and Tragedy*, Volume VI, by Winston S. Churchill. Copyright 1953 by Houghton Mifflin Co. Copyright © renewed 1981 by the Honourable Lady Sarah Audley and the Honourable Lady Soames. Reprinted by permission of Houghton Mifflin Co.

Quotations from *Marlborough* and *The World Crisis* are made by permission of Curtis Brown on behalf of the Estate of Sir Winston S. Churchill. Copyright the Estate of Sir Winston S. Churchill.

A Harmony of Interests

1
The Polemist

The War of Words

MODERN public figures are rarely conversant with literary matters. Gladstone may have been an amateur classicist, but twentieth-century politicians, certainly in America, lack both the cultivation and the time for such unworldly, almost suspicious, pursuits. In Britain, Asquith, Churchill, and perhaps Macmillan, while in America only Teddy Roosevelt, were notables familiar with current culture. The case of Churchill is unique for several reasons. A professional writer as well as a politician, he made his living by the pen and helped to save his nation no less in his capacity as a writer-speaker than as an administrator or strategist. He was highly self-conscious of his way with the written and spoken word, of making his mark as a stylist. As a young man, he had some literary ambitions. Publishing a novel and several short stories, he talked also of writing plays, and "literary excellence" remained his goal even when his writing ambitions narrowed in scope. In later years, he had a brief fling at film scrip writing, albeit for documentaries only. He even presumed to see a common denominator between poets and politicians: both were among the lucky few whose work is their play.

Such personal qualifications and interests aside, Churchill was close to literary society in many ways. He came from a cultivated family that had numerous literary contacts. His father not only loved Gibbon's writings; he wrote a book on travel in South Africa. Through his father, young Churchill had as a friend the old poet, W. S. Blunt. Churchill's mother, the equally famous Jennie, wrote magazine articles and founded and edited a short-lived journal, the *Anglo-Saxon Review*. (Her son contributed an article to it; alongside pieces by such notables as Edmund Gosse and G. B. Shaw, it was typically on a military rather than literary subject: "British Cavalry.") Being, in her son's words, "always in agreeable contact with artistic and dramatic circles," Jennie brought Winston together over dinner with, on separate occasions, such men as Galsworthy and Shaw.

In later years, Churchill made even more contacts through his long-time private secretary, Edward Marsh. As the critical H. G. Wells put it in the transparent satire in the novel *Men Like Gods*, "Freddy Mush," belonging in an Academy with the likes of Gosse and Beerbohm, had good taste and dug up poetic and literary figures. A patron of the arts, Marsh knew, among others, Rupert Brooke, Siegfried Sassoon, George Moore, and D. H. Lawrence. (Thus it was that Churchill was the only one among a gathering of political notables in 1929 who had heard of the books of Lawrence.) From Moore, Marsh knew about James Joyce, and the prospectus of *Ulysses*, mailed by Sylvia Beach to hundreds of prominent persons, obtained a reply, one is surprised to learn, from Winston Churchill.[1]

That he was a politician proved to be no handicap. In late Victorian and Edwardian England, as in Augustan Rome and as not in modern America, military, political, and literary figures were part of the same milieu. Yet Churchill characteristically brought his own style to such fraternization. He had, unlike the politic and placid Asquith, a knack for going beyond mere chatting in drawing rooms to crossing swords in public with literary intellectuals no less than with politicians.

This is not to say that he was a literary intellectual himself. For one thing, as a result of his loose education, his awareness of English literature was rather spotty and of world literature virtually nonexistent. He was, moreover, closed to the modern sensibility, with its roots in the thought of Darwin, Frazer, Marx, Freud, and Einstein, and oblivious of the great modernist masters—Yeats, Pound, Eliot, Henry James, Joyce, Proust, Kafka, Rilke, Mann, Faulkner—the writers who, in the main, are "difficult" in manner and "pessimistic" in matter. A major obstacle was his tendency to esteem literature for its public values, to politicize literature. No two viewpoints could be more mutually exclusive: the great modern writers were apolitical both in their writings and their lives, while in his own writings, Churchill shows a boundless indifference to the inner life, to the part of the psyche governed by—to use Yeats's distinction—poetry rather than rhetoric, or by—in Frost's distinction—grief rather than grievances.[2]

It therefore follows that the intermittently bookish Churchill would be well read in—and have dealings with—the second and third rank of writers, in Kipling, Galsworthy, Wells, Shaw (and also be aware of E. M. Forster and George Orwell), in those who were more social than private, more popular than avant-garde. This group constituted the outermost limit of his ventures into contemporary literature. Unlike the modernist masters, whose tragic vision was corroborated by World War I, some of these writers happened to have been incurably meliorist, optimistic—in short, leftist. And since young Churchill underwent his own meliorist phase, he was on speaking terms with them. Later, he moved to the right (though still thinking of himself as a Tory Democrat) while they, in the wake of the Russian Revolution, which then seemed to be at long last the Great Experiment, in effect moved even further to the left. The crossing of paths and, given Churchill's temperament, of swords became inevitable. (Though Churchill often spoke like a meliorist, he, with characteristic inconsistency, thought and wrote more like a pessimist.)

The story of their friendships and quarrels has been almost entirely left out of the never-ending official biography of Churchill written by his son Randolph and by Martin Gilbert, no doubt on the legitimate ground that it is unimportant in the chronicle of events. But it happens to be more than a little interesting in the history of ideas.

As a traditionalist and conservative, Churchill was, at least from his forties on, suspicious of social (and artistic) innovation, design, planning, system building. His scorn therefore fell heavily on those committed to such an approach, the leftist intellectuals, the socialist thinkers and writers, the fellow travelers, all of whom sometimes seemed to him to be congruent with the British literary establishment itself. He could be respectful of intellectuals and their role when it fitted his purposes to be so. In Russia, he noted in the 1930s, no knowledge of the truth was available as a result of the destruction of the intelligentsia. In the same period, he praised France for being filled with vital ideas because of her "agitated intellectualism." He respected, while disagreeing with, the opponents of capital punishment as carriers of the "Victorian lamp," as men from "the literary age." He even briefly grew to like contemporary British "intellectuals of Socialism and Radicalism" and the growing body of the "intellectuals of the Left Wing" when in 1936 they came to agree with him on the need for strong defenses.[3]

More often, however, he attacked the literati as, in effect, bleeding hearts. In the post-World War I period, when his estrangement from the intellectual left, with whom he had been vaguely associated in his reformist period in the 1900s, began, the target of his shafts were often the "thin-blooded pacifists" and cosmopolitans who saw all races as equal except their own British race. They favored the League of Nations, the Russian Revolution, and the Indian nationalist movement, whereas he placed Britain over the League, was a diehard on the Empire, and saw the Revolution as the end of Western civilization, fearing that it would spread to Britain. The battle was joined.

In the interwar period, he railed at sentimental liberals, pacifists, calling them "very high-brow writers," "highbrow sentimentalists and chop-logic feeble minds."[4] The English race is tough, but the intellectuals are not a true part of it. They are rather responsible for a sad fact of English life: national self-abasement, "vague internationalism and the promise of impossible Utopias." They would cause Britain to throw away the fruits of the struggle after each victory; they would strip Britain of her glory and make her a fifth-rate power. (By this he did not mean, he hastened to clarify, the British military and scientific minds, which are the best in the world.) He exhibited once a bit of *schadenfreude* over the advent of Hitler because that discomfited the British intellectuals, among whom it had become fashionable to be compassionate—inordinately so, he implied—to Germany. Even during World War II, he defiantly declared his right to use the world "Empire" though it might shock "certain strains of intellectual opinion."

More frequent and bitter-sounding were his attacks on the post–World War II intellectuals who supported the historic Labor Government of Attlee. He veritably ranted against the "stay-at-home Left Wing intelligentsia," "the crack-pate elements . . . the crypto-Communists and pacifists and other trends of Left-wing opinion," that "breed of degenerate intellectuals who have done so much harm," who have, in an unguarded moment, "hag-ridden" Britain with "Party fads and slogans, long-term visionary roads to Utopia." Britain's only weakness is this group of "very brainy" people who seek only to give away or pull down everything noble at home; "collective ideologists and professional intellectuals who revel in decimals and polysyllables." This "tribe of highly intellectual left-wing scribblers," of class-conscious and exhibitionistic "intellectual highbrows," delights in imposing "rigid, symmetrical" doctrines on a nation which has grown by "indulging tolerance rather than logic." Such men, however well intentioned, have deluded themselves and the voters by their un-British emphasis on abstraction and theory at the expense of experience and tradition. The Labor Government consequently concerns itself "with so many intellectual exercises" in lieu of pressing problems.

There was a good deal of posturing, winking, and good-natured chaffing in all this. Churchill used a few intellectuals as straw men with which to belabor the party in power. In ringing all possible changes on a few basic terms, moreover, he rarely availed himself of any proper nouns. His targets were probably such Laborite intellectuals as Harold Laski and R. H. S. Crossman. When he added that experience has vindicated the Conservative belief that there is no "quack cure-all for the tribulations of human life," he may also have in mind fellow traveling Socialists and dreamers of Utopia like G. B. Shaw and H. G. Wells.[5]

This is the rhetoric one expects, if with less grace and style, from a Nixon, Agnew, McCarthy, or George Wallace, but not from a Churchill. Yet his attack on the style of the left-wing intellectuals was not peculiarly a politician's or a reactionary's. It parallels that of one of the intellectuals themselves, one hard to locate on the political spectrum but certainly more social democratic than conservative—George Orwell. One recalls that the jargon-ridden, evasive English attacked by Orwell in his "Politics and the English Language" and caricatured by him as the Newspeak of Ingsoc (English Socialism) in 1984 was forged by idealistic professors and intellectuals on the left. Perhaps it is no accident (as the Marxists would say) that the doomed hero of 1984, the last human being, is named Winston.[6]

So intense sometimes are Churchill's feelings on the matter that they manifest themselves even in his relatively detached historical writings. While ostensibly telling the story of Britain, he rarely resists making sallies at intellectuals wherever he finds them, often turning these gibes into oblique glances at contemporary leftist intellectuals.[7] Thus he indicates that when the British Navy attacked neutral Copenhagen to forestall Napoleon's invasion of Britain, "Whig political and literary circles" raised a storm against the government, but the action was soon vindicated to Churchill's satisfaction. Or when, under Melbourne, "the Poor Law was reformed on lines that were considered highly advanced in administrative and intellectual circles, they did not prove popular among those they were supposed to benefit." In most times and places, in short, the intellectuals can be securely relied on to be on the wrong side. "The hearts are as trustworthy as the brains" is a tell-tale and telling sentence from his early period.[8]

From Collaboration to Controversy

Such intellectual wars may have been carried on with anonymous men, past and present. Churchill did not, however, know the intellectuals and literati merely through books and journals. He met many of them. He was, after all, gregarious by nature. Though himself famous from very early on, he always retained a naive celebrity-seeker's awe of Very Important Persons in all fields. He had a politician's compulsion to make acquaintances and connections; he belonged to the right clubs and country-house sets. H. G. Wells speaks in his autobiography of how, at the turn of the century, "philosophers like McTaggart mingled with politicians like Churchill, trying over perorations at dinner" at places like Lady Sassoon's house at Sandgate.[9]

In one such literary and political salon, he had brief encounters with a leading figure of the English-speaking literary scene. Henry James was an acquaintance of Claire Sheridan, a cousin of Churchill's on his mother's side. James contributed a short story to Jennie Churchill's short-lived *Anglo-Saxon Review*. He was also a friend of Asquith, with whom Churchill had been working from 1904 on. The novelist would come to Margot Asquith's weekend gatherings at Walmer Castle, Kent, and to lunches given at 10 Downing Street for notables from the military and the arts. A fascinating meeting between the seventy-two-year-old Anglo-American master and the forty-year-old half-American British politician took place on a January 1915 weekend at Walmer Castle.

James, curious about British war leadership, eagerly awaited the arrival of "The Great Winston." Expectations, as usual, exceeded reality, for there appears to have been a collision between these two, the most articulate men at the gathering. Churchill, used to being the center of attention, found James displacing him and, according to one observer, "was at his very worst." He had never read James's writings; he was impatient with the old man's slow manner of speech; he was jealous of the homage that the other received. He interrupted his long sentences and used slang which grated on the fastidious novelist. This meeting of the two strong personalities, each with his own large sense of dignity and authority, left the Asquiths unhappy. Upon leaving, James informed Violet Asquith that the experience was interesting, for it was "very encouraging to meet that young man. It has brought home to me very forcibly—very vividly—the *limitations* by which men of genius obtain their ascendancy over mankind."

Then James apparently hunted for the *bon mot*, in this case some argot à la Churchill: "It bucks one up."[10]

James must have been fascinated for nonpolitical reasons as well. Here was an offspring of the typical Anglo-American marriage of New World money and Old World blood that dots the landscape of his writings, most recently and esthetically satisfying in the *Golden Bowl*. Though Jennie Churchill was perhaps more like Daisy Miller or Charlotte Stant than like Maggie Verver, Lord Randolph might in some ways pass for Prince Amerigo. At any rate, Winston was the next generation, the one beyond James's experience and artistic reach (in the subject matter of politics, as well as in time). James's curiosity may have sprung at least as much from the preoccupations of his art as from the political fame and infamy of Winston.

A few years earlier, Churchill's lineage had also been on another famous American author's mind when he introduced Churchill at Carnegie Hall. During a 1900 lecture tour in America, Churchill, on learning that one of his perennially favorite authors, Mark Twain, lived at West 10th Street, phoned to ask the novelist to introduce him. The sixty-five-year-old Twain was delighted to do so. After the lecture, they had a chat, and, despite an argument over the Boer War, Twain said, "I like you very much." He autographed twenty volumes, and on Churchill's favorite, *Life on the Mississippi*, he wrote, "To Winston Churchill from his devoted friend, Mark Twain."[11]

Among other literati with whom Churchill had dealings briefly were W. B. Yeats, Rupert Brooke, and Rudyard Kipling, and, more extensively, Arthur Conan Doyle and T. E. Lawrence. Of greater duration and interest were his relations with three other British literary figures—relations in which politics played a major role—Galsworthy, Wells, and Shaw.

Churchill had entered politics in 1900 as a Conservative but by 1904 had switched to the Liberals. During the next seven years, he became a leader of the left wing of the party, a loyal lieutenant of Lloyd George in espousing the cause of the New (or social welfare) Liberalism. His latest values found literary expression in a long sympathetic review he wrote of the American muck-raking novel, Upton Sinclair's *The Jungle*. A few years later, Churchill moved further to the left and into government posts. During the transition period between his stints as president of the Board of Trade and as home secretary, literature closer to home suddenly meshed with politics. John Galsworthy was writing problem plays that drew attention to glaring flaws in British social institutions. These plays (*Strife, Justice*) made their impact; *Justice* especially created a stir in Parliamentary circles and led to cooperation between a member of the government and a member of the intelligentsia.

In 1909, Galsworthy had first met and liked Churchill "better than I expected. . . . [He] impresses me with a sort of cold force." Galsworthy had written an article on prisons for *The Nation*. Churchill expressed great interest in the article and admiration for *Strife*: "It is a fine piece of work which will long survive the silly chatter of the day." Then in early 1910, Churchill saw *Justice* and became home secretary, almost concurrently. The combination of alert play-goer and sensitive politician, of the man and the hour, was fortuitous, and Galsworthy sensed it. In congratulating Churchill on his new post, he wrote, "How glad I am that you have been appointed to that department of Government which most requires a man, not only of judgment and decision, but of sympathy and imagination." He apologetically asked Churchill to attend quickly to the solitary confinement issue. Churchill responded in kind to Galsworthy: "I greatly admire the keen and vigorous way in which you are driving forward a good cause. I am in entire sympathy with your general mood." He promised to study the whole question of imprisonment and to arrive at his own conclusions.

By June, Galsworthy, expressing admiration for Churchill's general welfarist activism, asked for an appointment with him on the prison question. "You have given a real example of what can be done by a Minister who is truly stirred to a sense of national needs." The writer, he explained, is the nerves, feelers, and eyes of a people, the first part of the animal to receive impressions. "You have much of that temperament yourself, and will understand." At the meeting which soon took place, Churchill revealed to Galsworthy the prison reforms that he would announce in Parliament. In his subsequent speech to Parliament, Churchill said, alluding to Galsworthy's letters in the press and to *Justice*: "That subject has also been brought before our notice by the various able writers in the Press and by exponents of the drama, who have brought home to the general public the pangs which a convict may suffer during long months of solitude." The classicist Gilbert Murray, congratulating Galsworthy on Churchill's announcement and on the clear allusion to *Justice*, rejoiced at the way art and life had come together, as they properly should.

Galsworthy published letters in the press supporting the reforms, which were "admirable" and exceeded his expectations.

Privately he wrote that he had always esteemed Churchill's pluck and capacity and now saw that Churchill also had a very warm heart. For his part, Churchill wrote the playwright a letter which bears directly on the relationship of literature and politics, as he liked to envision it, and which reveals his own modesty:

> Your admirable play bore a most important part in creating that atmosphere of sympathy and interest.... So far from feeling the slightest irritation at newspaper comments assigning to you the credit of prison reform, I have always felt uncomfortable at receiving the easily won applauses which go to the heads of great departments whenever they have ploughed with borrowed oxen and reaped where they have not sown. In this case I can only claim a personal interest which has led me to seek the knowledge of others.[12]

A literary figure had galvanized the government into action, but that change took place mainly because someone sensitive, activist, and imaginative like Churchill was in government. The home secretary had a right to share in the glory of Galsworthy and the joy of Murray. Though Galsworthy regarded his play as mainly criticism of life, not just of social institutions, Churchill characteristically had extracted from it the practical, political rather than the philosophical, psychological kernel. Working together, artist and politician, playwright and home secretary, had made a difference they could not have made separately.[13]

The incident with Galsworthy was a brief encounter, after which, except for a last meeting at a house party, each went his own way. Far more lasting, sometimes acrimonious, sometimes chaffing, always ambivalent, were the relations Churchill had with two perdurably prominent literary celebrities, Wells and Shaw, who were not just liberals but vocal socialists, and, later, defenders of Soviet Russia. These incidents constituted, after his apostacy from meliorism, skirmishes between liberalism and conservatism on the frontiers of politics and literature.

Churchill and Wells had early entered into a friendly correspondence in the 1900s. Wells zealously backed Churchill in the 1908 election, calling him statesman-like and speaking of his rapidly developing career and his vivid and brilliant personality. For his part, Churchill read Wells's many books, enjoyed and admired them, and even regarded the author a seer. In the 1930s, he credited Wells, "that vivid modern philosopher," with having foreseen two decades earlier the horrors of modern war and with having warned that modern men may be swept back to chaos.[14]

The two men were certainly linked by common tastes. In his autobiography, Wells confesses to having had, until the age of sixteen, reveries of being a military leader. Even in his early adult years, these fading memories remained in the form of a love of war games. Hitler and Germans, he now saw, were only adolescents who did not grow up, who lived for nothing creative, only for bloodshed. Even civilized notables like Churchill and Trevelyan were men "whose imaginations were manifestly built upon a similar framework and who remained puerile in the political outlook because of its persistence." Only when confronted with real war, in 1916 and thereafter, had Wells begun to think of war in the way a responsible adult should.

Such obsession with martial matters, however unfortunate, immoral, or puerile, proved terribly relevant in the twentieth century insofar as it helped lead to a major technological breakthrough in war-making and may have been another link between the two men. Wells reveals that he had been eager to help the Allies win the war but not as a soldier. Instead he would contribute his mind. An old idea of his, the Land Ironclads (broached in a 1903 article), was being worked out in the form of tanks. Wells thought it absurd that his imagination was not mobilized in planning the structure and use of these contrivances. He met Churchill, aired his grievances about the tanks, and was able to "get going with him" about a mobile system. Churchill "saw my points and put me in touch with capable men to supplement my mechanical insufficiency". At Churchill's instructions, the Trench War Department set in motion and worked out an apparatus which (as in the case of Galsworthy) made a "reality of my dream."

A truly novel war accessory had been invented—Wells having contributed the original idea and some further observations, Churchill having again listened and acted—and it would have saved vast numbers of lives if only the "tin hats" had liked it. But Kitchener dismissed it as a toy, and his first use of the tanks frittered away all the benefits; "these obvious weapons were forced upon the army by Churchill against all the conservative instincts of the army."[15]

One notes that Wells writes much like Churchill here: the emphasis on mechanical ingenuity, the losing battles with the conservative army brass, the pages-long critique of the army mentality. The only difference is that Wells, for reasons of both personal origins and ideology, makes his condemnation along class lines, while to Churchill the incident is just another example of the benightedness and lethargy of bureaucracies. One of Wells's biographers, Antonina Vallentin, points out that the housemaid's son and the duke's grandson had not a few things in common: energy, obsession with new ways of making war, impatience with routine, with fools, with slow movement, and especially with the military leaders.

To this one might add that during World War I both had a sense of terrible waste caused by obsolete tools, methods, and thought processes. Both looked for, as the hero of Wells's wartime novel *Mr. Britling Sees It Through* puts it, a hard strike through the air, across the sea, or at Gallipoli "instead of dribbling inadequate armies thither." Both men looked to the tank. The role of airpower in destroying cities and quickly winning wars had, moreover, first been dramatized by Wells in 1908, and, of course, Churchill pushed the development of a fighting air arm in Britain a few years later, again over the resistance of the brass, who saw no military use for the plane. It is curious, remarks Herbert Howarth, that posterity may see the two antagonists bound together by a somewhat idiosyncratic love of titanic warfare.[16]

It is curious because of what took place between them thereafter. So far, Churchill the warmaker had as carefully read and hospitably received Wells for deliberations on reforming war technology as Churchill the liberal, a half dozen years earlier, had carefully read and hospitably received Galsworthy for deliberations on reforming the prison system (and as he was imminently to be hospitable to T. E. Lawrence on the subject of Middle Eastern strategy and diplomacy). World War I ended with the rise of the specter of communism in the East, however, and a great barrier sprang up between Churchill and Wells. Churchill had, as is well known, tried to mount an abortive Western crusade to strangle Bolshevism in its cradle. Wells not only opposed the crusade but sympathized with the new regime. The ideological battle lines were drawn; the days of political and military collaboration were finished.

In late 1920, in a newspaper article Wells urged the sending of Anglo-American help to the nascent Bolshevik regime in order to establish a new social order and to prevent the collapse of Russia. Churchill at once responded in a fury by calling Bolshevism a cancer which devours the body, the revolt of the single cell against the body's discipline and subordination; Wells, as a great imaginative writer and "philosophical romancer," would feed the cancer. Russia was one of the granaries of the world, and yet Wells has the temerity to blame the famine on the Allied blockade. When Wells persisted in ascribing the Russian debacle to capitalism and imperialism, he "of course has to vindicate his theories," but, thundered Churchill in a speech, that is "arrant nonsense! The Bolsheviks did it."

Then, as larger wars also have a way of doing, the fight spilled over into adjacent areas—in this case, the personalities of the combatants. During the following weeks Wells replied that he was not anti-Churchill. He had known the minister for twelve years and found much to like in him (even as Shaw was to declare that everyone found Churchill cordial). The minister's imaginative liveliness was both rare in politics and personally "unusually" amusing. But all that aside, Churchill simply should not be entrusted with any public office; his presence embarrassed and tainted the Government. In a time of scarcity, Churchill was a great waster who had "monkeyed" with the British Eastern policy for two years. He concluded with some of the irony which Shaw was to use on the subject: "Mr. Churchill has many resources. He would, for instance, be a brilliant painter."[17]

Then the debate moved beyond Russia and personalities to such delicate subjects as patriotism and personal allegiance. In "Mr. H. G. Wells and the British Empire" (November 1923), Churchill remarked that men often plunge into fields other than their own specialty. So, with unfortunate results, Wells had done. A great romancer and prophet, whose *Time Machine* was reminiscent of *Gulliver's Travels* and *Erewhon*, he was erratic on political questions. This presumably wise man was ready to dissolve the British Empire into a vague federation. He carped against the monarchy, although, according to Churchill, Britain had the best democracy and the king was the keystone of the Commonwealth. Filled with the "intellectual superiority" of "advanced thinkers" (familiar phrases now to the reader of this chapter), Wells remained undaunted by the flop of the "Great Experiment" in Russia. He cleaved to abstractions at the expense of verities like family and country, tradition and experience, and the British inheritance.

George Orwell believed that in this "interesting controversy . . . Wells accused Churchill of not really believing his own propaganda about the Bolsheviks being monsters dripping with blood, etc., but of merely fearing that they were going to introduce an era of common sense and scientific control, in which flag-wavers like Churchill himself would have no place." To Orwell, Churchill was the prescient one.

A decade later, Churchill again attacked Wells the man and the thinker while admiring the writer. He confessed himself to be a voracious reader of Wells, able to pass an examination on his works. Wells's achievement had been to carry on the tradition of Jules Verne, and, unlike his predecessor, to see his numerous prophecies—about tanks, planes, aerial bombing, the Great War, and atrocities—come true. But the same man was filled with ill-conceived and imaginary grievances against Britain over his being born poor—even though it was precisely the British institutions which enabled him to overcome this disability. In fact, Churchill lamented, Wells had singled out for attack the most humane of civilizations, one which needed gifted men like him to help rather than carp at her.[18]

Wells did not take these criticisms passively. Even in World War I, when they saw eye to eye on some things, he had come to have his doubts about Churchill and wanted him locked up to play with his war toys without danger to the nation. Later he remarked on Churchill's obsession, in the *World Crisis* (Churchill's version of the Great War), with a world of one hero (Churchill himself) and many villains. Churchill apparently suffered from a Napoleon complex.

During World War II they seemed to put aside their differences over Communist Russia, true patriotism, the class system. But then, late in the war, even after the heroic climax of 1940, the quarrel broke out anew. In December 1944 Churchill and Wells were eerily reenacting the drama of 1920, the only major difference being that the scene of incipient communism was Greece instead of Russia. Here Churchill was again mounting an anti-Communist crusade, and Wells was again attacking him for it. A subsidiary difference was that this time, Churchill, as prime minister, was to have his way. He was also too busy or important as a statesman to reply to a mere literary man; Wells therefore had to satisfy himself with hearing only his own words.

Wells now called Churchill a "would-be British Fuehrer"; a man with ideas limited to "the adventures of British political life"; a man who never thought extensively and who lacked "any scientific or literary capacity"; a man of pampered political infancy who had overlooked everything that happened since then; a man whose ideology was picked up "in the garrison life of India, on the reefs of South Africa, and the conversation of wealthy Conservative households"—in short, a jumble of nonsense. Like Shaw, Wells spoke of how the country had turned to Churchill when the "old gang" had been disgraced and how his pugnacity brought him to the fore and made him a national symbol. Churchill was a "romantic militarist" who kept up British spirits in the war but who, in peacetime, was dangerous because, far from being a hypocrite, he actually believed his own nonsense. Wells concluded that Churchill "has now outlived [his role] . . . has served his purpose," and, in the Greek crisis, has lost his head altogether.

These were Wells's last important dicta on Churchill. When Wells died soon thereafter, Churchill paid tribute to him by saying, "Few first class men of letters have more consistently crabbed and girded at the national scene and the social system in which they have had their being. Fewer still have owed so much to its ample tolerations and its magnificent complications."[19] This judgment, swelling with typical Churchillian patriotism and national pride, seems rather more to praise Britain for tolerating Wells than Wells for making himself an unexpendable gadfly to Britain. Churchill was quite prepared to carry on the quarrel beyond the grave.

The Case of Shaw

It is against the background of this perennial war between Liberals and Conservatives that one can best appreciate the skirmishes between Churchill and Wells's ideological ally, George Bernard Shaw. Here was another artist whose ideas Churchill disliked but whose art he revered. In the early 1900s, the aristocratic nascent politician and the Anglo-Irish writer had already achieved fame, as *Punch* and others readily parodied and caricatured them. The two men seemed to have a joint destiny in the world of letters, and near the end of their incredibly long careers they were in a sense still together when Dean Inge rated Churchill as Britain's most eminent native and placed Shaw second.[20]

Churchill's "almost first literary effusion" was his 1897 "ferocious onslaught" (unpublished) on Shaw, prompted by what he, as a subaltern, took to be slur on the army in *Arms and the Man*. Churchill therefore had to overcome one of his "earliest antipathies" when a few years later his mother took him to luncheon with the playwright. "I was instantly attracted by the sparkle and gaiety of his conversation." In later years, they had several pleasant and, to Churchill, "memorable talks on politics, particularly about Ireland and Socialism." Their chaffing relationship was the occasion of a famous apocryphal witty exchange: When Shaw sent Churchill a pair of complimentary tickets for the opening of his latest play with the remark, "bring a friend, if you have one," Churchill allegedly replied that he would not be able to attend the premiere but would be there on the second night, "if there is one."[21]

The banter took place in public as well as in private. In a speech of 1906, Churchill compared Shaw to a volcano spouting smoke, inflammable gas, electrical flashes, scalding water, mud and ashes. Amid all the "extravagant nonsense" there occasionally appears "a piece of pure gold smelted from the central fires of truth." Churchill did not dislike "this continually erupting volcano," but Shaw's proposed solution for social ills was "to cut off the Lord Mayor's head." This "blind paroxysm of undisciplined anger" at organized injustice is of dubious value. And in a 1924 election address, Churchill solicited the inevitable Tory cheers and laughter when he noted that the Socialists had behind them that "brilliant intellectual clown," George Bernard Shaw.

As Peter de Mendelssohn observes, Shaw, who took nothing seriously, and Churchill, who took everything seriously, got on famously. They had more than a few things in common—a sense of the "contradictions in human conduct," a love of exaggeration, and an intolerance of conceptual ambiguity. Both men had serious reservations about democracy, its "trumpery" politicians, and the electioneering process itself (with which they even proposed to tamper). Both noted the irony that ruthless dictators without traditional restraints had replaced the hereditary monarchs, whom Shaw regarded as harmless but useful and Churchill regarded with reverence.[22]

Common tastes and good vibrations notwithstanding, political differences eventually came into play, as Shaw, ever the severe critic of the status quo, directed his fangs at the increasingly conservative Churchill. In a 1914 essay, he declared Foreign Secretary Grey to be an incompetent Machiavelli carrying out the programs of militarists like Churchill better than they themselves could. Though "Junker" was a scare word in Britain, Shaw considered most British political leaders to be Junkers. Then he could not resist some wordplay at Churchill's expense: "Mr. Churchill is an odd and not disagreeable compound of Junker and Yankee. His frank anti-Germanic pugnacity is enormously more popular than the moral babble of his sanctimonious colleagues. He is a bumptious and jolly Junker."

Elsewhere Shaw contradicted himself by denying that Churchill was an "ist" of any sort. Instead of holding an ideology, Churchill simply subscribed to the popular view that, if threatened, "you should hit out." Shaw's criticism became entangled in grudging admiration: "Had he had the conduct of affairs, he might quite possibly have averted the war (and thereby greatly disappointed himself and the British public) by simply frightening the Kaiser," for Churchill was spoiling for a fight, and the "British public had all along been behind Mr. Churchill." After the war, Shaw saw Churchill as not only a militarist but also a leading member of the party of "robber barons." In a lecture of 1920, he baited him by lumping him with, of all people, Lenin. The Soviet revolutionary, he said, had been too smart or impatient to wait for public opinion to come round to him. No, Lenin believed rather, like Churchill, that things are done by an "energetic minority which has got a conviction" and is intent on carrying it out. The Socialists, Shaw himself included, "do not go to work in the practical way of Mr. Winston Churchill and Nikolai Lenin. I take off my hat to both gentlemen. It appears to me until we get to work in their ways it will be all talk, talk, talk, and nothing coming of it."[23]

Churchill appears to have licked his wounds quietly for almost a decade. Then in a magazine article written in 1929, he took the offensive on a broad front. His essay was actually a balanced appreciation of the merits and failings of Shaw. Churchill saw in him less the Irishman or the late nineteenth-century aesthete than the adherent of the "New" movements of the time—the New Journalism, the New Politics, the New Religion. These radical ideas had sociological and psychological roots; Shaw, like Wells, had had to fight his way up from poverty and obscurity. Having grown up with a distaste for religion, respectability, "custom-made morality," and conformity, he finally made his mark "as a herald of revolt, a disconcerter of established convictions, a merry, mischievous, rebellious Puck, posing the most awkward riddles of the Sphinx." He was an "energetic, groping, angry man of about thirty." Tired of God, Shaw "invents the Life-force, . . . twists the Savior into a rather half-hearted socialist, and estab-lish[es] Heaven in his own political image." All this is no credit to Shaw, and Churchill finds particularly odious such Shavian dicta as that "there are . . . good reasons for burning a heretic at the stake."

Yet, though Shaw's ideas might be dubious, Churchill conceded that his artistry was not. His praise of Shaw's literary work exceeds even his praise of Wells's: Shaw has succeeded with a series of plays that have eclipsed Oscar Wilde in every way and have captured a worldwide audience second only in size to that of Shakespeare. He has destroyed the well-made play and turned drama into a study not of character or circumstance but of ideas. His characters are there for what they say, not for what they are or do. "Yet they live." *Major Barbara,* for example, seen long after its premiere, clearly has withstood the test of "the most terrific twenty years the world has known." Despite vast social changes, it is still "the very acme of modernity."

Who then is the essential Shaw—the intellectual rebel or the consummate artist? Neither, according to Churchill, for Shaw is actually a licensed jester laughing "his sparkling way through life, exploding by his own acts or words every argument he has ever used on either side of any question." The jester's impartiality saved him; "everyone was so busy rubbing his own shins that none had time to kick the kicker." During the Great War, to be sure, Shaw's clowning was not very helpful but with the return of peace, his presence again seemed apropos.

Now it was Churchill's turn to bare his fangs. He wrote that not only does Shaw seem to lack patriotism in wartime and convictions at any time, but he is terribly inconsistent. Churchill revels in the numerous self-contradictions in Shaw's life: worshipping Soviet Russia but living comfortably in capitalist England; propounding heretical, radical, and subversive ideas while leading a prim, respectable life; exploiting liberty of speech in order to advocate the abolition of Parliament and the establishment of dictatorship; arguing for the equalization of all incomes, yet, as an "already wealthy Fabian," making the loudest "squawk" over some mild new high-income supertax. Adept at eating the hand that feeds him, Shaw is, finally, "at once an acquisitive Capitalist and a sincere Communist."

Yet Churchill is compelled to conclude with high praise indeed: Britain rejoices in someone who has caught the essence of his age, who is "saint, sage and clown," who is the recipient of, "if not the salutes, at least the hand-clappings" of people, and who is nothing less than the "greatest living master of letters in the English-speaking world." What Churchill could not bring himself to say in his eulogy of Wells, he did say of Shaw in 1929: "Certainly we are all the better for having had the Jester in our midst."[24]

Churchill must have been proud—and rightly so—of his sketch because he reprinted it two years later on the other side of the Atlantic, in *Hearst's International-Cosmopolitan Magazine.* It was reprinted yet again in 1937 in the *Sunday Chronicle* and in both the English and American editions of his new book, *Great Contemporaries*. For some obscure reason, this latest version bestirred Shaw into a rebuttal over inaccuracies that he had not felt compelled to make at the time the allegations were first printed in 1929. To Churchill's assertion that Shaw "was dragged to Low Church and chapel" as a child, Shaw replies, "Never"; far from being Dissenters, his family members were "derisive freethinkers" and Shaw himself was an atheist as a matter of deliberate choice at an early age. If Churchill said that Shaw "speaks at hotels and at street corners," Shaw insisted that he rarely spoke at hotels. Churchill's pseudoscholarly pinpointing of 1889 as the year when Shaw "shows for the first time a little Marxian influence" is, Shaw insists, off by more than six years, for a Shavian novel of 1883 "is pure Marx." Churchill's following sentence, "Later on he throws Marx over for Mr. Sidney Webb," is flatly denied: "I never threw Marx over. In essentials I am as much a Marxist as ever." What did happen was that he found Marx to be ignorant and unreliable on certain questions in economics, while Webb was brilliant, independent, and saintly. As for the putative anomaly of a wealthy Socialist like Shaw complaining over the "slender beginning" of a supertax, Shaw patiently explains that he had merely carried out the policy of some Suffragets, who had urged wealthy wives not to "disclose their incomes to their husbands for declaration to the Inland Revenue as part of his income." As a result of Shaw's principled refusal to reveal, or even ascertain, his wife's income—what Churchill had crudely aspersed as a "squawk"—a new law, "The Bernard Shaw Relief Act," now allowed husband and wife to make separate returns. In any case, he opposed all taxes (e.g., on capital or inheritance) other than those on income.[25]

The critique of Shaw in Churchill's *Great Contemporaries* was larger than the original 1929 version because, in the meantime, a new bone of contention between the two men had come up. As the British moves against emergent communism in 1919 and 1944 created a donnybrook between Wells and Churchill, now a certain conversation in which Shaw participated involved Churchill in a similar uproar.

In the summer of 1931, Shaw and Lady Astor (as well as others) visited Soviet Russia and eventually met for over two hours with Premier Stalin. In a newspaper article, Shaw reported on the colloquy that took place in the rarefied atmosphere of the Kremlin. According to him, Stalin had asked why Churchill was so anti-Soviet. Shaw had replied that it was a bee in Churchill's bonnet and very old-fashioned of him. When Stalin indicated a high opinion of Churchill's ability, Shaw demurred. Churchill, Shaw asserted, "would probably lose his seat at the next election and anyhow would never be Prime Minister." Thinking it salutary for Churchill to visit Russia so that he could blow off steam on the spot, Shaw asked whether Churchill would be welcome as a private guest. Stalin agreed that it might be a good idea. Then, alluding to the abortive British attempt to crush the Russian Revolution, he sarcastically declared himself "grateful" to Churchill for having unintentionally equipped the Red Army by way of the defeated White Army in 1920.

Churchill did not take kindly to this discussion which took place, as it were, behind his back. He promptly wrote a newspaper article which derided the visit: "The Russians have always been fond of circuses and traveling shows. Since they have imprisoned, shot or starved most of their best comedians, their visitors might fill for a space a noticeable void. And here was the world's most famous intellectual Clown and Pantaloon in one." Shaw—Churchill continued—was an excellent traveling companion for a Conservative lady who was as inconsistent and unpredictable as he was. And both persons had been shamelessly duped by the hypocrites who presided over a hellish society.

As Lady Astor's biographer puts it, Churchill's scalding, eloquent, and justified attack was an overreaction to an insignificant incident, but the leader of the anti-Bolshevik crusade of 1919 would naturally be outraged that two world-famous British celebrities so casually fraternized with a butcher and said kind things about the society he tyrannized. What is amusing and ironic about this tempest in a teapot is that Churchill was, of course, reelected to office, did become prime minister, and eventually became far more chummy with Stalin than the Socialist Shaw could ever hope to be.

In the following week's issue, Shaw came right back at Churchill. They had tried, Shaw said with exasperation, to undo Churchill's Russophobia. They had tried to show it to be merely Edmund Burke's bathetic tears over Marie Antoinette. The skirmish having turned into a battle royal, Shaw, in a lecture later that year, kept up the fire on Churchill by using Russia as a stalking horse. He observed that Churchill had tried to turn the Great War into "a war against Russia" until he had been forced to stop by a "Hands Off Russia" movement (whose viewpoint was articulated by, among others, H. G. Wells). Stalin had recently told him in person that one reason Russia kept a large army was that Churchill "was still going very strong," and the recent election proved it.[26]

The 1937 essay in Churchill's *Great Contemporaries* therefore was longer than the 1929 journalistic appreciation of Shaw because it incorporated a good portion of the 1931 attack over the visit with Stalin. In turn, Shaw's critique of the critique also dealt with that now famous conversation in the Kremlin. Shaw called Churchill's mocking description of a large street demonstration and parade which had allegedly greeted Lady Astor and Shaw as "pure imagination." Shaw, to be sure, had been treated as if he "were Karl Marx in person," but with a refreshing "absence of ceremony and platform bunk." Stalin had received them "as old friends." After a discussion on child rearing and on politics, "I asked what about inviting Mr. Churchill to Russia. His geniality became, I thought, slightly sardonic as he replied that he would be delighted to see Mr. Churchill in Moscow."

To the cultural historian, the details of the Astor-Shaw-Stalin summit meeting take on a *Rashomon* effect, for, according to Lord Astor's notes of the event, nothing important at all was discussed. And according to what Churchill claims in 1950 (in the *Hinge of Fate*), Stalin told him in 1942 that in 1931 Shaw had said little or nothing of consequence! Lady Astor was the one who blamed Churchill rather than Lloyd George for the intervention of 1919, who told Stalin that "Churchill is finished finally," and who thereupon received the prophetic reply that was balm to Churchill's ego—or a figment of it: "I am not so sure. If a great crisis comes, the English people might turn to the old warhorse".[27] Clearly the name of Churchill was brought up, probably by a Stalin who appeared anxious over the possibility that the arch British anti-Bolshevik might return to influence. But, considering the selectivity of memory and the swelled egos of all concerned, it would take a bold man to assert definitively who said what to whom.

Even when the "old warhorse" came to his rendezvous with the destiny that Shaw was so egregiously unable to forsee, Shaw was not about to put aside decades of criticism and derision. He could join the chorus of universal praise for the heroics of 1940 only on his own terms. Churchill—Shaw noted in a preface of 1945—maintained his popularity by "his long cigars and the genial romantic oratory in which he glorified the war." This is not quite the way most people would describe the withstanding of Hitler's worst. On the other hand, some would agree with the succeeding remark, familiar Shavian rhetoric though it be, that Churchill was defeated in 1945 because his election platform "was a hundred years out of fashion." But when Shaw adds that Churchill induced heroism in the British people in 1940 by hiding from them the truth as to how ghastly the situation really was, Shaw does not give Churchill sufficient credit for the magnitude of the achievement and the courage it involved. Churchill's feat is the greater when one considers that Shaw himself, already shown to be fallible as a prophet, was among those who lost their nerve and who urged the government in a letter of March 1940 to seek a truce and a negotiated peace with Nazi Germany.[28]

Shaw had one more sally to make. At the request of one Charles Eade, he replied again to Churchill's piece in the *Great Contemporaries* even though he had already ceased his professional writing career. In an appreciative, if fragmentary and mischievous, set of notes (published posthumously in 1953), he called Churchill "the most brilliantly talented Minister on the Treasury Bench." He also found him decent; if in 1901 Churchill had been "impressed" by Shaw's "eating only fruit and vegetables and drinking only water," now a half century later Shaw was impressed by the fact that Churchill's "recreations are civilized: painting and bricklaying, not hunting and shooting."

But the main event was 1940. This man who initially had exhibited the military distinction of the young Marlborough was chosen in old age by a frightened and desperate Britain to confront the "new Napoleon" on the rampage. All the other politicians were party hacks, "safe men" who, long preferred over Churchill, "were evidently no match for a live wire of Herr Hitler's voltage." Had peace prevailed, Churchill would never have risen to the top because he did not act like a normal politician. He was "suspected of wanting to do something," and he had the temerity to change parties merely on principle or on the merits of a particular bill. Even so, the political system made sure to hobble the prime minister by placing reactionaries at his side who would keep "his Tory Democracy active in its Toryism and paralyzed in its Democracy."

With all his talents, therefore, Churchill—according to Shaw—had made the wrong vocational choice. At a similar juncture, Shaw himself had had better sense, as he had turned down a chance to run for Parliament because it was far better to be "The Amazing Shaw . . . than to put my head under the Westminster extinguisher. Was I not right, O Winston?" He pushed hard on this point. "What I want Churchill to tell us is whether if he had his life to live again he would waste it in the British House of Commons as it has been wasted by the party system." Then Shaw peremptorily dismissed a half century of politicking and the heroics of 1940: "His real career has been as a soldier and an author."[29]

Coming from so accomplished an author, this was no mean praise. Certainly Churchill saw no insult here. On being given the Nobel Prize for Literature in 1953—for once Shaw was on target as a prophet—Churchill made a brief comment that serves as his valediction to Shaw. He noted that earlier recipients of the prize had been Kipling and Shaw, two writers with whom he felt he could not compete. Why, one may ask, cite those two of so many other prize winners? In order to propound one last paradox: Churchill had known both men "quite well," and his ideas were usually more in line with those of Kipling than those of Shaw, but Kipling "never thought much" of Churchill, whereas "Mr. Shaw often expressed himself in most flattering terms."[30]

"Often"? Well, not in the sense of "every day" but in the sense of "almost always."

Churchill Portrayed

Churchill's personality was so marked and his controversies with the literati so spirited that his opponents could hardly resist turning their attention to him in their literary productions. They were, after all, not merely essayists, who jousted with their friendly adversary in discursive prose, but artists. They could avail themselves of other, less blunt, weapons on which to impale the bulky, formidable, and therefore tempting figure of Churchill.[31]

A lifelike version of Churchill appears in a novel by a man who was not a party to the intellectual wars surveyed above—Arnold Bennett. Moving through the world of clubs and restaurants where the political and literary celebrities mingled, Bennett ran into Churchill periodically and noted how he excelled as a talker. He also believed, in the face of qualifications expressed at one of the clubs about the reliability of Churchill's *World Crisis*, that it was "a remarkable achievement." But he had his reservations about Churchill, and his novelistic eye was not closed to the ridiculous side of the man. Observing Churchill with military medals dangling on the lapel of his dress coat, he confided to his diary that he had never seen such a thing before, except on the dress coat of the hall porter of the club. When someone criticized Churchill's rhetorical style, as in the phrase "pistols drinking blood," Churchill, after citing as precedent "arms against a sea of troubles," said that when he had written the passage he had had pistols actually by him; needless to say, this explanation left Bennett in the dark.[32]

As one of the writers whose voices counted, especially on the left, Bennett was busy with the war effort during 1918. He was at the Ministry of Information, where Beaverbrook put him in charge of British propaganda in France. He thereby obtained acquaintanceship with such wartime men of power as Churchill and Lloyd George, and in 1925 Beaverbrook fed him much more inside information on the power struggle among the wartime Cabinet members. This material—which, after Bennett's converting it into fiction, was double-checked by a Beaverbrook thrilled by its political accuracy—was richer than what any other political novelist, except Disraeli, ever had, and it resulted in the then much talked-of political novel, *Lord Raingo*.[33]

The protagonist, Sam Raingo, a self-made millionaire, in 1918 joins the wartime government, and through him, at a Cabinet session, the reader meets Tom Hogarth, "in a lounge suit, short, bald, blonde, and challenging." In subsequent scenes, Hogarth's eyes often "blaze" or "twinkle"; when speaking, he does things like raising his "massive shoulders" or marching away to a corner "in triumph." Working "sixteen hours a day, seven days a week," he displays at public meetings the "bellicose pugnacity of John Bull in unsurpassable oratory." His "pure and impassioned oratory" lays a "magic spell" on people.

The Churchillian character traits are as much in evidence as these physical resemblances. He is described as "irrepressible." One of the youngest members of the Cabinet, he "had reigned in seven departments of State, fought, written, and fought; he was the most brilliant advocate in the House, and one of the finest polemical and descriptive writers in the country; he had every gift except common sense, and he could rise victorious even from the disasters imposed upon him by an incurable foolishness." Hogarth's words and actions often have a melodramatic truculent, self-centered, almost sinister ring to them. He applies tongue lashings to military officers, rails at "dagoes," urges the suppression of certain newspapers, lectures everyone, and monopolizes all conversations. His brain is "tireless, greedy, tremendous."[34]

Despite the ambiguity of the presentation, Churchill liked *Lord Raingo*, cheerfully acknowledged the portrait, and congratulated Bennett on the description of the Cabinet meetings and surroundings: "You must have been a fly on the wall." On the other hand, Lord Birkenhead, who feared for a while that he was the leading character in the book, attacked novelists like Bennett and Wells in a newspaper interview for using real persons, living or dead. Bennett replied that Raingo was not based on a real person. Soon thereafter, at the Other Club, Bennett ran into Churchill, who said to him, apropos the row with Birkenhead (who was a close friend of Churchill's), "Receive the congratulations of Tom Hogarth."[35] This was, like Churchill's treatment of Shaw and Wells (and theirs of him), part of the good humor and tolerance with which, as Churchill frequently boasted, political debate is carried on in Britain.

If *Lord Raingo* portrays Churchill enmeshed in wartime politics, a novel of the following year, H. G. Wells's *Meanwhile*, presents him during peacetime. If Bennett describes events at a remove of a half dozen years, Wells writes of them on the day after. If in *Lord Raingo* Churchill appears, however thinly disguised, stage center, in *Meanwhile*, he appears in his own person on the periphery.

The setting is, in part, the General Strike in Britain. Some right wing chauvinists wish that Churchill were at the War Office just now. Others, such as the protagonist of the novel, Philip, fear rather that he is out of control. Someone talks of man's ultimate reasonableness, but, thinks Philip, that is weak "when some atavism like Winston collars all the papers for his gibberings and leaves you with nothing to print your appeals to the ultimate reason." A dreamer of Utopia (probably Wells himself) says that this world is only a prelude to real civilization; then Philip asks how to get on with it, how to "get by Winston?" The conclusion is that he is "probably certifiable [i.e., mad] but no doctor can get near him to do it." Philip believes that the heart of the matter is the inability of the unintelligent majority of Britons to understand or accept the decline of British imperial greatness. Churchill is their man.[36]

In *Meanwhile*, then, the focus has shifted from Churchill as unideological in-fighter to Churchill as a comfortably ensconced politician leading, or a front for, the forces of reaction. This novel, moreover, carries through on another idea already broached. The implication that Churchill stands for the irrational, primitive, uncivilized side of man had been developed by

Wells four years before in another, more famous novel, *Men Like Gods*.

This earlier book centers on Churchill himself, for the man so haunted the imagination that Wells had to resort to the writer's peculiar form of self-therapy—fiction. He not only made Churchill a character in a *roman à clef* but made him the major antagonist in a work of fantasy. He brought a sordid political reality into the dreamscape of his science fiction. He thereby was able to write, like the authors of *Gulliver's Travels* and *Metamorphosis*, about—in Aristotle's distinction—the impossible probable rather than, as was done in *Lord Raingo* and *Meanwhile*, the possible and historical.[37]

On a planet called Utopia is a world which has left its Age of Confusion—that is, earth's present mode of life—far behind. One of the visiting earthlings is Mr. Rupert Catskill, the "well-known" secretary of state for war, a resolute little man who orates with hands on hips and head thrust forward. When a Utopian girl says that Rupert "thought romantically—but he did not look romantic," the liberal protagonist, Barnstaple, replies: "He has lived most romantically. He has fought bravely in wars. He has been a prisoner and escaped wonderfully from prison. His violent imaginations have caused the deaths of thousands of people." And one of the earthlings (the thinly disguised A. J. Balfour) concludes from such facts that "it would have been better for all of us if Rupert had taken to writing romances—instead of living them." And in fact Catskill soon undertakes to lead an abortive rebellion against the rational and pacific Utopians.

This tale anticipates the much more subtle *Brave New World*.[38] Catskill, like the Indian John in the Huxley novel, presents the claims of human complexity against the simplifications and velleities of the socialist planners of Utopia. But where the sympathetic John is the author's spokesman, the obnoxious Catskill is his author's *bête noir*. Where John's implicit critique is psychological and theoretical—can man live in a world without Shakespeare and without guilt?—Catskill's is both ideological and political. He spouts ideas of laissez-faire economics and social Darwinism and diluted Nietzscheism. Harping on the spiritual losses caused by the absence of adversity, contrast, risk taking, and adventure, he prefers life to be "titanic" rather than "tidy"; he celebrates the intensity of an existence marked by struggle. Beauty comes from "competition and conflict," and man is molded in hardship. Abolishing these by means of their socialism, the Utopians "have altogether cut out the bracing and ennobling threat and the purging and terrifying experience of war." Everything is secured except for "degeneration." There being no stimulus to activity, Utopia's success is only inertia and autumnal glory. Adapting Tennyson's lines, Catskill prefers fifty years of Earth to a cycle of Utopia.

A representative Utopian responds that Catskill's alternative is to leave things to God or to Nature: "If only we submit to her freaks and cruelties and imitate her most savage moods! . . . [Catskill] preaches the old fatalism and believes it is the teaching of science." The ideological and dramatic clash between Catskill, on the one hand, and the Utopian, on the other, turns upon a fundamental, insoluble philosophical question: Are the ills of life mainly due, as rationalists and meliorists aver, to an inept social arrangement which can be remedied by a reordering? Or are they, as Conservatives hold, constants in human nature and the products of the innate imperfectibility of man? Is change possible but temporarily blocked by malevolent vested interests—such as Catskill-like politicians—or impossible because of an ineradicable flaw in the universe itself? Are the Utopians, as Barnstaple finds them, supermen, or, as Catskill finds them, degenerate—3,000 years "away" from, not "ahead" of, earthlings? Have they reached a permanent summit or merely passed a transitory prosperity?

Catskill's conservatism manifests itself in ways peculiarly Churchillian. He dissents from the paeans of these earthlings "bitten by the Socialist bug." Life being a permanent flux, any image of permanent social perfection must be a will-o'-the-wisp. Then, when an epidemic among the Utopians seems to justify his contention that Nature is on his side, Catskill resorts to activism—the reactionary kind of activism. Having expressed esteem for policemen and pugnacious aristocrats resisting social change, he is not only going to take advantage of the Utopian's gentleness but will also prove thereby their inferiority in those matters that are his yardstick: martial and strategic prowess, the will to fight and endure, adventurism. Finally, from the desire to justify his philosophy of human nature and to defend traditional notions of dignity in the face of novel notions, he slips insensibly into his habitual rhetoric of British, imperial, Anglo-Saxon, Western chauvinism. He will treat Utopia as Britain or any Western European power treated Africa and Asia in the nineteenth century. The portrait is that stock image of Churchill which hobbled him throughout his career, that of imperialist, warmonger, and militarist, of perpetual *enfant terrible:* "the puerile imagination of Mr. Catskill . . . [his] incurable craving for fantastic enterprises."³⁹

Lord Raingo and *Meanwhile* are novels in the realistic mode, vignettes of life set against the background of contemporary events; *Men Like Gods* is a philosophical romance. In all three novels, the Churchill figure is seen from the outside rather than as a hero. In *Men Like Gods*, he is indeed the leading antagonist to the hero. In *Lord Raingo*, he has a considerable niche carved out for himself, and not all of his doings are necessarily baneful to himself or to nation. In the two Wells novels, he is a menace to Britain or to mankind, a major obstacle to progress.

The portrait of Churchill varies with the setting and the plot. If *Lord Raingo* is about politics as seen by an outsider (Raingo) who becomes an insider, a novice who learns the ropes of politics, Hogarth-Churchill is in many ways the incarnation of the art. In *Meanwhile*, he is a reactionary on the domestic front. He (like his "class") has no real ideology, only a blind striking out, a desire to hold on nakedly to privilege. In *Men Like Gods* he is an ideologue.

Men Like Gods is about Utopia spoiled or rejected by the presence of the old reflexes as these are embodied in Churchill. In other words, Catskill-Churchill does not merely, *as a philosopher, posit the existence of an ineradicable Old Adam in man; he is, as a politician-militarist, a classic instance of it.* The novel adheres to the pattern, as Orwell pointed out, common to all of Wells's books: the clash between men of science working for a planned world state and the reactionaries trying to restore the messy past. To this one might now add that *Men Like Gods* differs from the paradigm only in that a quarter century of criticisms and complaints about Churchill by Shaw, Wells, and lesser left wing literary lights is packed into the colorful portrait of Catskill.

It is merely one of history's ironies that the man who had cooperated with Galsworthy on peacetime liberal reforms and with Lawrence and Wells on ways of triumphing expeditiously over German barbarism should come to seem so barbaric himself. And it is an even more delicious irony that the man who was viewed by the literary intelligentsia in the 1920s as "The Adversary" to civilization would be viewed by everyone in 1940 as the savior of Britain and perhaps of civilization itself.

If many of the Churchillian traits in *Men Like Gods* parallel those recorded by reporters, observers, and critics in essays and letters, we yet turn to literary artists for an imaginative depiction, a credible rendering that is from within the man written about, that is fully rounded. The artist, unlike the journalist, works under the obligation of being sympathetic and fair minded—if he is to be an artist at all. He also has the means of dramatizing what essayists remark on only in a few sentences or paragraphs, that is, the means of presenting a coherent picture of a human being, not a one-dimensional polemical adversary who exists only by virtue of one or two ideas of his, and wrong ideas at that. His dismissal of Churchill is the more persuasive—and lasting—because of that. While it is as fair to attack the intelligentsia as any other section of society, Churchill may have gotten more than he bargained for when he started up with Wells. He had, one now sees, a personal as well as a partisan and an ideological reason for railing against these "very high-brow intellectual scribblers," who had not only attacked him in essay but derided him in fiction.

And yet the last laugh is not at Churchill's expense. Had there been no Hitler, World War II, and prime ministry, *Men Like Gods* would have been the definitive word on a brilliant but erratic minor political career, on a lost leader, on a man of great promise who burned himself out unfulfilled. But as it happened, Churchill is now remembered by everyone (save some historians and scholars) mainly as the hero of 1940, and the portrait of him in *Men Like Gods*, however justified in its time and fair from a certain perspective, has been rendered somewhat eccentric, archaic, pedantic, hysterical, and irrelevant. Life and art may indeed go together, as Gilbert Murray thought, but sometimes life has the upper hand.

2
The Conservative

THE mélange of liberal and conservative ideas which one sees in Churchill's relations with the literary intelligentsia whom he at once admired, feared, and resented raises the question of what was his ultimate political and philosophical affiliation. This matter is not easily resolved, for not many political figures have had such diverse objurgations as "radical," "sincere Liberal," "reactionary," and "fascist" hurled at them during their lives. It happened to Churchill as a result of his eccentric political zigzagging during an unusually long career. Now that, with the passage of time, we can see his words and works in perspective, the question arises: What, then, finally was he?

Previous discussions have approached the matter chronologically and arrived at the conventional wisdom that Churchill (like many another soul) was liberal when young and conservative in middle and old age. This finding, somewhat too neat and schematic, runs roughshod over numerous subtle discriminations. The question must be rephrased: How did Churchill stand on different areas of human experience, only some of which were directly political? The new categories of judgment brought thereby into play will be found to cut across chronology—Churchill in some ways undergoing change, in other ways remaining impervious to time.

Party affiliation proves to be of little help in solving the riddle. Remaining through most of his career an outsider—no matter what party label he happened to be carrying—he may, like Milton in religion, be said to have finally formed (in the 1930s) his own party with a membership of one. His defense was that he remained consistent amid changing circumstances by altering his ideas or parties and not, as did the parties and their leaders, his "dominating purpose"; that he in fact changed parties in order to not change principles.

Certainly his views on foreign policy brought him into conflict with the party to which he belonged—the "new" Liberals, when overnight (in 1911) he changed from dove to hawk; the Conservatives in the 1930s, over India, Russia, and Germany. He could be quite anomalous on foreign affairs, becoming a reactionary on the question of Empire but being by turns dogmatic and pragmatic on Soviet Russia, depending on the balance of power in Europe. As a young man, he declared his will to devote his life "to the maintenance of this great Empire of ours." Even though he had noted that Europeans walking in one Indian city would be spat upon by the natives, he did not draw any inferences from that with reference to the British imperial mission.[1] When, a decade later, he entered the government, his first official memo was, Ronald Hyam observes, a classic statement of the code of the Victorian ruling elite, "the principle of timely concession to retain an ultimate control." His current domestic liberalism found an echo in his imperial vision. He wanted no further territorial expansion and opposed an incident of British adventurism in Tibet. He would retain the Empire, not to exploit the natives, but to fulfill Britain's civilizing mission and to maintain her world position.

Despite initial jingoism, he soon took an enlightened view of the Boers; he would give South Africa back to them as "great act of renunciation and justice" rather than "frittering it away piecemeal." When in the Colonial Office, he tried to improve the quality of governance in favor of the governed. He spoke of the "disgusting" butchery of natives and miscarriages of justice as part of the tyranny against which the "unfortunate" Zulus were struggling; he reprehended the "chronic bloodshed" in Africa as "odious and disquieting" and easily interpreted by observers as "the murdering of natives and stealing of their lands."[2] He favored loosening all the imperial bonds; autonomy would, as in South Africa, make for better members, and freedom would promote loyalty. In conversations before World War I, Churchill struck W. S. Blunt as persuadable on the idea of letting go of costly India and on the noxiousness of racism. He seemed to hint that were he prime minister he would carry out Blunt's anti-imperial ideas.[3]

During World War I, however, Churchill did not want Britain to be left out if the victorious allies made a rush for territorial spoils, and after the war, though he had seen the light on Ireland, he resumed his prewar litany on Egypt, "We should hold on to Egypt as we hold on to India . . . whatever happens."[4] In the early 1930s, because of the unusual political consensus that, after the lesson of Ireland, concessions in India would be best,

Churchill's solitary and fruitless opposition to the demand for liberty by nonwhite people confirmed his reputation as a reactionary. In an essay of this period, "If Lee had not won the Battle of Gettysburg," Churchill presented many historical events as though they had been merely a hideous possibility. Among them was the Emancipation, "followed by some idiotic assertion of racial equality" and attempted grafting of "white democratic institutions" on the "simple, docile, gifted American negro race belonging to a much earlier chapter in human history."[5] Churchill was clearly not only passing strictures on mistakes in the past but giving a cautionary tale to his contemporaries who were eager to dismantle the British Empire and grant colonies in Africa and Asia immediate independence.

No wonder that to liberal and moderate American leaders throughout World War II he seemed mainly concerned with preserving Britain's position in Europe and the European empires in the Pacific. Nor did his triumphant wartime visits to the United States dispel the American sense of him as a reactionary from a dim past. Much as he might prate about self-determination in either war, he could cavalierly spurn such principles when it came to possible territorial booty in the wake of World War I, fighting Bolshevism, or carving out spheres of influence with Stalin. Though he was, concludes Vladimir Dedijer, clear-eyed at the beginning of World War II, he could not foresee the imminent end of the empires or Europe's forfeiture of hegemony.[6] The loss of India and Burma after World War II strikingly symbolized for him Britain's "rapid decline"—as if imperial holdings were the only way to gauge her greatness. As postwar prime minister, he vainly tried to revive Victorian grandeur by making Britain a nuclear power.

Unlike his gradual ossification on the imperial question, Churchill's responses to Communist Russia were more complex, pragmatic, and sensitive to altered conditions. He had been suspicious of Czarist Russia in the late 1890s, especially of her intentions vis-à-vis India. Then in 1911, with war clouds hovering over Europe, he reversed himself and emphasized the importance of an alliance of France and Britain with Russia. During the war he forwarded (or rationalized) the Dardanelles expedition in part as an effort to help the secretive and crippled titan in the east. When Lenin took over, Churchill suggested that the British government guarantee the survival of the Bolshevik Revolution in return for Russia's remaining in the war against Germany. Since that proposal went nowhere and the Allies won without

Russia, Churchill then veered to the other extreme and became the linchpin of a halfhearted Allied attempt to mount a military crusade against the new regime.

In the 1930s, he reverted to his stand of 1911, urging a Western alliance with the Communist monolith against Germany. Stalin, he reasoned, now stood for "Russian nationalism in somewhat threadbare Communist trapping" and presided over a shift in "the axis of Russia" toward the army.[7] That the growing dependence on Russia ushered in his—and our—postwar troubles with the Communist state was probably made inevitable by Hitler, who first placed Britain in jeopardy and then plunged her into the unholy alliance. In the later 1940s, he again saw Russia as the major threat to civilization, and then in the 1950s he, softening once more, sought reconciliation and peaceful coexistence. Possessed now by the thought that a personal conference with Malenkov in the wake of Stalin's death would make all well, he yearned to round off his long story in war and peace, his career as a warrior, by being a global peacemaker.

Though for the sake of a non-Communist Russia, he had been ready enough in 1919–20 to sacrifice the small states at Russia's periphery, he generally held that the internal affairs of a country—Nazi Germany, Fascist Italy and Spain, Czarist and Communist (in the 1930s and 1950s) Russia—were "not our business" and should not impair friendships if no external ambitions were present. With Hitler, no compromise had been possible, but communism, he now thought, was susceptible to internal change and could be lived with. He even conceded that Russia had her legitimate security needs. He thereby seemed to fall into the same trap he warned others of, for had he not at various times (1919, 1938, 1944) criticized Lloyd George, Chamberlain, and Roosevelt for thinking they could talk Lenin, Hitler, and Stalin into reasonableness? At any rate, such Machiavellian flexibility for the sake of survival and stability transcends the categories of Liberal and Conservative. In either camp will be found the pragmatists and idealists, as well as men who are both by turns.

If on India Churchill grew reactionary and on Russia he seemed, depending on the circumstances, at times Liberal and at times Conservative, he managed to trace yet a third pattern of behavior on domestic policy, notably social welfare issues, on which he was static. He early established himself as a "progressive" and (except in the 1930s) adhered to his position even as events made it come to seem conservative. He grew up in an aristocratic family in which there had been occasional liberal forays, the most important and famous of which was that of his own father, Randolph, who adopted the Disraelian concept of Tory Democracy. Despite some radical sounding rhetoric late in his career, Randolph remained in his party, and young Churchill began at that point as a Conservative with liberal inclinations. Tory abandonment of Free Trade politics caused him to join the opposing party in 1904, and he became one of the most effective spokesmen of the "new Liberal" or "radical" wing, led by Lloyd George. To W. S. Blunt, Churchill confided that he would give his life to improve the lot of the poor, and his speeches of 1904, 1906, and 1908 increasingly urged a host of reforms and the need for a "Minimum Standard."

At the same time, however, he had reservations about many aspects of the "radical" 1909 budget, and he seemed not entirely at home with the Liberals. He favored nationalizing the railroads but not, as did Lloyd George, the land; he would have the state provide employment in bad times but not guarantee jobs for all. His attitude during strikes in 1910–11 was seen as "bloody"; although he disliked rich employers, he was impatient with the workers or at least the trade unions.[8] He nervously took note of Germany, where "militant socialism" had driven many into "violent Tory reaction," or of America, where giving the blacks the vote begot a "sinister reaction."

Some contemporaries and later historians therefore believed that he treated politics as a game, took up causes so long as they remained popular, and entertained opinions and ambitions in lieu of a considered philosophy. Others saw him as wanting reform for paternalistic rather than egalitarian reasons, for the purpose of preserving Britain as a powerful and stable state rather than for its own sake.

During World War I he favored an unprecedented war profits tax and argued for a mobilized, "socialized" nation (what has been called "war socialism"), and after the war he looked to the state to curb unmerited acquisition of property, to ensure that "the exercise of the self-interest of the individual conform[ed] to the general harmony of the nation," and to spend large moneys on building houses and relieving unemployment. Yet, though sympathizing with people's desire for better living conditions rather than great causes, he soon wanted to arouse the people to the great cause of antibolshevism, at home and abroad (as he would again after World War II). He worried lest an anti-British, anti-Empire Labor government be elected and in turn be overthrown by local Leninists. He separated the "unattainable ideal" of equality from the attainable Anglo-Saxon ideal of liberty. If in the early 1900s he saw the central issue as the Individual versus the Trust, now it was "national and individual conceptions" against "cosmopolitan and communistic theories."[9] After his initial flirtation with a radicalism of sorts, he seemed in the 1920s (years in which he little enhanced his stature as a statesman), despite some liberal gestures, to agonize more over the Treasury's needs than the workers'. And in the 1930s, he was preoccupied by foreign affairs. Thus he never found his way back to the domestic radicalism from which emergent international problems had deflected him, and his antiquated defense of the status quo helped prepare the way for his stunning 1945 defeat at the hands of a Labor Party promising postwar social restructuring.

During the Depression, he distinguished between relief and insurance and would purge the unemployment insurance rolls of those not belonging on them. Favoring a Means Test and opposing veterans' bonuses, he offered only the austere consolation that life for the plain man, harsh under either communism or capitalism, is better under the latter. While at first admiring Franklin Roosevelt as an explorer whose experiments would influence the world, he came to be critical of most of the New Deal measures. Dismissing the Socialist (nationalization of everything) and Liberal (gigantic borrowing and spending by the state) solutions, he insisted that nations should be made rich by individual enterprise, not by governments; that state expenditure was wasteful; that social insurance could be obtained only by prohibitive confiscatory taxes; that the modern state must not overdo the manufacture of credit; that an economic crisis must not be treated as though it were a war and so cause the state to grow too powerful. He disliked no less the New Deal onslaught, as he thought it, on millionaires and the Supreme Court than its zeal to legislate prosperity and to create a trade union movement overnight.[10]

Churchill saw himself, nevertheless, as a proponent of the via media. Employers who refused to deal with unions, he warned, merely play into the hands of extremists; a strong union movement is a bulwark against communism and therefore a benefit for employers. Just as a 1900 judgment imperiling the right to strike gave birth to the Labor Party, so could continued hostility to unions in America lead to the politicization of the unions and the rise of sinister forces.

During World War II and after, he was too preoccupied by

military and international matters to bother with domestic issues. In 1942–43, he responded reluctantly to the Beveridge Report for a postwar welfare state, which gave many people, in the egalitarian mood of the war, a domestic war aim. He nevertheless iterated after the war that, though opposed to socialism, he still favored the "immense social reforms, in many of which a free British nation has long led the world." He would try to close the gap with Liberals, especially as the Conservatives now espoused all the sentiments "which animated the great Liberal leaders of the past," whereas the Labor Party would, if in power, ruin both British industry and democracy.[11] When he was a Conservative peacetime prime minister, Churchill, listing with pride the welfare laws he had been responsible for "both as a Liberal and a Conservative Minister," adopted the Liberal program of 1910: "minimum standards" and "free competition upwards."

In sum, while he is no darling of the Libertarian Party, neither can Churchill be regarded as leftist. Despite his flaunting of his father's slogan, he did not "trust the people." He never in his long career turned his back on the welfare measures he advocated in 1906–11; he simply would not go much further. He was basically, as became evident with the passage of time, a conservative who held that mere amelioration of hardship was the best that could be done. He would not dream of a Utopia, of a profound change in the human condition. "The struggle for life is unceasing. There is no easy and pleasant road."[12] Social planners were bound to create a new hell even if they succeeded in creating a new heaven and earth.

While on social welfare issues, Churchill, by remaining ideologically inert, shows a narrowing of horizons; on constitutional questions he exhibited, as on India, a growing reactionary attitude. When large numbers of women, working class people, and the poor were enfranchised after World War I, he was not only himself victimized by these new political forces but also perturbed by the ramifications. Having as a young man declared himself to be completely against female suffrage, he still thought, a decade and a half later, that sex barriers were not a real grievance. When women's suffrage did come, he blamed it for such disreputable things as Prohibition in America.[13]

Churchill thought the "one man, one vote" principle valid only after everyone had been educated, as part of a "leveling up." Yet, if he complained about the large number of ignorant voters, he also dimly sensed that too much education for everyone might be dangerous. He wanted politicians in any case to distance themselves from the electorate. He objected to undue courting of popularity. The statesman should "have his eyes on the stars rather than his ears on the ground."[14] The masses of new voters, by demanding immediate action for economic dislocations which could be relieved only slowly, might blindly break the delicate old instrument of Parliament. The representative and parliamentary institutions seem to lose their authority "when based on universal suffrage." Nostalgic for the days when Britain had a "real political democracy led by a hierarchy of statesmen," that is, an oligarchy, Churchill invariably found elections to be disturbers of "social, moral, and economic progress" or even a "danger to international peace." Too frequent electioneering deprives Parliament of dignity, turning it into a vote-getting machine; "elections exist for the sake of the House," not vice-versa. Not for Churchill does the truth emerge from political brawls. Electoral campaigns merely cause both sides to exaggerate the facts in opposite directions and to obfuscate the issues.[15]

In the 1930s, Churchill blamed the extension of the franchise "far beyond those interested in politics" for Prohibition in America, the economic crisis, the socialist government, the decay of the Parliamentary institutions and the party system, and the desire to cast off the Indian empire. During the economic crisis of 1931, when no party had a majority and an election might recur at any time, nothing was being done because any way out of the crisis would, he thought, entail unpopular steps. The precious and adaptable Parliamentary institution, although assimilating a "large new party" based on "manual labor," seemed increasingly incapable of dealing with the Depression.

Churchill therefore sought conservative—or even reactionary—solutions. Since universal suffrage would not bring the right, and consequently unpopular, answers to the "intricate propositions of modern business and finance," he urged the formation of a nonelective "economic sub-Parliament" of experts. Another solution, proposed in 1935, was to so alter the franchise "as to assign due leadership to the more instructed and responsible elements." Having gone too far in broadening the basis of full citizenship, Britain must "retrace" her steps "for a short distance" by, for instance, giving more votes to heads of households.[16]

If he had tried, moreover, in his "radical" years to emasculate the House of Lords, he now wanted it made into a strong second chamber which would block sudden change. The anti-New Deal

Supreme Court in America functioned in the way in which the House of Lords had once properly functioned. Churchill warned those Americans complaining of the deadlock created by the Court's ruling certain social legislation unconstitutional that "to take the rigidity out of the Constitution" would be a disaster, for it is a shield of the individual, more a bulwark than a fetter. Yet he conceded that the letter of the law, archaic language, and pedantry must give way, as in Britain, to interpretations which conformed to new facts, lest violent plunges into Toryism be followed by socialism and then by fascism.

The pendulum swing was the pattern on the continent. In an age of universal suffrage, ignorant people, and mass media, the European parliaments established by nineteenth-century liberalism had, along with the older dynasties, been swept aside by dictators of the left or right, who, without the restraints of constitution, tradition, or a dynastic outlook, held much greater power than did kings. A constitutional (i.e., limited) monarchy, such as the one under which British democracy had blossomed, was his prescription for Portugal in 1910, Spain in 1938, and Italy, Yugoslavia, and Greece in 1944. With all its faults, he preferred Czarism to the alternative and defended Nicholas II from charges of tyranny and incompetence. If Americans therefore suspected that he backed "Right Wing governments or monarchies for their own sake," he in turn blamed the Allies for thinking, "under American and modernizing pressure," of the overthrow of dynasties as "a form of progress." His own views, expressed more than ever in a vein of sarcasm on modernity, progress, democracy, and liberalism, are, he realized, "very unfashionable." He had, after all, been almost alone in championing Edward VIII (though he fought against, often unsuccessfully, royal interference on such specific matters as the naming of warships in 1912–13, the prohibition of liquor in 1915, or his own participation in the Normandy invasion in 1944!), and after World War II, he, as a historian of the war and as a conservative, actually found the origins of the conflict in the driving out of Hapsburg and Hohenzollern dynasties in 1918.[17]

His reverence for monarchy distinguishes Churchill's European conservatism from the American brand. But like his American counterparts, he preferred, if he could not have a constitutional monarch, a right wing dictator in lieu of bolshevism. He believed that a society rent by civil strife can "only be reconstituted upon a military framework."[18] In the 1930s, he therefore exhibited an admiration for generals and strong men. And the anticommunism which predisposed him to fascist leaders like Mussolini, Hitler, and Franco also prevented him from seeing Gandhi, Lenin, and Trotsky as molders of a nation.

Despite his attraction to these modern rootless dictators, when it came to questions of culture and social institutions, Churchill's simple patriotism, nostalgia, and love of continuity mark him as almost reactionary, sentimental, antiquated. An unquestioning patriotism like his comes more easily to the conservative than to the liberal mentality. The only true values, he held, are tradition, experience, the British inheritance, "frequent recurrence to first principles," an understanding of what one fights for, a knowledge of the history of one's nation, a preference of custom over logic, and pride in the glorious achievements of the forefathers. Had he not declared as a young man that his political aim in life was to improve the British breed? Britain should not decline like Rome, he said in his first political speech, but carry peace and civilization to the ends of the earth. The "public schools," which produced the men who would administer the empire, inculcated not book learning but conduct, tradition, and standards of English responsibility. The manner in which the passengers and crew behaved while the Titanic sank proved to his satisfaction the humaneness, Christian piety, and democracy of British civilization, as against the ancient Greco-Roman, which could neither have built that ship nor lost it with honor. He often thanked his stars for having been born into his blessed land of freedom, fair play, and social services, a land unique in all history.[19]

But the greatness of England was created by her white males. Churchill's references to women and to race remained all his life colored by a Victorian paternalism. He found the sight of women involved in the war effort (in World War I) revolting and unchivalric; it was caused by forces (like the feminist movement) thought to be progressive but really part of the tide of modern barbarism. Visiting the Western hemisphere, he praised the "darky attendants" for being always a source of comfort and amusement on American trains; hurricanes in the Bahamas, he observed, are preceded by "instinctive premonitions of the Negroes and birds." In South Africa, though appalled by the Boers' treatment of blacks, he favored civil rights for white males, not for blacks or women. Indeed he expected the black peril to unite Boer and Englishman eventually. When he made the liberal statement that an intelligent community would rather govern itself ill than be governed well by someone else and that Britain did not have any knowledge of Boer problems, he meant by "intelligent" white—Irish and Boer—and was not prepared to apply this insight to Egypt and India. He spoke blandly of the "great white race all over the world." He feared that, as a result of contraceptives, the white people's desire for comfort and leisure in lieu of large families would, in conjunction with the fecundity of the yellow and brown races, cause a decline in civilization. Emancipation in America may have been noble, but the Fifteenth Amendment, which gave the blacks the vote, was to him only another example of a generous American ideal soured by implementation.[20]

In art also, Churchill veered toward tradition and the "disciplinarians." He was out of touch with modern painting and literature; his Victorian taste dismissed the new art by supposing its practitioners to be only after notoriety and profit or to be—in a false analogy he drew with politics—undisciplined and anarchic. In many things, he preferred the past over the present or future. He made a show of his adhering to the old spelling of "czar" and the old pronunciation of Latin. His mode of writing history was archaic. Believing capital punishment to be a deterrent, he would have executions open to the public.

In general philosophic outlook, he had, to be sure, his occasional liberal moments. In the settlement of the South African war, he did not mind if some Boers wished to have "Dutch teachers to teach Dutch children Dutch." He believed rather that the way to preserve the obnoxious *taal* dialect would be to proscribe it and so turn its illegal use into a deliberate and malicious protest against an act rightly regarded as intolerant. He likewise enunciated—but neglected to apply after 1911 to domestic policies—a liberal-radical principle: "When men are denied all status," as he later said apropos of the Spanish Civil War, "it is natural that in desperation they should prove their credentials by terror and show that force at least is on their side."[21] This observation anticipates Franz Fanon's and Hannah Arendt's definition of violence as the last resort of the powerless. So had he in his reformist phase used the radical argument that, if the obstruction of welfarist legislation by the Lords, Tories, and plutocrats incited the workers to resort to extralegal measures, the source of the violence will have been the former group and not the latter.

His first newspaper publication, an 1894 letter to the *Westminster Gazette* attacking a women's temperance society as "old women in a hurry," can be viewed as either liberal, in its thrust against the attempt to legislate morals and its argument that to improve by repression is counterproductive, or as conservative, in its preference for gradualism and evolution rather than legislation as a social corrective. Equally ambiguous is his assertion, in a letter of two years later, that governments should not sacrifice to posterity any generation for the sake of a principle. But more significant is Churchill's anxiety, recorded in a sympathetic and meliorist review of Upton Sinclair's *The Jungle*, a novel he saw as justifying the welfare laws Parliament was then passing year by year. He believed that if society was as bad and men were as selfish as the novel intimated, men would corrupt any system, and the most admirable system would merely transfer the social miseries from one group to another. Here is Churchill, in the midst of his radical phase, expressing philosophical reservations about the ultimate validity of his efforts.[22]

By the time of his conservative phase, in the 1930s and 1950s, Churchill came indeed to speak often with the voice of Edmund Burke. He insisted, for instance, that the onus always lies on the proposer of change, who must consider what is due to the past as well as claimed for the future. If the young, liberal Churchill liked to legislate and experiment, the old Churchill preferred social and legislative passivity. Relief to economic crises, he said, can be obtained only by cultivation. "Almost everything worth having here below is not manufactured but grown, and what is best usually grows slowly." He favored long Parliamentary recesses because a nation is "not built up like a scaffolding" or "fitted together like a machine" but grows rather like a "plant or tree . . . slowly and noiselessly."[23] Ignoring or postponing difficult decisions (in peacetime) may well be wise, because compromises and indeterminate courses, by satisfying various interests, often keep the nation undisturbed or allow apparently insoluble problems to fade away. He liked Henry II's and Henry VII's gradualist ways—cloaking innovation in conservative garb, respecting existing forms, opposing custom to custom, making hoary principle take on new meaning. He wanted to see modern principles clothed in the garments of the past; he enjoyed high-sounding titles. He even treasured legends and fables as having an importance in a nation's history.

Churchill repeatedly insisted that "all wisdom is not new wisdom, and the past should be studied if the future is to be successfully encountered." (Yet he had difficulty distinguishing the past from the legacy of the past; had he lived in the days of Buddha, Christ, or Mohammed, he once asserted, he would have opposed those teachers because of the turmoil and bloodshed they brought.) His conservatism as much as his British pride caused him to prefer the British unwritten constitution to the French or American written ones. Adverse to airy theorizing and abstract principles, to "theorists and doctrinaires," he preferred the gradual way, compromise, the respect for precedents and constitutional forms. His principle was that a venerable institution like Parliament should be altered only with great care: "In attempting to avoid an occasional anomaly, we might find that we had seriously affected the health and vigor of this famous, world-honored institution.... An innovation in our practice should be most carefully watched.... Sir, we must beware of needless innovation, especially when guided by logic.... Fortune is rightly malignant to those who break the traditions and customs of the past." He gave a characteristically idiosyncratic explanation of why he had the Commons building reconstructed after World War II in its apparently inefficient and unaccommodating shape. Even when someone proposed merely making the titles of two cabinet posts more descriptive, Churchill (who had in his youth made a similar suggestion about some army titles) asserted that tradition must not be flouted on behalf of logic.[24]

The young Churchill used favorably such words as "symmetrical," "logical," "complete," "fair," and "just"; the old Churchill preferred "tradition." Lord John Russell was not one of his heroes because of that worthy's "high devotion to the cause of liberty in the abstract, whatever the political consequences might be." Hence Churchill was not dissatisfied with the slow pace of the European Movement. Since under the pressure of danger and necessity many different nations will soon find it "obvious and inevitable," he would not attempt as yet "to define too precisely" its form. With his perennial Burkean bias against hasty system-building and "rigid constitution-making," he would have the union be, like the Anglo-American alliance or the British constitution, unwritten. Whether apropos of it or of the UN, he thought it better to proceed on a broad front not spelled out rather than attempting to obtain immediately by written treaties what is a "hopeless ideal." Nor should everything at issue between the Communist and Democratic states be settled at once; piecemeal and gradual solutions should be striven for.[25]

Churchill's philosophical conservatism is signally expressed by the major theme of the *History*, that of "disguised blessing," according to which, British liberty was frequently best served by those looking out after their own selfish interests, not by altruists and reformers. His conservatism also leads him to the justification, in the *History*, of certain forms of force and violence—

patriotic, defensive, legitimate—because they originate with those in positions of power and authority. It results likewise in a growing, explicit questioning of the idea of progress, in which he had, like a good Victorian, at first believed but which he came, as the twentieth century matured, more and more to question. When he declared that the minister in charge of postwar reconstruction cannot create "a new heaven, a new earth, and no doubt a new hell," nor "create a new heart in the human breast," the ideas that a new heaven and earth are elusive, a new hell is inevitable, and a new heart is impossible are central conservative assumptions.[26]

All this adds up to a picture of man with deeply conservative tendencies in every aspect of life, a man who yet showed glimmers of liberalism, moderation, centrism, or pragmatism at different junctures: in youth, toward domestic reform and certain imperial possessions and subjects; in old age, toward cooperation with Communists in the face of Hitler or the H-bomb. As a result, for many Britons, Americans, and Europeans, he was more often a part of the problem than of the solution—especially (and sometimes except) where war was concerned.[27]

3
The Warhorse

1

THE difficulty in pinpointing Churchill's political stance is mild next to the question of making sense out of his attitude to war. His long career, with its ups and downs, spanned periods of war (three major wars, in fact) and peace, and his attitude varied accordingly. He regarded war as, at first, a sporting affair; later, a challenge to one's wits, an enthralling theme for Clio, a means of establishing manliness and glory, a proof of personal honor, a preserver of the best virtues—courage, endurance, faith, determination, indomitability, patriotism—and sometimes the sole means of defending basic values, upholding or retrieving national honor. But did he do so in a humane or perverse fashion? Was his interest rooted in yet another legitimate conservative axiom or in a personal eccentricity?

Because his warnings in the late 1930s and his inspired leadership in 1940 have given Churchill a niche in history as the savior of Britain and of perhaps much else, some people overlooked the many failures in his earlier career, the hostility he often aroused, the ill repute he bore much of the time. Memories stirred, to be sure, in 1944–50, when his pronounced anti-Communist stand prompted his political opponents to pin the label of "warmonger" on him. This charge was not merely left wing apologetics but a revival of an accusation long hurled at him, even at the time of his philippics against Germany; Hitler himself only echoed British critics of all persuasion in calling him a blood-thirsty amateur strategist and warmonger, while those who esteemed him expressed their feelings with morally ambiguous phrases like "a man of war," "the god of war," "the old warhorse."[1] Throughout his career, Churchill was considered by many as a jingo eager to send military forces here or there, a saber rattler not only against bolsheviks but against just about anyone. We may well wonder now at the moral paradox that someone who finally stood up to a real warlord like Hitler should himself be considered a "warmonger"—unless this was a situation requiring homeopathic treatment, fighting fire with fire.

In grappling with the complex question of whether Churchill was in fact a power-hungry war lover, one must first acknowledge a profound correlation between Churchill and military life. He was mainly a politician and a writer, but these two vocations began with, and during the rest of his long life revolved around, war. His "first coherent memory" was of soldiers and volleys, even as his first passion was for toy soldiers and, later, for tracing military or naval campaigns on maps. As a boy he loved such activities as building sand forts, blowing up a haunted house, or reading about the American Civil War; when in school, he relished the Harrow "army" maneuvers and drew a sketch map of the war. These might be the diversions of all youths, but in September 1894, the nearly twenty-year old man wrote to his parents, who were traveling in Japan at the time of the Sino-Japanese war, "It must be interesting to be so near the seat of war"; he was signally curious about the Japanese naval and military operations, the brilliant timing and effect of a rare night attack.[2]

His father, impressed by his obsession with toys soldiers and not regarding the boy as good for anything else, dispatched him into a military career. Attending the Royal Military College of Sandhurst, Churchill at last found a school environment to his liking. Desirous, after graduation in 1895, of some extramural military education, he rushed off across thousands of miles to the only war this impoverished world could offer, that between Cuban insurgents and the decadent Spanish empire. There he made shrewd observations, wrote newspaper dispatches, and enjoyed himself thoroughly. Then, within less than four years, he garnered medals as an adventurous junior officer and correspondent in the three British imperial frontier wars that rounded out the century—in India, the Sudan, and South Africa. As he later put it, he had dreamed of war very early and had, as a young man, risked court martial in search of it. Thoughts of oratory and politics were temporarily eclipsed by the excitement of bullets. He would not prematurely leave the army for a political career lest he lose his self-respect and he always believed thereafter that military service was essential to a political career. He certainly had more military experience than any other civilian leader of a nation, and he is at his best as a historian when writing on wars.[3]

He shifted eventually to his father's vocation of politics, which he said, is almost as exciting as war and quite as dangerous because in it one can be killed often. As his politics became liberal (in 1904–11), he drifted somewhat away from his military interests. Yet he attended maneuvers and war games in Britain and in Europe even while holding nomilitary posts in 1906–10. He studied the battlefields of the past—Blenheim, the Franco-Prussian War, the American Civil War. Then, with war clouds gathering in 1911, he went to the Admiralty and a succession of similar posts. What Churchill was to say later of Mountbatten, that he had thrived in the four elements of war (land, sea, air, and fire), was true of himself: five years in the army, as an officer; five years as civilian head of the navy and as head, indeed one of the founders, of the air force. He thus spent nearly a decade of his life in, or at the head of, each military service and, as he reminisced, "had the good fortune to be in all the wars that Great Britain has been engaged in in one capacity or another during my lifetime." His was, conceded J. M. Keynes, "the most acute and concentrated intelligence" to observe war from up close.[4]

What impelled Churchill into these commitments was, of course, in good part, love of country. Combat seeming to be the definitive altruistic gesture, Churchill found great joy and fearlessness in fighting to the death for a noble cause. In World War II he would have the army appeal to men "who wish to fortify their lives by a special sacrifice for our country," and he reminded everyone that they were fighting for a cause even "greater than a country . . . that of freedom and justice." Far from dismissing war as an evil, he made a characteristic distinction between "the curse of war and the darker curse of tyranny," and he always scorned mere survival. Insisting that he loved life but did not fear death, he saw nothing idiosyncratic in his stance; "the one thing" which people cannot forgive, he asserted, "is being shut out of their honorable and legitimate chance of taking part in a supreme national struggle."[5]

Wedded to this patriotism, however, was an undeniable love of combat for its own sake. He loved it for being "action, energy, and hazard." He celebrated such "intense experiences of war" as the minutes immediately before the "unknowable situation" of a battle and the unique "thrill" of "a surprise attack at dawn." He enjoyed the experience of combat, the testing of will and courage, the garnering of medals, and even the look of uniforms, rather as others enjoy football, war movies, or paintings of the crucifixion—that is, scenes of cruelty transmuted by esthetic distance. This taste for war, out of fashion in our century, found brilliant if naive expression in his very first writings, the frontier war books of 1897–1900.[6]

Subsequent wars, to be sure, lost much of their charm. They had become a matter of "Men, Money, and Machinery," of "entire populations" fighting in "brutish mutual extermination." Yet Churchill found things to cherish even amid the impersonality of modern war. His ambivalence revealed itself in the phrase, "the stimulating but disagreeable conditions of war," no less than in the only half-ironic regret over the failure, in the 1930s, of the hope in electro-magnetic waves which would detonate all explosives from afar and which would return war to "the crude but healthy limits of the barbarous ages. The sword, the spear, the bludgeon, and above all the fighting man, would regain at a bound their sovereignty." Or in the "shock" with which he heard, after World War II, the new classification of warfare into "conventional" and "unconventional" (i.e., atomic)—as if something precious were being taken away from him.[7]

Though on the eve of World War I, he saw conflict as vile, foolish, barbarous, wicked, as an appalling calamity for civilization, he yet confessed that it attracted him greatly. (In 1912 he proudly called a memo on military matters a "prose poem.") Excited by crisis and action, by the movement of troops, by battles and important military results, he felt ashamed about the horrible "levity" of his hideous fascination with the preparations for, and the advent of, the Great War. A colleague had thought that should war come, Churchill would beat Lloyd George "hollow," and when it did come, Churchill, alone calm and prepared, seemed indeed to flower. Finding it ignoble to cheer the rowers from the bank and having a taste of shelling in Antwerp, he wanted to leave his high government post "to go to the War and fight and be a soldier." While he congratulated Lloyd George on his baptism of fire during a visit to the front, he added that "the taste forms if not cloyed by surfeit." As he watched a bombardment, he spoke of his "splendid" view of the "whole entertainment." To his wife he wrote that shells did not make him jump or quicken his pulse, and to Margot Asquith he confessed with glowing eyes and guilty conscience that he would not be out of "this glorious delicious war for anything"—not even for the once-coveted vice-royalty of India. When he joined the army on the front lines, he appeared to his officer colleagues as a fearless man who regarded war as a game to be played with a smile, who reveled in it, and who led a charmed, carefree life amid bullets. More exhilarated by the sounds of combat than are most professional soldiers, Churchill, like no other European minister, could stand and smoke a cigar calmly in the midst of the shellfire.[8]

Machines of war, whether the new gunboats of the River War, "remarkable in every way," or the newest battleships in either world war, always excited Churchill. A characteristic picture is of his impressing everyone (as first lord) at a Cabinet meeting with a model of a newly developed photoelectric cell to be used in mines; or, during a visit to Normandy, proudly timing with a stopwatch the debarcation of tanks from the landing craft he had helped develop.

His writings during the interwar years—the huge *Marlborough* and *History*—exhibited this peculiar compound of sangfroid and excitement. In passages on the American Civil War, the words and accent of several quotations may be Southern, but the emotions clearly belong as well to the author. For example, during a desperate battle at dawn, Jackson muttered to his companion, "delicious excitement"! And Lee, surveying a field of carnage, observed reflectively, "It is well that war is horrible—we would grow too fond of it."[9]

During World War II Churchill came close to making the British people enjoy war as much as he did. Subject to the Blitz, the students of Harrow and Malvern should be, he lectured them, "very proud of having had the honor of being under the fire of the enemy at such an early age—a very great privilege and a piece of good fortune." The Churchillian posture in the wartime speeches, of determined resignation, is spiced in the retrospective narrative of the *Second World War* with a joie de vivre, a delight in the challenges and adversities of combat. Nor was this mere posing. Just as in World War I someone observed that Churchill "gets younger under the strain instead of older," so now acquaintances remarked that he had not seemed so fit in the previous years, that "being Prime Minister and a historic figure" rejuvenated him (at least at first, during the lean, heroic years), that "his responsibility seems to have given him a new lease on life," and to have brought out greatness of soul. In 1944, Churchill seemed ten years younger at a Cabinet meeting, "all due," surmised one of his leading generals, "to the fact that the flying bombs have again put us into the front time."[10]

In postwar years he gloried in the achievements of 1940 and would choose to relive that year more than any other of his life; likewise he was prouder of his military decisions than of his speeches in that crisis. Had not his very first book spoken prophetically of making a gallant last stand at London and of those who thrive better when confronting disaster and defeat rather than victory? Churchill was in fact criticized, then and since, for conceiving "of the war in medieval terms," talking "of it as if it were a tourney," swathing the terrible human suffering in poetic terms and sentimental rhetoric about epic glory, exhibiting "adolescent irresponsibility" in using words like "fun" and "the good things" about combat. Where Hitler and Mussolini, comments G. K. Lewis, saw war as the moment of apocalyptic destruction and most people see it as the expression of the worst in us, Churchill thought it was noble chivalry.[11]

II

The love of the sheer panorama of combat—the sensuous excitement, the gamble, the adventure—is to be distinguished from the special intellectual pleasure available only to the few: that of generalship, leadership, strategy making. Churchill not only sought to participate in battle but, confident of his own military judgment, he also desired to shape the battle and to handle large forces. What T. E. Lawrence was to do informally, Churchill dreamed of in 1911: commanding during the next war an army in a decisive victory in the Middle East and returning triumphantly. With the advent of hostilities he soon wanted to organize a "heroic adventure against Gallipoli and the Dardanelles"; hence his commitment to the Dardanelles expedition that eventually materialized and that, coming to be regarded as his foster child (early successes gave him an ascendancy), seemed to be fulfilling his dreams. Throughout the war, Churchill, scorning the political life, saw in himself the potential for a great soldier because he alone could visualize large movements and combinations. If he could not be made a general, he would not take any governmental posts except in a military department; like Pitt, he believed that only he could save the nation.[12]

Not content with guiding the fleet at the Admiralty, he played at being a general by building up his Royal Naval Division and sending it hither and yon. It came to be known as "his own little army" (or, to Asquith, as the "Winstons"), which he often inspected in France while wearing a uniform of his own design. He managed to make himself for a few days, during the defense of Antwerp, the chief of the Belgian government and armed services. When his offer to resign the Admiralty post for the sake of a general's hat was turned down, he continued to visit the French front on matters not connected with the Admiralty, infuriating Field Marshall Kitchener, then secretary of state for war, for meddling (as he would again in World War II when first lord) in military matters. Although really happy to be able to have the power at the Admiralty to control events at the storm center, he seemed to be only waiting for the expected big sea battle which would destroy the German fleet and so release him for service on the main front. He later hoped, in vain, for a command of British forces against Germans in East Africa. The command of a mere battalion in Flanders, which he actually obtained for a brief period, left him with a gnawing sense that his war-making talents were being squandered.[13] After the war, his attempts to coordinate and mastermind the abortive allied effort to destroy the new Bolshevik regime gave him the chance to play for large stakes; he must have had visions of bettering Napoleon when he traced on a map in his office the forces converging on Moscow from all directions.

Never achieving field command of entire armies or fleets, Churchill tried his best to simulate being a general by bombarding his cabinet colleagues, notably the prime minister, before and during World War I, with memos on land strategy. Some of these, like the one of 1911, which saw fulfillment in 1914, were highly praised by civilians and military men alike. By means of a political career, he also achieved vicarious command without having to put in long periods in rank: he got himself appointed civilian chief of each of the services—the Admiralty, the war and air offices, the munitions ministry—and, finally, prime minister in wartime. In modern war an official position connected with the services, he reasoned—or rationalized—is like, or even superior to, the leadership of an army. If he could not command armies, he could at least command the commanders. To ensure that this was the case, he, the only British prime minister in history to wear a military uniform in office, chaired the chiefs of staffs committee and, making it directly responsible to him rather than to the Cabinet, personally supervised military strategy as no prime minister (or Roosevelt) ever did. Domestic matters or postwar aims bored one who liked to think of placing twenty divisions there, a battle fleet here, or who was eager to halve British rations in order to attack Italy. But even that did not suffice: rushing to the front at every opportunity, he confessed to General Alexander that he envied him his victorious command. As Birkenhead pithily said of Churchill in World War I, "not one Department, hardly one war, was enough for him." To be at long last prime minister in a great war—to direct the Cabinet, the services, the House, and England herself—was "beyond even his dreams" noted an observer. "He loves every minute of it."[14]

He certainly consorted in his imagination with the likes of Napoleon and Marlborough. He impressed many people as overly convinced that he inherited his ancestor's military genius. Delighted to have generals, admirals, air marshals, and dominion leaders in attendance at his various conferences abroad, Churchill appeared to be playing to the hilt the role of Marlborough "riding the whirlwind and directing the storm" (in the oft-quoted words of Joseph Addison's 1704 poem on Marlborough, "The Campaign").

This aesthetic love of combat and attraction to leadership positions in the extreme conditions of war cannot be extricated from a personal belligerence, a character flaw, a Yahoo streak. Not for nothing do the words "military" and "militant" have common roots. From early on, Churchill irritated people by being dictatorial and demonic, a man "closed to the gentle gradations of the human mind" and driven by blood lusts against his foes and brainstorms against his rivals. In his zeal for the empire, he struck people, when he was in the Colonial Office, of being capable of annexing something in Africa or of leading Congo rebels against King Leopold. During several labor strikes, he exhibited what seemed a "bloody"attitude, an impatience with both workers and their rich employers. On the eve of World War I, he was "very bellicose and demanding immediate mobilization"; as the leader of the "war party" in the Cabinet, he longed for a sea battle and for violating the neutrality of certain states. His attachment to Napoleon struck some observers as ominous; he appeared to them "such a personal force for evil," a man of blood who prayed against peace, a would-be führer who delighted in fighting, a soldier-strategist who threatened to write his name in blood, who had long sought World War I as a chance for gaining glory without regard to the misery he would cause thousands of men. Relishing a good fight, he declared in old age that the spectacle of his middle-aged opponents "in a state of uproar and fury is really quite exhilarating to me. I have not had fifty years' actual service in this House without having got used to the rough-and-tumble of debate."[15]

His instinct for the melodramatic blossomed in wartime into truculence and megalomania. He always favored harsh measures, like shooting at ships bearing white flags; retaliating with gas and with terror bombing; billeting workers as if they were soldiers;

using seventeen-year-olds in the military services; letting the Belgian population starve and so distract the German occupation forces rather than admitting it to Britain. He often wanted domestic issues grappled with by means of quasi-military organizations. Ever ready to apply military force to civilian problems, he thought that a little bloodshed during the General Strike of 1926 would do no harm. In some circumstances, "force has to be used to save life as well as to take life. . . . Pugnacity and will power cannot be dispensed with." Oblivious on numerous occasions to the realities, he demanded street fighting to the last man, and he wrote an essay on "Great Fighters for Lost Causes," which expressed, among other things, the beauty of having men fight a quarrel to the end.[16]

Churchill was, to be sure, neither a warmonger nor a sadist. He loved a scrap, not a slaughter; his maxim for war conduct was "vigor, not rigor." He acknowledged that excesses of good sentiment could beget evil reactions, that militarism, loyalty, humanism, patriotism, and imperialism could become brutality, tyranny, maudlinism, cant, and jingoism. He warned that government, secure in the knowledge that it can always use force, must yet "avoid such hateful conclusions," for once blood has been shed, "that makes a different tale." He could ironically note that to a child (and therefore to the adult world) a "very great man" is someone who "had blown up all sorts of things." As a young man he praised Britain's way of expanding her influence by such nonmilitary means as subsidies to tribal leaders; "silver makes a better weapon than steel." He noted that in war "both sides lose whoever wins the victory." He bemoaned the arms race in an eloquent, apparently deeply felt speech of March 1912. Keynes pointed out that Churchill was, to a degree little known, a "persistent advocate of appeasement" and a moderate toward Germany, Ireland, and Turkey in pre-World War I years. And he did help bring peace (for a while) to Palestine and Ireland in the early 1920s.

Writing about himself in 1936, he maintained that though he had studied, served in, prepared for, and written about war, he did not delight in it and often tried to prevent it. Had his proposed naval holiday of 1912 been accepted by the Kaiser's government—he naively insisted—there would have been no conflict. As long as war can be avoided, Churchill advocates all sorts of diplomatic initiatives (such as his wish in July 1914 for a conference of all the major European monarchs to prevent disaster), always coupled, of course, with military preparedness.

Once war is inevitable, however, the peace-making Dr. Jekyll is abruptly replaced by his Mr. Hyde counterpart—the bellicose man who found war exciting, strategy challenging, and all-out attack necessary. Most politicians are proficient either at seeking peaceful resolutions through negotiations or at cold-bloodedly making war. Churchill was one of those rare persons adept at both.

On the other hand, one should not rule out the existence of a streak of violence. As a young man he spoke candidly of an "aboriginal desire" to kill the odious Dervishes and of his delight in doing it. In *Savrola* and the Frontier War books, the lust to kill, briefly revealed, is said to be ingrained in the human heart. He speaks of "those deep-seated instincts of savagery, over which civilization has but cast a veil of doubtful thickness," of a "cruel devil" who lurks in men's hearts and is "awakened by bloodshed and danger." His private utterances, on various occasions, about the filthy, vile Germans, Frenchmen, Turks, or Communists can be related to his periodic fantasies of bombing people who annoyed him.

There is an unholy zest in his continual casting about for enemies—and Britain's enemies are always, conveniently, against the liberties of the world. (He forgets that during the Napoleonic Wars and World War I the Irish rebelled *against* the British in quest of liberty.) To one seeing everything as a pragmatic question of the balance of power—when it pleased him to set sentiment about "common causes" aside—there was always another enemy in the field, and the problem was simply ascertaining who was the leading enemy. Having sided with Mussolini against bolshevism in the 1920s, he came to side with bolshevism against Mussolini (and his partner) in the 1940s. Just as after World War I he feared an alliance against the West of Germany and Russia (and possibly Turkey), along bolshevik or anti-bolshevik lines, so could he calmly contemplate at the end of World War II the possibility that the wartime alliance would be replaced soon by a new confrontation, this time of the European imperial powers (Britain, France, et al.) against the non-European non-imperial power (the United States, Russia, China). The advent of the Cold War in the wake of the hot one shows that "intolerance and persecution are no sooner overcome than they return in new shapes"; something or someone always seems to come along—"these tribes of nationalists, ideologues, revolutionaries, class warfare experts, and imperialists with their nasty regimentation"—with the result that homes are bombed instead of built. To Hans Morgenthau, who sets aside the ideological rhetoric, this awareness of power politics was a strength of Churchill's and much preferable to American naiveté. But others found it difficult to set so much rhetoric about country and cause easily aside; they surmised it to be rationalization for unseemly national greed or personal blood lust.[17]

III

Churchill's enjoyment of all aspects of war came to dominate his voluminous writings and his philosophy of history. In lieu of being a general, he made himself a military historian, and he later admitted himself fully qualified to receive an award for the "writing of books about war." One reviewer even complained that his books dwell more on anarchy than on culture. Certainly Churchill's mind was suffused with wars. In 1929–33, for instance, he was busy writing of recent battles (finishing the last volumes on World War I), studying remote battles (Marlborough's 1704 campaign in Germany) and unwittingly preparing for future ones by warning of German rearming and the rise of Hitler.

Even when deflected from military matters, he brought his military obsession with him. His paeans to painting and writing are so affected: the painter's application of colors or the writer's assembling of material is likened to the general's disposition of military forces. When he spoke of the need for hierarchy, he found the analogue not in church, business, or government, but in the army. Indeed in all his writings, no matter what the subject—be it be a drug for pneumonia or the organization of the UN—military imagery, some critics complained, came too easily to him. He even planned, in 1900, to write an essay on "The Ethics of Slaughter." As A. G. Gardiner remarked long ago, "He sees life in terms of war, and his high and turbulent spirit is entirely happy only when politics and war are merged in one theme."[18]

War therefore tempered his approach to every question. Though moved in December 1901 by Rowntree's *Poverty*, he wrote a review of it in which the worst he could say about social squalor was that it was bad for army recruiting. He admired the Israelis mainly for establishing "the best army in the Levant." He regarded Julius Caesar as the greatest of all men because he was a magnanimous conqueror. "The prizes of war," he wrote in 1901, "are the greatest that a man may wish," and much later he called the battles of Crecy, Blenheim, Waterloo, and of the summer of 1918 as—without any humane qualifications—the "four supreme achievements."[19] He spoke smugly of the "sublime function of military genius." By the "glories of the past" or "the glories of the Napoleonic era," he too often seems to mean the battles that Britain fought, putatively for human rights and freedom.

Other wars were no less glamorous. The "agonizing" American Civil War was "forever illuminated by drama and romance"; it was an "immortal struggle" that celebrated "the martial virtues and civic fidelity of both sides." World War II is "one of the greatest" to "have ever glorified, torn, and dignified the human race."[20]

War is the commanding reality, and all other institutions and endeavors have to be subordinated to that fact. In 1919, he did not share the widespread conviction at that "enthusiastic moment" that hostilities were ended forever. Rather, as he reminded his readers on the eve of World War II, the history of man is mainly a tale of wars, with a few uneasy intervals of peace; although everyone now was against war, it yet drew ever nearer. Nor is the fashionable pacifism historically correct: Churchill mimics contemptuously, "Let men bleat, 'war settles nothing.'" On the contrary, notwithstanding modern opinion that battles are mere incidents in the greater drama of social and economic forces, he insists that battles are "the principal milestones," changing the entire course of events, creating new standards and conditions in every way; the victory of Blenheim, for example, settled the destiny of Europe for a century. Churchill sometimes even sounds curiously like Chairman Mao: "In the advance of culture, precedence was regulated by gunpowder." The Maxim gun, for instance, enabled Christianity to survive its encounters with Islam. Since nations cannot survive without knowing the art of war, the French army is, as the shield against invasion from Germany or Italy, "the highest expression" of the soul of France. He also—rather simplistically—ascribed the fall of the British Empire in Asia to "the loss of influence inherent in our early defeats in the Far Eastern war."[21]

War and its appurtenances are not only unavoidable and influential but even salutary. If the modern literary sensibility regards military service as brutalizing, mindless, and authoritarian, Churchill does not. He insisted that the British navy is one of the finest schools of manhood in the world; that, were they to serve in the wartime army, sixteen-year-olds would garner rich experiences and increase their professional value; that the education of any young man can only benefit from a period of military training, especially if the "bonds of discipline are genial" and the "background of service great." The military way is often the civilized way, and so highly did he think of military discipline that in 1935 he wanted to see it introduced into the great universities to curb the prevailing (and in the 1960s again familiar) "long hair, untidy clothes, and subversive opinions."[22]

Like military routine, combat itself may be less barbaric than heuristic. As but another of the challenges of adversity, it can paradoxically humanize men and societies. Only the soldier at war, living at the top of his bent, discovers or realizes his inner self, perhaps his best self. In Churchill's Machiavellian vision, the "crunch of war" is seen as a healthy catalyst. It is a harsh school teaching men to discard unessentials, grasp realities, and establish organization. Exacting great exertion, it ushers in "superior solutions" which help the world progress, however fitfully. The "hardest of teachers," it is the "only one to whom attention is paid," and he was proud of his people for being, "once compelled to go there, ... attentive pupils" and learning "under [its] rod.[23]

Hence young Churchill exonerated the rebel leader, the Mahdi, who was blamed by Europeans for arousing the Sudanese from their torpor. The Madhi's greatness lay in his having animated his countrymen and freed his land of foreigners, and to the philosopher, the consequent destruction of trade, property, and life has, Churchill believes, a certain value in contributing to the development of men's souls. Savrola, the hero for Churchill's early novel, concedes reluctantly that "might is a form of fitness, ... a low form, but still physical force contains the elements of human progress"; technology will enable an effete Europe to preserve moral ascendancy against the "valiant savages." For in this wicked world, right must sustain itself with force or threat of force, and Churchill only slowly, with the advent of the A-bomb, outgrew his youthful celebration of the role of force in the advancement of civilization, Christianity, and scientific progress. On the frontiers, he had said, apparently without a hint of irony, "the religion of blood and war [Islam] is face to face with that of peace. Luckily the religion of peace is better armed"; as a result, "credulity and fanaticism [are] now happily passing away from the earth, under the combined influence of rationalism and machine guns."[24]

War simplifies. Churchill often remarked on how the problems of peace are more difficult and (as only he could think!) even more perilous than those of war; they require more "patience, courage, and perseverance." War limits choices, simplifies questions, and unifies people, while peace does the reverse, opening up a diversity of aim, clatter, minor turmoil, even as it limits the power of government; peace offers no "clear-cut objective of victory", no "unity of purpose."[25] He dismisses as drab certain periods of security, prosperity and peace in English history, periods in which "apathetic tolerance prevailed." War is the test of greatness, individual or national.

The "lash of disaster," he had early noted (it became a refrain of his books), is unfortunately "always needed before victory is won." In the 1930s he wondered why conscription, coalition government, unified commands, and a war cabinet were not instituted at the beginning of the Great War but had to wait for the carnage and the terrible experience which taught men much. Then in the Spanish Civil War, new structures and possible unity were again being erected in "blood, sweat, and tears"; the Loyalists had become disciplined and had repressed the wholesale butcheries, for "when the structure of civilized life is destroyed by atavistic hatreds, the State can only be reconstructed upon a military framework." War is inevitable because man is otherwise unteachable. As a student of war, a proponent of firmness, and a believer in strong men, Churchill concludes as he had in his earliest works: "War, the hardest of all teachers, is the only one to whom attention is paid."[26]

War, he declared decades later, has brought about the boon of modernity, and "it may be that the hard teachings of war are one of those instruments by which these changes [of automation] are forced upon us." Among the good things that war, the fear of war, and modern military preparedness may finally bring is peace itself. As early as 1947, he asserted that the A-bomb is a guarantee of peace, shocking though that be to those born in the nineteenth century and mocking though it be of their pacifist dreams.[27]

Such a conclusion naturally coincided with the great paradoxical philosophy of his career—that lenity, legality, and humanitarianism merely increase suffering. In 1915 he remarked that President Wilson's criticism of harsh British naval measures not only prolonged war and destruction but overlooked a lesson from America's own past: the North's scorched earth policy in Georgia proved that sometimes severity is the quickest and most humane way of terminating hostilities.[28] Later, in India, the British government's soothing sentiments had to be followed with rough measures like the jailing of twenty-four thousand natives. From the first Britain should have arrested and tried agitators like Gandhi and concurrently advanced the "material conditions" of the masses.[29] If Foreign Secretary Grey raised the standard liberal objection to Churchill's wish to retaliate in kind on the Germans for bombing open towns in World War I—that such actions only put Britain on the same moral plane as the perpetrators—Churchill made the equally typical rejoinder that Grey would in time have to change his mind. Since, whatever the claims of moralists, men are often governed by force, fear, and the desire to be on the winning side, he insisted at various junctures that people (like the Turks or the Dutch) who were the objects of harsh British measures would in the long run be better off.[30]

Hence his famous, lifelong antiappeasement stance. Yet Churchill is careful to distinguish his policy from an advocacy of violence. Through the decades he saw the issue as, given the ironies of human nature, between his own long-range pacifism and the government's pacific rhetoric and inept action, which would lead unintentionally to severity and violence. Platitudinous speeches and "short-sighted optimism" are useless, he believed, for the idea that aggression can be stopped only by the resolve to use force is a "mocking paradox" but true. Passive resistance tempted the dictators into imprudent steps from which withdrawal by them was impossible. Had Britain armed in time in the 1930s, war would have been averted. To dwell on the horrors of war would not prevent a foe from beginning one, and Hitler's policy of aggression without war succeeded because the mere threat of force sufficed. So also, in the postwar years, did the Soviet leaders admire strength and despise weakness. If the hostile camps were equal, war would follow, but only a preponderance of force could avert war. Had there been peacetime conscription in the past, Britain's attempt before each world war to be a peacemaker would have carried more weight. He therefore opposed unilateral British nuclear disarmament, because a hearing can be gotten for one's views—as Churchill puts it—only if one has "a stake in the balance of world power" and such stakes "are still measured in military language."[31]

Though he saw himself as a figure easily mocked, a "pacifist who is ready to fight for peace," he insisted that safety would be gained only by the "pacific nations" amassing great powers and being ready for the sacrifice, even ruthlessness, of the "warrior mind." Justice must have her sword, and peace its constables. His greatest admiration was reserved for defenders of their nation, who are praised—in a typical Churchillian distinction—for preferring peace, not for avoiding war. The very depravity of man, which some would invoke as an argument for turning the other cheek rather than going to war and loosing worse evils, Churchill implicitly uses as reason for toughness, for the paradox of peace through might, because only militancy can control the Old Adam.

Thus it was that he, while deriding Stalin's contemptuous remark about the Pope's divisions, really thought in similar fashion. He ignored the possibility that such a hawkish attitude may be applied where the nation's vital interests are not at stake and thereby may lead to fruitless wars; or that it may, by hardening in turn the other side, become a self-fulfilling prophecy. His militaristic swagger and masculine machismo appear in such remarks as the one about Nietzsche preaching the gospel of violence while not being able to "wield even a peashooter" and in his contempt for the intelligent but pacific Chinese (his epithets) for regarding war as uncivilized and soldiers as despicable.[32]

IV

Churchill so rejoiced in soldier's honor, battlefield vistas, the challenge of strategy, and the exercise of war power that, as many remarked, he often overlooked the purpose of the fight or forgot to be glad when hostilities were concluded with a victorious peace. Without anything to fight for in peacetime, he often became spiritually unemployed. One colleague found him "so brave in war and so cowardly in peace."[33] He always sides in his books with militancy against allegedly self-defeating peace parties, for war exists for its own sake, while peace, in Violet Barbour's words, "must give sureties for good behavior." Churchill yearned for the simple resolutions of the battlefield. He could see pacifists only as defeatists, cowards, or revolutionaries, not as men holding a legitimate philosophical position grounded in Scripture.[34]

Churchill's idiosyncratic interests, of course, helped make him the one man for the crisis of 1940 even as they made him out of place in many of the other peacetime crises during his fifty-five year career. They enabled him to provide the requisite national leadership, perfervid oratory, animating spirit, and will to win. In the simplified conditions of war, as not during the complex days of peace, Churchill, like Pitt, thrived. His words and phrases made Britons discover the heroism of which they were capable, and one auditor at least could say, "I feel so much in the spirit of Winston's great speech that I could face a world of enemies."[35] If, in World War I, Churchill, wishing "for a month of power and a good shorthand writer," was sure that more could be gotten out of him in two years of war than in one hundred years thereafter and that he would make an effective war leader, "better" than "any other living Englishman," he did not obtain the chance to prove himself till a quarter of a century later.[36]

Yet few of the politicians and generals who have advocated the "hard line" as a diplomacy which is ultimately compassionate did it with such persistence and eloquence over so long a period, and fewer still with such a suspicious background. His lifelong interest in military matters, quest for battlefield glory, love of the panorama of combat, delight in the chess game of war strategy, dreams of being a great general, proficiency in war administration, experience of many wars, devotion to country at all costs, acceptance of war as a policy, belief in firmness, in strong leaders, in the necessary bloodshed that makes civilization possible—like his bellicose temperament and the centrality of war in his books, metaphoric language, vision of history, and theory of education—have naturally caused his antiappeasement posture to be taken for war-mongering. That his values occasionally pushed him to a worship of extremism, authority, hierarchy, military discipline, truculence, and even an apparent love of battle for its own sake should not, however, consign him to the company of such overt, consistent, bona fide military adventurers and expansionists as Attila and Hitler.

Churchill is a man in whom a perverse twentieth-century civilization activated interests and abilities which—judging from his early years of commitment to domestic liberalism, social reform, and military retrenchment—might otherwise have remained dormant. War gave him a opportunity for the full employment of his potential, and one great war climaxed his career. Having always idolized great war leaders, he finally became one.[37]

At the beginning of the century and of his career he had himself predicted, moreover, that twentieth-century wars would be long and brutal. He was among the first to take note of the major new factors in modern warfare—the vastly greater firepower, the general indifference to the loss of life, and the impact of technology on modern warfare with the consequent existence of a scientific race invisibly paralleling, as well as feeding into, the contest on the battlefields. He was therefore right to complain that, in such conditions, to take an interest in, and to accumulate knowledge and experience of, military matters is to be regarded unfairly by the foolish as a warmonger. Nor can one hold against him his catalytic role in the development of some of the major weapons of the twentieth century—the tank and warplane in World War I, the tank landing craft and the artificial harbor in World War II—if such study and zeal led to the defeat of Wilhelmine and Nazi Germany.

His intuition, remarks Goronwy Rees, that war was the most important force shaping men's live in modern times and his acceptance of the consequences of this made him a statesman, gave him a tragic depth, revealed him to be more contemporary than anyone else, and set him apart from all other democratic statesmen of the age.[38] Given the complexity of human motivation, it is in the end impossible to separate his idiosyncratic, unhealthy fascination with war from his perfectly legitimate ideas about the unfortunate but undoubted role war plays in human affairs and the need to come to grips with the resultant problems. If war is inevitable, it is because of an ugly streak in human nature which showed itself all too visibly in Churchill, concurrently (and paradoxically) with some cogent arguments for preventing the onset of war and minimizing its danger—for coping with that same streak when, because of sadism or stupidity, it appeared in others in unadulterated form. Having been inoculated, he had only a mild and benign form of war fever, which he mostly put to good uses.

He was the man for extreme situations. The basic gnawing philosophic question is whether he compounded the problem or helped diminish it. The dour judgment of most people seems to be that, if Berthold Brecht pitied the nation that needs a hero, part of the tragedy of our times is that someone essentially archaic like Churchill, with his strident antiappeasement theme of the 1930s (and perhaps of the late 1940s), his indomitability of 1940, and rather special interests and obsessions, may still be indispensable at certain junctures.

4
The Dreamer

OTHER men, great and small, have been interested in—or obsessed with—war. Few, however, have had someone like the first Duke of Marlborough for an ancestor, a circumstance that invited a rich fantasy life. Churchill's dreams of participating, leading, winning in combat indeed threatened, in the eyes of many not unsympathetic observers, to go to his head. That he should eventually deliver a biography of his ancestor was therefore hardly surprising, and perhaps even therapeutic. But what resulted from the interplay of the biographer's velleities or intuitions and of contemporary events is more anomalous.

I

In 1929, when he left the chancellorship of the Exchequer, Winston Churchill's career in government may well have seemed to be petering out. Although he was soon made a member of the "Shadow Cabinet" of the Conservative Opposition, he resigned that position in 1931 because of dissent over the question of India. Estranged from the Conservatives for a second time, he had begun his years in the political wilderness. In private, he spoke of withdrawing from politics altogether.

Looking back then, he must have considered his public life with melancholy. Long ago, he had, after gaining fame during the Boer War, entered upon a brilliant political career. Moving in the highest political circles, he had in but ten years come to be considered, at the age of thirty-seven, dynamic enough to be assigned the task of putting the unprepared Admiralty—that British shield and sword—on a modern war footing. This he did signally. Then had come the Dardanelles expedition. At his post in the Admiralty he had not had enough power to push it through to its consummation, and it died amid irresolution, conflicting wills, the absence of a comprehensive directing intelligence.

Insisting that the disaster had not been of his making and could have been avoided in any of several ways, he felt himself abandoned by leaders who needed a scapegoat to appease public opinion. Though he went on later to hold most of the other prominent posts in government—in Munitions, the War Office, the Exchequer—it seemed that in the eye of public and press he would always be associated with the two hundred thousand British casualties at Gallipoli. He would never be entrusted with the post at the helm and, with it, the chance to redeem himself unhampered by others' power of overruling, the chance to show his mettle and fulfill the potential he surely had in him.

He had probably entered upon the composition of the *World Crisis*, in the decade after World War I, partly in order to justify his role in the disaster; Volume II of the work is mainly an apologia. Having finished that, having found renewed fame as author and been freed in 1929 of administrative responsibility, he now turned to writing the biography of Marlborough. This was an ambitious literary and historical project, requiring immersion in a remote age and in great masses of documents and books.

But why one million words and nearly ten years on Marlborough? The man had been, of course, not only an invincible general and a national hero but also Churchill's direct ancestor, the glorious founder of one of the great families of modern Britain. From childhood, Churchill had read everything about him he could lay his hands on. Perhaps he even had, from the time of his youthful and abortive entry upon a military career, secretly modeled his life on that of this "English worthy." If so, he had run into a check—a defeat such as Marlborough had never known. He seemed after all not destined to be another such hero. Perhaps, as his facility with pen and his early shift from military to journalistic and authorial endeavors intimated, he was destined to be remembered more as a man of words than action.

Very well, then; he would evoke for his age a figure from the heroic past and find satisfaction in vicarious heroic fulfillment. He would (to adapt his own words) choose to be "nailed" to the "cross of Thought" rather than of "Action" (MEL, 113)[1] or (to use Yeatsian language) strive for perfection of the work rather than of the life, content himself with dreaming of the "antiself," the projected image of what he would have wanted to be and the opposite of what he himself was. In writing, thirty years earlier, the biography of his father, Churchill had turned to the sources of his own being, had studied the man he revered, and the principles and values on which he based his own political career.

Then, in the just concluded *A Roving Commission: My Early Life* he depicted that career, which touched on minor wars. Now, by way of rounding out the familial picture and climaxing his career as author, he would turn to the family model of a military hero who thrived in a long major war. Hence, shut out from government and as he claimed—no doubt cavalierly—without resentment or pain "at being so decisively discarded in a moment of national stress" (SWW, I, 36), he retired to write *Marlborough*.[2]

Once Churchill became immersed in the project, Marlborough took on a sort of mystical significance. The preface of each of the four separately published volumes is dated August 13— Blenheim Day. In the *Second World War*, Churchill tells of beginning his first visit to Moscow on August 13, "to me always 'Blenheim Day'" (IV, 484), and in General Montgomery's autograph book he took almost superstitious note of the fact that the new Desert command of Alexander and Montgomery opened on "the anniversary of Blenheim," which may bring them "the fame and fortune they will surely deserve" (IV, 518).

The project was at first academic. Churchill set out to examine the causes of the "contrast between the glory and importance of [Marlborough's] deeds and the small regard of his countrymen for his memory" (M, I, 15). With a sense of familial responsibility, he undertook the "task of making John Churchill intelligible to the present generation" (I, 18). But as work proceeded, the significance of the book changed. During the decade of research and writing, the outside world provided many distractions. Churchill never became more than a part-time scholar; the rest of his time was taken up with steady observation of the European scene. Keeping well informed on developments in Germany in particular, Churchill soon found himself busy sounding the tocsin about German rearmament and a man called Hitler. By a curious historical irony, Churchill reached the climax of his narrative at the same time that the swirl of current events rose to a whirlwind pitch. The story he had to tell contained a number of parallels to the story of the Great War and of the postwar world, but it now took on a relevance he could not have seen in the late 1920s.

The prefaces to the volumes give glimpses of the difficulties in the world outside the silent library where the books were being written. By the time of Volume III (1936), he could say that the constitutional and European issues in that volume were apposite to modern times: the selfish, quarreling alliance that was fighting for its liberties against a central monarchy; the spectacle of England's "leadership of the Grand Alliance, or League of Nations, . . . of 26 signatory states finally overcoming a mighty military despotism [is] so moving for the times in which we live" (M, II, 491, 485). The last volume (1938) showed how peace-at-any-cost groups and discussions within the alliance caused the foe to resist; how England won the war and lost the peace. The dangers of British oscillation between heroic strife in war and indifference to lasting peace; of an uneasy peace and of future perils; of a well-intentioned pacifism, like the one which brought about Marlborough's downfall—all were being duplicated before his very eyes. Instead of a historical reconstruction, the *Marlborough* had become an exemplary tale with a depressingly familiar pattern.

The significance of Marlborough's stance vis-à-vis France was clearer now that Germany had taken over France's predatoriness and threatened the Empire in the same way. In a 1936 address explaining traditional British foreign policy, Churchill conjoined Marlborough's era with the current period. Against Philip II, Louis XIV, Napoleon, and William II, Britain—led by Elizabeth, William and Marlborough, Wellington and Nelson, Lloyd George—had opposed the "most dominating power on the Continent" and "preserved the liberties of Europe" (SWW, I, 208). Hitler was merely the latest in the line of would-be pan-European tyrants; by night Churchill wrote about Marlborough confronting Louis XIV, while by day he himself confronted (as yet in words only) Hitler.

Even minor parallels presented themselves. Some time between 1934 and 1936, Churchill wrote of the shock created in Commons when St. John revealed that only a third of the troops voted by Parliament for service in Spain had fought in the decisive battle of Almanza. As the government later confirmed this, "the crowded House sat for nearly half an hour dumb-founded" (M, II, 315). And now in 1935, he saw something similar happen when a hitherto complacent Baldwin confessed that Germany had achieved air parity with Britain. Perhaps the earnestness and resolution that Churchill discerned in the silence of that "long vanished Parliament" was still with this one.

But where was today's Marlborough? Churchill himself understood much of what was happening; he had the requisite experience, knowledge, confidence, and will, but would the nation see that? Or would it, still associating him with the now remote Dardanelles fiasco or with the somewhat more recent General Strike of 1926, go under by continuing to repose its trust in the likes of MacDonald, Baldwin, or Chamberlain? Was the story, both of himself and of Britain, to end here so ignobly?

Concluding the narrative, he laid down his pen in August 1938, the time of Munich—a dark moment in history. Soon the contemporary drama would have *its* climax. On the closing pages of the *Marlborough* he noted that after four more big wars with France during the eighteenth century, Britain finally against Napoleon "was at one time left alone to face the world. That the indescribable perils were surmounted by the valour and vigour of the descendants of those who fought in the age of Anne unfolds a series of new marvels and prodigies in our island story" (M, II, 995). Churchill wrote this with World War I in the back of his mind and perhaps an intimation that the world was on the eve of another large war and British heroic phase even as the sloth after Anne's heroic age was followed by new vigor. He could not have known, though, that Britain would again be all alone for a year; that something like a modern Marlborough—at least in his own eyes—would emerge; that Churchill would eventually write the story of that hero as well, but with himself as subject as well as biographer this time; that, in short, he himself would seem to be walking in the footsteps of his ancestor by leading Britain out of an impasse into a Grand Alliance and victory; that he would thereby bring the long story of Britain to the next great Churchill. All that was hardly visible in 1938—let alone 1929.

II

In the *Marlborough*, Churchill makes periodic reference to World War I in order to explain the remote with the familiar and to note "remarkable similarities." Many of these comparisons, it so happens, apply as well to the coming World War II. The threat facing Europe in 1688 was similar to that of not only 1914 but also 1939. Louis XIV, like the Kaiser and Hitler, threatened the religious and civil liberties of democratic states. All three wars saw the "peril that the supremacy of one race and culture would be imposed by military force upon all others" and the gradual, reluctant acceptance by Britain of the leadership of a Europe lost without her. In all three wars, a great European power allied with a weaker subordinate one (France and Spain; Germany and Austria; Germany and Italy) was encircled by an alliance, of which Britain was the mainspring, and by the sea, which she ruled. The central powers, with the advantages of developed interior lines, could throw their main force against various lands in any direction. They had an army "incomparable in power, numbers, organization and repute," and a War Lord who would choose the decisive theater, perfect his plans in secrecy, execute them without domestic hindrance, and annihilate the allies seriatim.

If Louis, by his aggression on Belgium, "called into being the beginning of the Grand Alliance which was to lay him low" (M, I, 74), Hitler did the same by his aggression on Poland and, later, Belgium. It "was fortunate that Louis's aggressions were universal" (M, I, 229), for the allies, loosely joined by slow and slender communications, "were liable to be struck down one after the other" (M, I, 557), even as it was fortunate that the Kaiser had, in attacking Belgium, forced Britain into war while Russia and France were still in the fight and that Hitler abandoned his "one at a time" policy by invading Russia while Britain still lived. In all three wars, "the reverberations of the main quarrel roused a giddy excitement in all minds" and sucked in (to their grief) other ambitious nations and rulers—Bavaria and Savoy in 1702–3, Bulgaria and Rumania in 1915–7, Italy and Japan in 1940–1—so that "the decisive struggle was transferred for a while to new theaters and more distant battlefields" (M, I, 634).

The truth of the matter was that Churchill wrote the *Marlborough* during what was only a peaceful interval between two related wars. Picking up again in 1947 his historian's pen, he could see the struggles of 1914 and 1939 as but one extended world war with a long truce—"another Thirty Years' War." So indeed had it been with the earlier world war: a first phase, 1688–97, and, following an armistice, a second phase, 1702–12. The behavior of Britain during the truce was similar in both cases. "She was, though she could not have known it, in an interval between two deadly wars" (M, I, 428), and after 1697 she lapsed into a dangerous pacifism, but the demands for disarmament, economy, and reduced taxes were to be "speedily followed by the greatest of the wars England had ever waged and the heaviest expenditure. . . . [The English] were only too soon to redeem their follies in blood and toil" (M, I, 427, 430). So it was in 1918–39.

When the truce period drew to a close and Louis's ambitions loomed over Europe, Defoe proclaimed, "Our all is now at stake, and perhaps in as great a danger as at any time since we were a nation" (M, I, 463), as Churchill iterated in countless speeches in the 1930s. Still England "hoped against hope for peace" (M, I, 476), and the second Grand Alliance must have seemed, after the ill fortune of William's eight-year first phase of the war, a desperate venture, even as the situation in early World War II seemed bleaker than in World War I. Former allies like the Spanish Empire and Italy had gone over to the side of Louis and Hitler; in 1702 "the Maritime Powers had scarcely a friendly government beyond their coasts" (M, I, 483), and in 1940 Britain was without the powerful Japanese, American, Italian, and French fleets she could count on in World War I.

Nevertheless, the military colossus would be checked once the patriotism and the resources of the "great islanders," the independence of the House of Commons, the hardiness of British soldiers and sailors, the political "genius of the English race" in adversity came into play. "But those forces would have failed without the man to use them" (M, I, 78)—in 1702, Marlborough; in 1940, apparently the man who humbly said he did not inspire the nation but merely, as one who had earned his living by his tongue and pen, expressed the resolute will of the nation with the right words, one who merely gave the lion's roar and suggested to the lion the right places to use his claws.

In both wars, moreover, Britain fought not only for her own survival and greatness but also for that of Europe, even the world. Churchill dwells on how, in numberless letters, Marlborough spoke of his devotion to the queen's service and the "good of the Common Cause." Churchill used the phrase "Common Cause" in both of the modern world wars and applied to the anti-Nazi powers the name "Grand Alliance" that had been used of Louis's foes. Britain was sole champion in 1940 of "the world cause . . . the good cause" (SWW, I, 217, 629). It excited him to think of the many nationalities—"English, Scots, Irish, Danes, Prussians, Hanoverians, Hessians, Saxons, Palatines, and Dutch" (M, II, 701)—acting in concord under Marlborough even as in 1944–45, the British army in Italy was unique for including Americans, New Zealanders, South Africans, Indians, Poles, Jews, Brazilians, and liberated Italians. The England of 1705 elicited Churchill's admiration, as would the England of 1940: "What a contrast our country now presented"—the "pacifist island" determined never to fight on the continent again had been turned by Marlborough into the "drill sergeant of Europe!" (M, I, 981).

III

By Marlborough—and by Churchill? Not only were the crises, the alignment of states, the historical, ideological, and geographical circumstances at least superficially similar but so also—

according to Churchill—were the minds of the two men who stepped into the power vacuum, took the helm, and transformed the war. They seemed to think alike on many questions of strategy and policy.

Marlborough stood out among contemporary generals and irritated his Dutch allies by his unorthodox methods, which, his biographer assures us, were far advanced for his time. He disliked the traditional cautious methods of making war: the passive protection of the frontier; the slow, methodical reduction by siege of this or that fortress; and the protracted delays until the foe ran out of bread and money. Ignoring geographical prizes, textbook sieges, and military chess, Marlborough wanted to annihilate the French army in a great battle.

Thus, too, Churchill in World War I continually criticized the allied military staffs for thinking in terms of trench warfare, for ignoring the possibilities of flanking movements, for adhering to doctrines of the offensive rendered obsolete by the increased firepower of the defensive. This was the modern version of barren eighteenth-century sieges. He sought alternatives to the philosophy of attrition, but "the dangerous prudence of conventional opinion" dismissed these as "eccentric" (WC, II, 425). Even as Marlborough once declared that a battle would be of greater importance than the taking of twenty towns, so Churchill thought that such strategic considerations as keeping the French and British armies joined during the critical 1918 German offensive were more important than sentimental concern that Paris might fall. Churchill's description of Marlborough's strategy follows his own emphasis on the importance of victory in the "decisive theater," which may not be the same as the "main theater" where the largest forces are.

Marlborough preferred a mobile, improvising army rather than a static, besieging one, just as Churchill opposed the set allied offensives on the Western Front in 1915–17 on the ground that they merely led to an allied army that was "sprawled." What was wanted was a "crouched" army, the bulk of whose force served as a central reserve that threatened to attack anywhere along the line. In defense, as well, Churchill's abiding strategy in both world wars was not to wear one's power thin by trying to defend every inch of frontier, coastline, or sea with everything one had but rather to withhold a strong central mass of highly mobile reserve which could be brought into play wherever the enemy entered in force. This may be an elementary military principle, but it was overlooked, as he surmised, by the French generals in

1940 and by Hitler in 1944. When readying Britain for invasion, Churchill probably recalled vividly the oracular passage he had but recently written in his *Marlborough*: the only recorded remark brought back from the partly paralyzed Marlborough during the 1716 preparations against French invasion was, "Keep the army together; don't divide it" (M, I, 649).

In sea warfare, Marlborough wanted the fleet used in conjuntion with the land forces and not just for the protection of trade routes. Churchill had similar difficulty prodding the Navy out of its defensive posture and getting it to take offensive action in both wars. The alternative which he most desired was an amphibious operation. With the deadlock in trench war along the whole front in World War I, such an overseas effort was the only possible turning of the enemy's flanks. Instead of useless offensives in the West, he wanted daring strokes like the Dardanelles expedition, which seemed inevitable because "the Navy was a gigantic instrument of offensive war, capable of intervening with decisive effect in the general strategy, and it must bear its share of the risks. . . . The advantage of the command of the sea should not have been neglected" (WC, II, 541; IV, 48). This strategy would avoid the terrible firepower of the defensive in modern war, put to use British naval supremacy, force the strong land power to disperse its forces while giving the sea power the choice of the place of attack, and return to the offense the momentum and advantage of surprise. His ardor undiminished by the Dardanelles disaster, Churchill was to press (nervously) for amphibious operations all through World War II in the theaters of North Africa and Burma.[3]

Here again Marlborough, before the age of massive firepower, showed the way. In 1706, he became interested in an exiled Frenchman's plan to land a strong force north of Bordeaux. This would have circumvented the fortress barrier of the Low Countries and taken advantage of the absence of French troops in the body of the kingdom. Although the operation never materialized, it remained in his calculations for three years, and a force was even assembled in 1708 on the Isle of Wight. Then it was replaced by another amphibious plan to descend from Wight on Abbeville in Northern France in conjunction with his army's invasion of France from Holland and Belgium. Such a flanking operation, by cutting French land communications, would have avoided the tedious reduction of the great fortresses on the French frontier and rendered impotent the coastal garrisons and naval bases. It was never undertaken because it frightened even his heroic compeer, Prince Eugene of Savoy, a "land animal" who did not see that it—like the ones Churchill wanted in the Dardanelles or in North Africa and Burma—was made practicable by Allied sea mastery and the consequent desire to put the navy to greater use. Yet the French general Villars feared such a move because he "saw as clearly as Marlborough that here alone could the Allies make use of their command of the sea in supplying their forces or in establishing a new base" (M, II, 571). So sure was Churchill of the worth of amphibious operations that he declared the unwillingness of the allies to accept Marlborough's Abbeville plan as a cardinal point of the war, forfeiting victory and triumphant peace in 1708 even as the many woes of the protracted World War I were to be attributed to allied hesitation at the Dardanelles.[4]

Essentially, Churchill depicts Marlborough as a "modern" general. Before storming the Schellenberg, Marlborough drew troops from every battalion to form a special force of six thousand which "would now be called 'storm troops'" (M, I, 793). Marlborough's putative adaptation of technological progress became Churchill's keynote as well. "In nearly every great war there is some new mechanical feature introduced the early understanding of which confers important advantages" (M, I, 564). Orthodox military opinion is rigid and slow to adapt, but Marlborough quickly learned to exploit the greater firepower provided by the flintlock and the ring bayonet which enabled the soldier to be both pikeman and musketeer. Infantry tactics were changed thereby. In the same way, Churchill presents himself as the spirit behind the invention of the tank and the military use of the plane in World War I and as wholly committed to the "Wizard War" in World War II. Curious about gadgets, open to scientific innovations, he was ever alert to the vast changes brought by air power, armor, and radar in military strategy and international diplomacy.

Understandably anxious about such military independence and about the outcome of such bold encounters with the world's best army, the Dutch clogged Marlborough's steps with deputies and generals who held a veto power. Brilliant opportunities were thereby forfeited time and again, for the command system paralyzed all offensive action. Similarly, in World War I, the Dardanelles expedition was doomed amid a babel of voices, and, early in World War II, Churchill's various ideas for seizing the initiative from Hitler foundered, he lamented, in the elaborate committee system, in the veto power of the Foreign Office, the French Allies, and others.

A contemporary of Marlborough's remarked that under the constitution of the Dutch Republic, with each alderman having his say on military matters, everything would stay in confusion until a "true head would take over conduct of military affairs" (M, I, 680). Churchill observes, "Louis XIV was absolute Commander in Chief. Marlborough was only an informal chairman of a discordant committee" (M, I, 291). Such was the contrast, as Churchill construed it, obtaining as well between Germany and Britain in both later world wars. The "very lengthy processes of argument and exhaustion, the divisions of opinion to be overcome, and the number of persons of consequence to be convinced caused delays and compromises" (WC, II, 402, 445). Under Neville Chamberlain, the British government was overrun by committees.

Churchill quotes from the general of an enemy army facing Marlborough the avowal that the Dutch veto had at one point saved the French from a debacle, and likewise from the German records to reveal vulnerable spots left unexploited by Britain in World War II despite his urging. Thus at about the same time that Admiral Raeder had presented Hitler with plans for the invasion of Norway, Churchill had suggested mining the Norwegian waters. While the Germans immediately implemented the plan, the British let theirs lapse amid the countless committees, scruples, and vested interests. His idea for mining the Rhine took a half year to be approved, by which time the initiative was lost. "One can hardly find a more perfect example of the impotence and fatuity of waging war by groups of committees" (SWW, I, 580).

What most men did not see was that risks had to be run if the war was to be won. Churchill's Marlborough understood that, and Churchill's Churchill had tried to inculcate this message in his admirals in World War I and generals in World War II. These military men, like the Dutch deputies, lacked the comprehensive view of war. Marlborough "held the whole panorama of Europe in his steady gaze" (M, I, 692; II, 20). Thus he had to prod the Dutch into action while France was threatening the shaky German Empire. "If the Dutch will not venture some thing at this time," Marlborough reported back to Whitehall, "I am afraid Germany will have but too much reason to be angry with us. The Enemy being superior in Italy, and in the Empire, and being outnumbered no where but here, the Eyes of all the Allies are fixed upon us, and they will have cause justly to blame our conduct, if we do not do all that is possible to relieve them . . . do something striking. [Also] people would be in a bad humor at home this winter" (M, I, 669, 678–79). For his part, Churchill had to deal with generals, especially in the Middle East command, who seemed worried over only their own sector and ignored his pleas for offensives in the desert to help relieve the pressure on tottering Greece and Russia and to raise home morale: "Collapse of Greece without any effort by us will have deadly effect on Turkey. No one will thank us for sitting tight in Egypt with ever-growing forces while the Greek situation and all that hangs on it is cast away. . . . It is impossible to explain to Parliament and the nation how it is our Middle East armies have had to stand for four and a half months without engaging the enemy while all the time Russia is being battered to pieces" (SWW, II, 538; III, 543).

During combat, Marlborough kept a close eye on front-line conditions, either personally or through the eyes of a trusted officer, and sometimes he himself went into the thick of the fight. Churchill likewise often insisted on visiting the combat zones in both world wars to see at first hand what was going on, for, he noted, many generals "did not know the conditions with which their troops were ordered to contend" (WC, II, 346) and were thereby guilty of grievous errors. He thought he would imitate Marlborough's habit of establishing a rapport with the army. Napoleon used to spend entire days with a division "studying their condition, hearing complaints from all ranks, and becoming personally known to the men. Marlborough may well have been his exemplar in this" (M, II, 339). So Churchill in turn, in a memo written as prime minister, expressed the desire to spend a day with a typical infantry battalion in training in order to see for himself whether the British army division—whose size was swollen in comparison with Russian and German ones—was operating efficiently.

Such direct exposure to men and events was important as well in diplomatic matters. By his presence at The Hague, Marlborough was able to keep the alliance going through ten campaigns, and his tent was a clearing house for many diplomatic problems. His arrival in spring before the campaigns, like his one to two thousand mile trips to European capitals after the armies entered winter quarters, often served to patch up an alliance that threatened to fall apart. "When great projects have been brought to maturity, a personal touch is needed to set them in action" (M, I, 75). Churchill credits the Marlborough-Charles XII conference with causing the feared Swede's invasion of Russia rather than of central Europe. "Whatever effects could be produced depended upon personal contact" (M, II, 223).

Churchill functioned in the same way in World War II. He was the one who took frequent journeys to Paris, Washington, Moscow, and Cairo. In person, he mediated—or so we see him in his memoirs—between distant allies, patched up schisms in Italy or Greece, reshuffled command hierarchies. He urged and arranged summit conferences. "Only the heads of States face to face could settle the fearful questions that were open. . . . There were many things I could settle on the spot, and more which I needed to see with my own eyes" (SWW, IV, 666, 699). The mistake of the 1919 Peace Conference had been to postpone for two months "the heart-to-heart and frank conversation between the three men on whom ultimately everything rested" (WC, V, 142).

Though the bulk of Marlborough's correspondence was handled by his secretary, Cardonel, the letters sent to the German emperor or to the other ruling sovereigns were written in his own hand, even as Churchill composed himself the letters to Roosevelt and other rulers "on the basis that they were intimate and informal correspondence with friends and fellow workers" (SWW, II, 22). Personal contact made for a great alliance between the two "Princes of war," Marlborough and Prince Eugene. Once they joined efforts in 1708, "their perfect Comradeship and preeminence established a higher unity of command than had ever been seen in the war" (M, II, 331); theirs was a partnership and friendship—according to Churchill—"of which history furnishes no equal example" (M, I, 773). A similar unique relation seemed to exist in World War II between Churchill and Roosevelt, both of whom had been heads of their countries' Admiralties in the earlier conflagration. Churchill uses phrases like "absolute brotherhood" and "complete unity." When, for example, during one Churchill visit to wartime Washington, Roosevelt went to Hyde Park for a weekend rest, he left Churchill the run of the White House; the Briton presided there over a conference of the Combined Chiefs of Staff, "an event in Anglo-American history" (SWW, V, 138).

On substantive political and diplomatic questions, too, Churchill's thinking allegedly coincided with—or followed or was superimposed on—Marlborough's. Thus at one critical juncture, Marlborough enunciated a paradox which is a *motif* of the *Marlborough* and the *Second World War* and can be said to be the great theme of Churchill's career and writings. When the Tories, newly come to power, began to press in 1710 for an end to the protracted war, Marlborough noted that such behavior merely encouraged the French and renewed their war effort, "so that our new Ministers will be extremely deceived, for the greater desire they shall express for peace, the less they will have it in their power to obtain it" (M, II, 758). To appreciate the poignancy of these words we must recall that they were probably recorded by Churchill during 1937–38. Clearly, St. John, the Tory peacemaker, stood to Marlborough as Chamberlain stood to Churchill.

This approach is enlarged upon in each of Churchill's major works. Of the balanced allied behavior in 1709, under Marlborough's firm stewardship, he says, "We must admire the dual process to which the Allies were now committed of earnestly seeking peace while at the same time preparing for war on a even greater scale. Nearly always governments which seek peace flag in their war efforts, and governments which make the most vigorous war preparations take little interest in peace. The two opposite moods consort with difficulty in the human mind, yet it is only by the double and, as it might seem, contradictory, exertion that a good result can usually be procured" (M, II, 522). Once the Tories came to power in 1710, Britain lapsed into behavior akin to that of the 1930s—ignoring its allies, seeking a separate peace at all costs, appeasing the predatory tyrant. As he had said in the *World Crisis*, "In any quarrel among men, if one side proclaims its complete impotence of will and hand, there are no bounds to the evils that may ensue" (V, 448). The sole remedy in 1710 as in 1914, in the postwar Irish troubles, or in 1936–38 was "a remorseless punching at the heart of the foe" (M, II, 805). But the Tory government, like the later Conservative one, paraded "convenient words as a substitute for necessary deeds," while Louis, like Hitler, thought "not of peace, but victory."[5]

This peremptory manner was necessary not only with a ruthless foe but sometimes also with one's allies, for the approach of victory brought new difficulties with it. The Dutch, the most staunch, consistent, and powerful ally England had, provided Marlborough with continual, albeit changing, vexations. Early in the war, he had a hard time overcoming their fears of the powerful French army, as well as discouraging them from thoughts of a separate peace. With the improvement of the allied position under his leadership and with a tired England in turn seeking a separate peace, "we see them [the Dutch] during the last four years of the war the most steadfast and unrelenting of the Allies" (M, II, 631). Churchill faced the same problem with the Russians. At first, "a common opinion about Russia was that she would not continue the war once she had regained her frontiers, and that when the time came the Western Allies might well have to try to persuade her not to relax her efforts" (SWW, VI, 508). When the time in fact came, however, Russian offensive zeal redoubled and she began to encroach on the states of Eastern Europe. The common enemy had been the "sole bond of union" (SWW, V, 456); friction was generated as the fruits of victory ripened on all sides.

In the face of the Emperor's opposition, the Dutch laid strong claims, with "that kind of rough justice which asserts itself among allies in war whatever the parchments say" (M, I, 686), to rule of the Barrier (Belgium) freed from French domination. Marlborough, whom Churchill portrays as free of vindictive feelings, resisted this. "If the Grand Alliance was to continue," his biographer explains, "this seizing of territory as booty wherever the armies marched, without regard to treaties and hereditary rights, must be stopped" (M, I, 686). Churchill, similarly subscribing to principles of reconciliation and magnanimity rather than of revenge, had (though only for a while) during World War I asserted, amid premature Allied claims to territories under the control of the Central Powers, especially of Turkey, that the settlement of all territorial questions was to be left to the end of the war.[6] And in World War II, he attempted to resist the Russian encroachments on Poland and the Balkans. Britons and Americans could not "allow their allies to engage in uncontrolled land-grabbing or tactics which were all too reminiscent of Hitler" (SWW, VI, 555). The eighteenth-century Dutch were much hated by the Belgians, who returned their cities to the French as soon as they could, for they, like the Poles in 1945, "though liberated, had merely exchanged one conqueror for another" (SWW, VI, 331).

Marlborough and Churchill are depicted as acting decisively in the name of future peace conferences. Marlborough withstood the Dutch demands because, as Churchill puts it, "Peace can never be established between great civilized countries upon the brutal execution of the rights of one side over the other. . . . The unending cadence of history shows that moderation and mercy in victory are no less vital than courage and skill in war" (M, II, 556, 996). Thus it was that Churchill spoke out against the Versailles Treaty's heavy reparations demand, and wanted to avoid the same error with reference to Finland and Germany after

World War II. To avoid "having a poisoned community in the heart of Europe," he wanted a policy of "putting poor Germany on her legs again. . . . Experience shows that large indemnities do not work" (SWW, VI, 350; V, 400).

On similar grounds, Marlborough, though implacable in war, stressed magnanimity in victory. Rather than tearing provinces from France "to enrich others," he would, to ensure peace, have had Britain insist on the French being governed again by the Three Estates. Churchill finds this "one of the most revealing insights into Marlborough's state-craft" (M, II, 550); he is staggered to think how much the world might have been spared if a Parliamentary regime could have been substituted for the despotism. The French Revolution would have taken place gradually and there would have been none of the four wars with France during the eighteenth century and no Napoleon. "How far in this respect he stood ahead of his times—and our own" (M, II, 550).

It is interesting that Churchill, whose claims to being a prophet are well known, attributes a similar gift to Marlborough. "Profound and clairvoyant," he measured men and affairs so surely "that he seems almost gifted with prophetic powers. Every word of Marlborough's had come true" (M, II, 752, 275); Churchill would often say of his own warnings, "This was certainly justified by what happened. All came true. . . . I had seen it all before. Then, as at this time, I understood the world situation as a whole" (SWW, II, 198; VI, 570). Some of their prophecies are even similar. Marlborough thought in 1707 that Charles XII should be allowed to pursue his aim in Russia, for he would "never reach his end" in Moscow but "will ruin himself to such an extent that he will not be able to do any more mischief" (M, II, 275). Prince Eugene thought differently, but Marlborough was proved right. So too Churchill, during the dark days of the Nazi-Soviet *detente*, reassured a depressed Britain "of the profound, quenchless antagonism between Russia and Germany" (SWW, I, 448). Two years later he was vindicated: and then, with the example of Napoleon to add to that of Charles XII, he prophesied further that Hitler, who "forgot" about what every schoolboy knows, the Russian winter, had gone off to his doom.

IV

The European military and political situations, then, were arguably not dissimilar, and the minds of the two Churchills who stepped into the breach seemed to work in tandem. Given the continuity of European history, particularly of British insularity, that is not so surprising, but that the two careers should have been strikingly alike is curious.

Both men began active military service in minor frontier wars mainly in Africa—Marlborough in Tangiers and the Mediterranean, Churchill in the Sudan and South Africa. "Everyone agreed" early in his career that Marlborough "could not fail to make his future" (M, I, 79); the young and famous Churchill was greeted in the United States at the turn of the century by such notables as Mark Twain and with effusive descriptions like "the hero of five wars, the author of six books, and the future Prime Minister of England."[7] Each aroused suspicions as well. The French general Villeroy spoke in 1705 of Marlborough as an "adventurer" (M, I, 990), while Churchill, regarded first as an exhibitionist and then as a radical, in the 1910s gained notoriety as a "warmonger" and later was called by Ribbentrop "a political and military dilettante" (SWW, II, 580).

The connection between Churchill and Marlborough was, furthermore, made from the beginning of his career, by himself and by others. G. B. Shaw noted that young Churchill had compiled as good a military record as his ancestor had at the same age. The *Atheneum* saw in Churchill's very first book the genius of the author's father and of his progenitor. One of Churchill's first biographers, A. MacCallum Scott, noted in 1905 that a portrait of Marlborough was in Churchill's study, that he consciously modeled himself on the general, that neither man had had a university education, that both had had early army experience and showed a knack for statesmanship, and that both were hard-hitting attackers. The only difference was that, without a large war imminent, Churchill left the army.[8]

That war came in good time, and Churchill eventually found himself in the army and on the front-lines. Attached in November 1915 to the Second Battalion of the Grenadier Guards, which, he wrote his wife, "once the gt d of Marlborough served in and commanded," and facing combat in the Low Countries as Marlborough did, Churchill addressed his wife in a letter as "my dearest soul," self-consciously adding that this was how "the gt d of Marl" addressed his Sarah from the field. His ancestor's military instincts, noted a contemporary, replaced his father's political legacy in his interests, and shrewd observers like the journalist A. G. Gardiner and the politician Beaverbrook thought that Churchill now perceived himself as a Marlborough (or Napoleon). In 1923, wishing Churchill would turn from politics to writing, Shane Leslie, greeted the first volume of the *World Crisis* by urging the author to do a book on Marlborough, something appealing to his pride and genius. Tempted to do so from early on, Churchill was in fact sure he would live to write it.[9] And, he having written it and then becoming wartime prime minister, the emulation—or illusion—grew.

If, in April 1936, Churchill said in Parliament that Britain must retain command of the Mediterranean first established by "Marlborough, my illustrious ancestor" and if a 1938 cartoon in *Punch* conjoined Churchill and his ancestor, the idea that he inherited Marlborough's military genius was often forwarded during World War II, sometimes on Churchill's behalf, far more often sarcastically and satirically. His head, many thought, was filled with nonsense about being a "modern Marlborough" who, with a series of Blenheims, would end the job the duke had been unable to end. He seemed, as in a Cairo conference, to be self-consciously playing Marlborough's role, "riding the whirlwind and directing the storm." He even fondled a velleity about his troops charging in red coats![10]

In their personal lives, both had had an unhappy childhood, and both lived happily with their wives during a half century of wedlock: Marlborough's love, at least according to his biographer, "lasted forever" (M, I, 108); Churchill "married and lived happily ever afterwards" (MEL, 370). Both longed amid their wartime travails for rest and peace in the bosom of their families but would take no shortcut to achieve these.[11] Both suffered a series of strokes in their last years which partially disabled their speech but allowed them to continue attending Parliament, where they were revered presences, relics of an earlier, heroic age. Though both were soldiers (at least some of the time), they would know not death in combat but the anguish of gradual physical degeneration, as Churchill's father had known it prematurely, prompting the author's words, at once retrospective and proleptic: "What experience can be more painful than for a man who enjoys the fullest intellectual vigor to feel the whole apparatus of expression slipping sensibly from him?" (RC, II, 482).

The important parallels in their careers, however, involve the middle period, years in which each made his mark on the world stage only to be sent into a kind of long exile, then returned for a relatively brief climatic triumph capped with renewed exile. Each man was the only one in a commanding position in the second phase of the protracted world war who had played an important, if subordinate and confined, role in the first phase.

Marlborough's apprenticeship under William III found England, without coordination or planning, doing badly in 1688–90, rather as was Churchill's experience in 1914–15 and again in 1939. Despite his brilliant beginning as soldier and general, Marlborough had to wander through "a desert, a whole generation of small years, a quarter of a century" (M, I, 79) before reaching his heroic phase—like Churchill as warrior, from his leaving the Admiralty in 1915 until his return in 1939. "For many long years his genius seemed unlikely to carry him through the throng of securely established notabilities who then owned the fullness of the earth" (M, I, 80). After some minor military actions in 1691, "ten years, when the chances of a lifetime seemed finally to die, were to pass before he was again to exercise command" (M, I, 309). These correspond to Churchill's critical decade "in the wilderness," from the time of leaving his government post in 1929. (Marlborough had even to put in some time in the Tower; Churchill was to know political isolation in 1904, 1915, and 1929.) The words used of Churchill's father applied as well to their hard years: "Never was politician so utterly isolated, so totally repudiated, so signally rebuked, by all those persons of influence and position upon whose support he must depend" (RC, I, 245). The years of Marlborough's exile were years of war, of opportunities wasted. He had to watch the excellent army he had developed being mismanaged by others, even as Churchill had had to watch his Dardanelles expedition go under in others' hands or the phenomenon of Hitler being reacted to in precisely the wrong way time and again.[12]

But Marlborough in exile lived in "tranquil retirement, seeming not to fret" at the opportunities and the years of his prime which were being consumed, and Churchill spent *his* exile painting in Cannes, laying bricks at home, and, of course, writing, ironically enough, the *Marlborough*. Even as Marlborough had been in his exile "happy with Sarah and his children" (M, I, 431), so, "with my happy family around me, [I] dwelt at peace within my habitation" (at Chartwell) (SWW, I, 79)—at least outwardly at peace.

This very sequestration in fact was a blessing in disguise. Marlborough formed strong associations with his friend Godolphin and the Princess Anne, on whom Fortune also frowned, as well as with his future invaluable military aides, Cadogan and Cardonel. "In these fires of adversity the links were forged by which the smallest and the strongest executive our country has ever known was to be gripped together. . . . Thus when the occasion came, he was not only ready himself, but had at his disposal both a military and a civilian instrument which he had long selected and prepared, and which were so perfectly adapted to his needs that they were never changed" (M, I, 349, 466). At the very time he wrote this, Churchill was himself forming a circle of military and scientific advisers under Professor Lindemann, who interpreted his private intelligence information on German rearmament and whom he brought into the government when he assumed power. This small circle of officials, which was, he asserted, a model of efficiency, held together through the war. "The actual war direction soon settled into a very few hands. The machinery worked almost automatically" (SWW, II, 17) and gave England, as he thinks, the best government it ever had. Here again he took his cue from, or followed in the footsteps of, Marlborough, whose entourage was small—"it is best to have to do with as few people as possible"—and nearly unaltered through ten campaigns. Under Marlborough, "never was the English Constitution found more flexible . . . [in] the greatest government that had ever ruled in England" (M, I, 503; II, 789).

The exile was perhaps advantageous for other reasons as well. While Marlborough was unemployed and a prisoner of state in England, Count Solms ineptly cast the English army away at the battle of Steinkirk (1692). Churchill conjectures that Marlborough might, were he better treated, have been in command and, amid half policies and half control, have fared no better than Solms, have "been found unable to free himself from the stifling cloak of circumstance" (M, I, 364). As it was, he returned to the service later without any blemishes on his record. In like manner, Churchill came to feel it fortunate that he had been kept out of the governments of the 1930s and been left free thereby of all blame for their lame rearming in the face of danger: "Mr. Baldwin knew no more than I how great was the service he was doing me in preventing me from becoming involved in all the Cabinet compromises and shortcomings of the next three years, and from having, if I had remained a Minister, to enter upon a war bearing direct responsibility for conditions of national defense bound to prove fearfully inadequate" (SWW, I, 201).

Churchill therefore inquires, with reference to Marlborough's ultimately fortunate exile, "Did some protecting genius of England" watch over him (M, I, 349)? If some genius did, perhaps it was the same one that gave Churchill himself the sense "of being used in some appointed plan. . . . I felt as if I were walking with Destiny, and that all my past life had been but a preparation for this hour and this trial. Eleven years in the political wilderness had freed me from ordinary party antagonism. . . . Over me beat invisible wings" (SWW, III, 671; I, 667, 181).

Even in exile Marlborough grew in influence "and at the end of his lengthy period of eclipse was felt by everyone around the summit of affairs to be one of the greatest Englishmen of the day" (M, I, 431). Churchill, too, waxed in stature and esteem as his prophecies about Germany were being fulfilled; by 1939 Chamberlain noted in his diary, "Churchill's chances [of entering the Government] improve as war becomes more probable and *vice versa*" (SWW, I, 356). Indeed, when war broke out, Churchill was immediately returned to the Admiralty, and when, soon after, the government fell, he was (except for Halifax) the only man for the prime ministry.

Churchill paints the return of Marlborough in somewhat melodramatic terms. William died on the eve of war, having woven Marlborough into the texture of his policy and passed the leadership on to him, "the only man to whom in war or in policy he could bequeath the awful yet unescapable task. . . . [Here was] a new champion of the liberties of Europe. In his last hours he commended him [Marlborough] as the fittest man in the realm to guide councils and lead armies" (M, I, 484). The rhetoric is perhaps no more heightened than that which Churchill applied to himself in more subtle fashion. Though no one man thus hand-picked Churchill, various prominent personages have a way of exiting from the stage of history in *The Second World War* prophesying greatness for him. Thus a Foreign Office official rendered prostrate by his government's flaccidity in 1936 declared, before his death, that "Winston has always, always understood, and he is strong and will go on to the end" (I, 198); the French Minister Champinchi died in 1941 with mind fixed on the Briton: "His last words were of hope in me" (I, 500); even Count Ciano, Mussolini's right hand man, wrote shortly before his execution, "You will not be surprised that as I approach the hour of my death I should turn to you whom I profoundly admire as the champion of a crusade" (II, 130).

The new sovereign, Anne, at first relied solely on Marlborough as her ablest subject. He became "an Olympian figure making head against innumerable difficulties and opponents in every quarter" (M, I, 493). By his "genius and exploits," he, more than anyone else, forged the coalition. Virtual prime minister, he preserved the political foundations of England, procured military action from the discordant allies, and defeated the French in the field. The military, political, and diplomatic functions were harmonized by one who was but a "private man" in an aristocratic age. Nearly all this would seem to fit Churchill who, even when he was at the Admiralty, took it upon himself to advise Chamberlain (as he had Asquith and Lloyd George) on all sorts of matters outside his purview and thus readied himself for—by sheer momentum and zeal wove himself into—the prime ministry. While he did not lead armies in the field, he certainly oversaw as prime minister their formation, deployment, supply and use.

Churchill compares Marlborough as a warrior-statesman-diplomat to Napoleon. In his own imagination, Churchill's own claim to fame—whether or not deserved—is ultimately no smaller. Marlborough, to be sure, had attained political eminence by his military achievements whereas Churchill's climb had been through political and administrative channels. But Churchill had had five years of military schooling and experience in the field as young officer and war correspondent and had been a battalion commander in World War I. He remained an amateur military and naval strategist all his life. In World War I he often pressed cogent military advice on the Cabinet, pushed his own theories against the whole of the professional military and naval establishment, and sponsored the development of the tank, military plane, and chemical warfare. In World War II, he frequently intervened in purely military matters, with the rationale that in war political and military considerations are inseparable.

The joy Marlborough felt when in 1704 he at long last had freed himself—by secretively embarking on his daring expedition to the Danube—of Dutch and German interference and when he could direct his own army without reference to any higher authority was comparable to what Churchill felt on becoming prime minister. What Churchill says of Lloyd George vis-à-vis Asquith, he implies of Marlborough vis-à-vis others, as well as of himself vis-à-vis Chamberlain or Halifax: "Mr. Lloyd George had all the qualities which [Asquith] lacked. The nation, by some instinctive, almost occult process had found this out" (GC, 124--26). Because of his experience and knowledge, Churchill was pleased that at long last the welfare of the nation came to rest securely in his own confident keeping rather than being frightened by the impending peril. As he had put it many years earlier, "I could at that time give directions over a very large and intricate field of urgent and swiftly changing business which were acted upon immediately by a great variety of authorities who otherwise would have had no common connecting center" (WC, I, 348). Now could he, like Marlborough breaking loose from Dutch control, exact compliance with his wishes after a "reasonable discussion" and "give directions over the whole scene" (SWW, I, 667).

Churchill says of Marlborough at this juncture that he "felt the responsibility of proprietorship. It had become his war. He was the hub of the wheels. He had made the treaties" (M, I, 741). This is exactly the feeling the *Second World War* radiates, for, as Reed Whittemore has pointed out, Churchill writes his memoirs as though World War II has been all his own, as though he were a Shakespearean monarch triumphing personally over his enemy. Churchill's paean to Marlborough—"The scale of the new war was turned by the genius of one man" (M, I, 483)—he would have us apply to himself as well.

Sure of themselves, the two Churchills confronted criticism and political storms with equanimity. When a pamphlet writer disparaged his military efforts, Marlborough said, "I should have been very uneasy if the law had not found him guilty, but much more uneasy if he had suffered the punishment on my account. I should be glad he were forgiven" (M, II, 86), even as Churchill asked for reduction of a penalty given a woman who said that Hilter was a better man that the prime minister. In 1703, Parliament, while accepting the war policy, blamed the "corrupt" ministers for mismanaging it; Churchill in 1942 faced political crises in which opponents, while conceding Churchill's "emotional value," tried to take away some of his powers. The Whigs accused Marlborough "of acting defensively" and the Tories' attack took "the opposite form"; Churchill faced a Vote of Censure moved "on the ground that the Prime Minister has interfered unduly in the direction of the war; whereas the seconder seems to be seconding because the Prime Minister has not sufficiently interfered in the direction of the war" (SWW, IV, 398).

As a result, Marlborough came gradually to see the shortcomings of the party system at home. Although a Tory by origin, sentiment, and profession, he, having become the mainspring of Whig policy in Europe, ceased to be a party man. He wanted a government neither Tory nor Whig but unified to support the war, even as Churchill wanted Coalition or National governments in both wars. Marlborough's detachment from party prefigures Churchill's shuttling between Conservative and Liberal parties and his frequent falling out with both.[13] In fact, Churchill wrote the biography of his ancestor in part for the same reason that he wrote his own memoirs and the biography of his father—to undo the injustice that "neither party acknowledged him" and to establish that the hero acted on behalf of Britain rather than of party. Even Marlborough's deserting James II for William of Orange is presented as a mere crossing of the floor, of the sort Churchill himself did a number of times.

Their parallel careers reached a storybook climax as each was turned out of office at the height of his achievements and within sight—we are assured—of the promised land of peace. Marlborough was a victim of political intrigue, personal venom, and the hatred of a sovereign who had once been close to him; Churchill, a victim of the *de facto* sovereign in modern Britain, the electorate. But the pain of rejection was the same. The cause is to be found in human nature: an individual or a society can endure only so much of war, taxes, heroic striving. "Having made every sacrifice, . . . England, amid a babel of voices, dissolved in faction, disbanded her armies, and sought to repay the spites and hardships of war-time upon the man who had carried her through" (M, I, 427). So was it in 1697, 1712, 1763, 1815, 1918, and so, for somewhat different reasons, would it happen to Churchill himself in 1945. "Here again the tale is rich in suggestion and instruction for the present day," Churchill wrote in August 1936. "Here in foretaste we may read how England won the war and lost the peace" (M, II, 23). England's desertion "of her leadership of the Grand Alliance, or League of Nations," cast away victory, as did the machinations of a "victorious War Party" exacting heavy reparations in the 1920s and "the intrigues of a pacifist reaction" in the 1930s.

By 1709, Marlborough felt himself somewhat restricted when, after three decades of war, so many states sent contingents and generals that the British were a mere seventh of his army. Rather than insisting on his own plans, he deferred to Prince Eugene and others. "The fear of being defeated and destroyed had joined the allies together. Now his own victories had destroyed that fear. At the moment when his work should have given him the greatest authority, he found himself alone" (M, II, 555). Churchill came to know this feeling at first hand in 1945. " 'We have only a quarter of the forces invading Germany and the situation has thus changed remarkably from the days of June 1944. . . . It is not so easy as it used to be for me to get things done.' . . . The destruction of German military power had brought with it a fundamental change in the relations between Communist Russia and the Western democracies" (SWW, VI, 460, 267, 456).

But the major hindrance was lack of support at home. Marlborough, pained by this, often spoke harshly of the party system, of the "base ingratitude of my countrymen" (M, II, 25); he would not blame the future George I "for not caring to have to do with so villainous a people" (M, II, 752). To Churchill these last words seemed a "bitter phrase," but seven years later he would discover the truth of them and would, by innuendo, make a similar indictment of his countrymen, when, in describing his own coming to power, he glanced ahead to war's end with a scarcely concealed bitterness.

In explaining the capriciousness of the queen in dismissing Marlborough, Churchill spoke truer than he knew with the analogy he used: "It was as useless to reproach Queen Anne with fickleness and inconstancy as it would be to accuse a twentieth-century electorate of these vices" (M, II, 563). Of either leader could it be said, *if* one ignored the legitimate grievances of a war-weary populace, that "after having lifted Britain to a height hitherto undreamed of, he came home to a society which could have treated him no worse if he had ruined, instead of rebuilt, the state" (M, II, 783). It is the oldest story and the newest, and as such it, like a literary motif or frame, quite properly graces the opening pages of the World War II memoirs (the fall of Clemenceau) even as it climaxes the tragic closing pages.

Both Churchills were chagrined to be dismissed when there was still much to be done. Marlborough foresaw no peace "unless France was reduced to a definitely restricted power" (M, II, 995); Churchill thought that tensions would remain as long as Soviet expansionism replaced the Nazi kind, and that he alone had the experience, vision, and will to checkmate it with the necessary toughness. As he put it in explaining to the modern reader Marlborough's fervent desire to remain in office: "The will to rule was strong; to rule, to conquer, not to lose the game for self or Empire. . . . No man of spirit cares to have a task of which he is master taken from his hands while still unfinished. . . . The pursuit of power with the capacity and in the desire to exercise it worthily is among the noblest of human occupations" (M, II, 784, 915, 919). Or as he said in speaking of his own earlier controversial actions: "I believed that the special knowledge which I possessed and the great and flexible authority which I wielded in this time of improvisation, would enable me" to effect something (WC, I, 348). If his removal from the Admiralty spelled the eventual defeat of the Dardanelles operation he had fostered, his removal from the prime ministry more disastrously ruined things at Potsdam, where his policy had been to let various issues accumulate in order to bring them to a head after the British election that everyone thought his party would easily win. But "the destruction of the British National Government and my removal from the scene at the time when I still had much influence and power rendered it impossible for satisfactory solutions to be reached" (SWW, VI, 674).

"Impossible"? Churchill's complete identification with the fallen hero of either narrative leads him to discern greater consequences that most historians would be willing to concede. For one thing, the 1945 election was not so much a repudiation of Churchill as of the Conservative party, the result not only of weariness with war but also of zest to undertake adventures and experiments in peacetime domestic social reconstruction. For another, he allows his imagination to rove freely over what might have been if—. Thus, had Marlborough had the powers of Frederick or Napoleon, the war would have been decisively finished before 1705 (or during 1705 at a place called, ironically, Waterloo) and he "would have made a more ordered and a more tolerant civilization for his own time . . . a wise and stable peace in harmony with the highest interests of England and Europe." So too *if* the world had listened to Churchill on the Dardanelles the war would have been over by 1915 and Europe would have had a lasting peace, and *if* in 1945 Churchill had been reelected, he would have forced a showdown: "The world has yet to measure the 'serious consequences' which I forecast" (SWW, VI, 667). In such passages Churchill seems to wander off into romance. He writes as though the Dardanelles expedition or his World War II Balkans strategy, if followed through on his terms, or his presence at Potsdam were guaranteed to be successful and to have wide-ranging beneficent results. This is pushing rather far his confidence in his own and Marlborough's charisma.

In any case, the heroes accepted their fate with dignity. At least Marlborough no longer had to risk his invincibility with each battle; he could at last relax after so much turmoil. And Churchill, returning to his role of historian, came to see the fall as perhaps again "a blessing in disguise."

Both men were granted a restitution and happy ending. Under a new monarch, Marlborough was restored in 1714 to all "the highest military and political functions" (M, II, 1024) and became an august member of a government run by friends and followers, even as after six years Churchill was again given the seat of power. The restorations were perhaps more symbolic and, for the nation, penitential than substantive. In 1715, the government was carried on by a Cabinet in which Marlborough was the foremost, but not most active, member: partly disabling strokes caused him to leave control in the hands of the younger men around him. No longer in the field, he "presided over, rather than conducted," the brief campaign against the Jacobites in Scotland. "It is an old man whom we now see once again installed in the highest authority; and the vigour of the government measures must be ascribed to Ministers in their prime" (M, II, 1027). These words apply as well to Churchill, prime minister again in 1951 at 77.

But with their physical disabilities, they were granted "a good and fair end to life" in the family bosom in ripe old age, their life work rounded off, its fruits and acclaim all about them. During Marlborough's difficult hour, Churchill reminded us in a prolepsis that the general would spend the last decade of his life in his "home in honor and splendour" (M, II, 904) while the villainous Bolingbroke would be disgraced, even as Churchill juxtaposed Mussolini's sneers at decadent England with a glance ahead to the happy end of the story: "In the end it was Ciano and Mussolini who went to their doom" (SWW, I, 341).

V

Thus the careers of the two Churchills, separated by two and a half centuries, unfolded along curiously similar lines, with the further link between them that the later one wrote the life of the earlier. This adds up to a fascinating paradigm of the interplay of character and history—and raises some important questions about the significance of it all; we are brought to the threshold of the larger mysteries.

Did Churchill merely describe Marlborough as the man had been, and history chose to unblushingly repeat itself by fashioning the same story anew in our century? Did he, that is, present us with an objective portrait of a Marlborough on whom he had been modeling himself, and sheer determination brought him through to a successful emulation?

Or did Churchill distort history, impose on Marlborough the values, thoughts, and gestures peculiar to himself and create a kind of autobiography; did he, in short, present us, as great men and dominating personalities often will, with a Marlborough refashioned in his own image, a Marlborough who, for example, is eager for an amphibious descent on France because Churchill is still fighting World War I battles, defending his strategic differences with the generals, and justifying the Dardanelles?

In a sense he did, and the parallelism is partly a figment of Churchill's mind. In the first place, there were important differences between the two men. Though some scholars have remarked on certain similarities in character—both men were aristocratic in demeanor and exhilarated by war, power, the applause of nation and sovereign[14]—many others have taken account of differences, such as Churchill's greatest weakness, which, by all accounts, was impetuosity. Lacking Marlborough's patience, he was a potential tyrant. He sometimes had an astonishing lack of vision. He depended on impulse and intuition rather than on a logical approach and a cool, farsighted sagacity. He was so sure of his military knowledge and yet so lacking in strategic judgment. He put his finger into everything and tried to do various things simultaneously rather than one at a time. Though some of his military ideas were brilliant, many more were wild and dangerous. Sometimes he became lost in some detail and could not see the influence of one theater or another; at other times he did not want to see the whole picture if it interfered with his wishes. He was unable to grasp the interrelation of war theaters—the very virtue he celebrated in Marlborough he himself lacked. He was sometimes carried away by the theater of operations under examination. In his daring ventures at Antwerp, Gallipoli, and Greece (in 1941), Churchill, unlike Marlborough, was weak on logistics. (The Dardanelles ventures accorded more with the strategy of Marlborough's political opponents than with Marlborough's.) In these attempts he, again unlike his revered ancestor, blundered into cases of "improvised muddle," took a gamble on political and sentimental rather than military grounds, and tried to do too much with too little. The result was ignominious evacuation and concurrent defeat on other fronts.[15]

Marlborough rose through the army, whereas Churchill soon abandoned the army and rose through politics. During wartime, Marlborough emerged undefeated from ten campaigns; Churchill knew defeat at Antwerp and Gallipoli and, in the later war, underwent three years of perhaps unprecedented disasters under his leadership. Marlborough evolved his own strategy and implemented it himself; Churchill interefered with, or imposed on, the strategy of his generals, with mixed results. If Marlborough was taciturn and secretive, Churchill felt compelled to write a multivolumed apologia at every historical juncture. If Marlborough was a commander who assumed—unevenly, according to historians—the role of statesman, Churchill was a statesman who *thought* he assumed the role of commander.

Secondly, the parallelism is strained (and yet, curiously, abetted) because Marlborough was not the invincible hero and saintly soul that Churchill makes him out to be. Out of a need to justify his ancestor, Churchill distorts, no doubt unconsciously, the historical record. Marlborough's relations with Prince Eugene and with Godolphin were not as unruffled as the chronicler seems to believe. (Though here the parallel is perhaps salvaged, for neither was the Churchill-Roosevelt relationship as pure, altruistic, and untroubled as he sometimes makes it appear.) Some military historians, morever, suggest that Ramillies, Oudenarde, and Malplaquet were not quite the glorious victories for Marlborough that Churchill presents—some even doubt that Malplaquet was a victory at all—but were rather bloody battles like Loos, Somme, and Paschendale, leading to a victory through exhaustion and that Marlborough was fortunately sacked by the politicians as Haig was unfortunately not. Nor was Marlborough an "easterner" in the World War I sense. Others think that his diplomacy was flawed, in good part because of his selfish interests.[16]

Nor can limits easily be set to the science—or game—of finding similarities in character and career. Because of his long career and many-sided personality, Churchill has been twinned, often speciously, with a host of notables. But when all such similarities with others and differences with Marlborough are taken into account, one recurs to the mystery, for the past reveals hardly any other such parallel, repetition, or symbiosis—at least externally, circumstantially, superficially—such a case of a man modeling himself on his ancestor amid monumental historical events. If Churchill had written the *Marlborough* after World War II, the reader would readily dismiss the parallels between author and subject, self and ancestor, as a classic case of projection. But it was written *before* the war, and even if he were producing a tendentious book, there remain many indisputable facts and events whose counterparts in his own career could not be of his own creation. No analysis of literary-historical *topoi* (themes applicable to diverse situations), of inevitable parallels and similarities because of the continuity of European history and the

British character can account for such close parallels—and in the same family, and with one man writing of the other.

Surely Churchill in 1938 did not sense in some occult way that a year later he would be back in the Admiralty and that after another year he, at long last, would be in the seat of power, would have a go at Marlborough's chance and task? It was late in the day, to be sure. His ancestor too had had to wait a quarter of a century, entering his destiny at the age of fifty-two. This made him older than any leading general of the day and older than Napoleon and Wellington at their zenith. At that age they had finished their military careers,[17] as had the late William III, Marlborough's exact contemporary and the man he replaced as commander. But Churchill took over at sixty-six—an age when most men retire and when Marlborough himself had finished his work and was close to the grave. "I was almost the only ante-diluvian. This might well have been a reproach in a time of crisis. I should have to strive my utmost to keep pace with the generation now in power and with fresh young giants who might at any time appear" (SWW, I, 420). Had the fates brought him belatedly this far along in emulation of Marlborough only to destroy him and make a mocking contrast between the eighteenth-century general and his twentieth-century descendant?

Churchill had been toying with, or was being "saddled with," the idea of writing a biography of Marlborough for some thirty years before finally undertaking it. How curious that he wrote it at that particular juncture, when, as T. E. Lawrence told him, he, having been deep in "affairs," could see around Marlborough and write a "practical" book.[18] By not writing it too early or after his wartime leadership, he produced much more than a practical book. Could Churchill have known when writing it that his own life—with so much to come after he finished the book—would yet run on a course parallel with his ancestor's? Could he, in writing the book and adumbrating the story of his own next two decades, have been indulging in the greatest of all his many predictions and prophecies, one hidden even from himself? It is as though, like other great men, Churchill informs the world in veiled fashion of what he will do—and then proceeds to do it. Some men are born great. They are aware of it from the start, continually inform us about it, and nothing that destiny can do seems able to stop the realization of their greatness. Of such mettle was Churchill—like, indeed, his opposite Hitler.

When, after coming through it all, he, unlike his ancestor, set about explaining all he had done, intended to do, and lived through, he refrained from making any explicit comparisons or pointing to the numerous parallels cited here. Posterity would see to that. However, he could not resist leaving some clues. Writing in the fateful year of 1938 of the greatness of Marlborough's genius and achievement, he had exclaimed, "Happy the state or sovereign who finds such a servant in years of danger!" (M, II, 492). A year later he himself seemed to be the found servant, and, in one of the very few references to Marlborough in *The Second World War*, he speaks of "the gracious intimacy" with which he himself was treated by the king as without precedent since "the days of Queen Anne and Marlborough during his years of power" (SWW, II, 380). The conclusion of syllogism is left to the reader.

There is additional irony in Churchill's remark that though Blenheim Palace cost Marlborough much travail, he had built it for posterity and, the Palace still standing, "Marlborough would probably regard it as having fulfilled its purpose if he returned to earth this day" (M, II, 755). It had done so, in a manner personal to the narrator: in it Churchill himself was born. The house is symbolic of the dynasty the general was so eager to found, and, though the line passed on through a daughter, Marlborough would seem to have had his dream of family greatness renewed and fulfilled in Churchill, his faithful biographer and emulator. In Churchill, the general could recognize his own heroic stature. Yes, Blenheim fulfilled its purpose.

But what finally was that mission? What was the ultimate significance of Marlborough's career? "John Churchill saw the rise of Britain to the summit of Europe" by crushing the overwhelming power of France. "He may even have seen at this early time the building up upon the ruins of French splendor of a British greatness which should spread far and wide throughout the world and set its stamp upon the future" (M, I, 264). Since Marlborough was taciturn in his utterances about anything except the immediate circumstances confronting him, this interpretation may be an anachronistic superimposition of Churchill's own philosophy on his ancestor. It conforms, though, to Churchill's role, in the wake of two hundred fifty years of British imperial primacy, of defending against a like tyranny all that Marlborough helped to establish.

Churchill's career thus becomes, in his reading of events, the climax of a three hundred fifty-year-old tradition of European-centered world wars, in which the survival of European liberties is at stake and in which Britain is the belated but potent leader of a Grand Alliance against a would-be tyrant. Three of these world wars Churchill treated in great detail by focusing on the leader—Marlborough and his alter ego, Churchill—who virtually singlehandedly (or so it seems) saw them through. If the *World Crisis* and the *Second World War* are about what Churchill did, the *Marlborough* is about the historical and philosophical bases of his actions, about the hero he imitated. Marlborough's story provides a historical clarification and justification of Britain's role in World War I, out of which she had had the option of staying, and the rationale for Churchill's own role in fulfilling Britain's destiny in the next war, a destiny born in Marlborough's time and under Marlborough's Churchillian vision.

Churchill, after all, was not just another politician but a leader highly conscious of his place in the developing tradition of the nation. No leader of Britain, perhaps, was so immersed in its history, so imbued with its values and its self-assigned mission, so conscious of his place in his family, his and his family's in Britain, and Britain's in Europe and the world. Churchill's greatness is due not only to his considerable talent but also to the clarity of his vision and purpose, the sense of design and destiny which being in a tradition gave him. Offering goals and values, tradition was to him liberating rather than confining. Political genius is perhaps not innate; the family and national traditions contained an exemplar of British *virtú* and charisma which fired the imagination of the young man who performed unevenly in school and seemed in danger of becoming a "social wastrel."

Writing history was thus not only Churchill's hobby or means of earning a living but a way of understanding his own and Britain's career. The *Marlborough* is a biography, history, family archive, and, in a manner of speaking, a proleptic autobiography. Even in the act of writing it, Churchill carries on a family tradition, for it was Marlborough's peculiar ability, in Churchill's analysis, to concurrently serve England, posterity, and himself in "a harmony of interests." So Churchill in this book presented the world with a portrait of heroism, Britain with a reminder of her mission, and himself with a model and prophecy. The *Marlborough* has a story as dramatic and romantic, a style as forceful, ironic, humorous, urbane as the much better known *Second World War*. It also has depth of personal relevance, a poignancy—even, in its proleptic qualities, an eeriness—which makes its perhaps more meaningful and exciting than the egocentric later work.[19]

But did Churchill know that he was rounding out a cycle? If

Marlborough suspected he stood at the beginning of the "greatness of Britain and her claims to empire," did Churchill suspect that he stood at the conclusion of it? If Marlborough picked up a small nation in the pay of France, a satellite to the Sun King, lifted it to the heights, Churchill, alas, set it down a nation dwarfed by hydrogen bomb superpowers, exhausted by the heroic exertions of two world wars, in seemingly permanent financial straits, overtaken by forces of history which caused the dissolution of old empires and the rise of new ones; a satellite now to a new sun, this time in the west, a sun he himself, ironically enough, had hailed memorably, with Clough's line, "But westward, look the land is bright!" Did Churchill see that fact, for all of his heroics about not having become the king's first minister "in order to preside over the liquidation of the British Empire"?

There they stand, the Churchills, at either end of Churchill's story of British ascendency, like the guardians of a great temple. Almost as much as the Caesars or the Romanovs, their family would seem to have been associated with the rise and fall of empire. And Winston Churchill comes at the close: leader, emulator—and, willy-nilly, prophetic scribe.

Or colossal dreamer.

5
The Semi-American

I

CHURCHILL is known to the student of history as, in politics, the young liberal and aging conservative, the scapegoat of Gallipoli and hero of the Battle of Britain, the war-monger and toiler for peace, the opponent of dictators and worshipper of strong men, the student of Napoleon, and, as we saw, emulator of Marlborough. To the student of style, he is a great (or at least famous) writer and a great orator, equally felicitous with phrase or thousand-page book, with quip or hours'-long speech. There was, however, another important element in his personality—his love of America.

It would be difficult to find another example in history of a statesman of one nation being taken so to heart by another nation as has been Churchill by the United States. The reason is not far to seek. The man who has often been called the greatest Englishman of the century also happens to have been half American. This fact did not escape either his contemporaries or himself.

From very early many have played the game—scientifically questionable—of apportioning Churchill's qualities according to his national origins. In March 1901, a Virginian writing to the *Westminster Gazette* saw in the political neophyte's oratorical skill and telling phrase-making a reflection of his Americanism, and since then his percipience, optimism, pragmatism, half-cynical ambition, stamina, elasticity, his self-advertisements, his interest in successful men, his love of hyperbole, and his humor have been related to the putative predominance of his American Jerome strain over the old world, melancholy Spencer-Churchill side. Some commentators were not so complimentary; the editor of the conservative *National Review* in 1905 called this grandson of a Duke "half an alien and wholly undesirable."[1]

Churchill made no secret of his mixed background. Often

declaring himself "very proud" of his American blood, he belonged to various American historical organizations, including, as a descendant of a captain in Washington's army, the Cincinnati. He especially flaunted his American roots during and after World War II. "Tell them," he is supposed to have said to emissaries during a wartime dispute with American officials and in reference to the Indian blood in him, "I was there before they were!" As a young man he toyed with the idea of writing a short and dramatic book on the American Civil War, a subject that remained a lifelong interest of his, as indeed was American civilization. From the first, his articles appeared in transatlantic magazines and newspapers, one American editor even introducing him as a half-American who kept a steady eye on New World affairs. Another editor marveled at the "feeling for the American audience" which Churchill had—partly because he was half American but mainly because he had visited and studied the country—and which caused him to select just the details that "could be of greatest interest to Americans." As an old man, amused by a certain liveliness in American English—or overcome by it against his better judgment—he loved quoting American phrases and verses.[2] His being made an honorary American citizen in 1963 certainly seemed inevitable. Indeed, many have remarked on the propriety that someone of mixed blood achieved, as did Churchill at the climax of his career, an informal and comprehensive Anglo-American alliance in World War II; celebrated—or deluded himself with—the idea of a more sophisticated and inclusive sense of patriotism based on the concept of the "English-speaking peoples"; and suffered, partly in connection with his mother's land, some of the great disappointments of his life in 1945 and 1955.

We have, then, the elements of a love tragedy, in an affair encompassing nearly seven decades and numerous meetings. The first of his many trips to the New World was taken by the twenty-one-year-old Churchill in November 1895. On the way to observing the Cuban guerilla war against Spain, he stopped off at New York to visit relatives and do sightseeing despite his mother's warning that he would be as bored by that expensive city as was everyone else. He found himself anything but bored, and among the results of this stay was a desire to write a book of short stories about a fictional New York journalist (combining thereby his new interest in his own nascent vocation and his continuing interest in America), and a friendship with Congressman Bourke Cochran, who, he claimed in after years, first taught him his oratorical style and the use of the voice as an organ.³

The next direct contact Churchill had with America came in 1900–1. In order to finance his incipient political career, he undertook a protracted lecture tour through Great Britain, the United States, and Canada. Five years earlier he had visited as an unknown, albeit well-connected, young lieutenant in quest of military adventure; now he came as a famous adventurer and writer. He met Governor Theodore Roosevelt (whom he was to resemble in many ways but who took a dislike to him) and President McKinley. His lecture manager, with typical American hyperbole—and to Churchill's proclaimed annoyance—publicized him as the "hero of five wars, the author of six books, and the future Prime Minister of Britain." Further, and, perhaps most exciting of all, his first New York lecture was chaired at Carnegie hall by no less a person than Mark Twain, whom he had adored since childhood. The sixty-five-year-old writer introduced Churchill as "by his father an Englishman, by his mother an American, no doubt a blend that makes the perfect man."⁴

But all was not sunshine. The "vulgar Yankee" lecture manager's lies to the press were embarrassing. Churchill was caught up as well in the stormy American sea of discussion. He denied to what he called the "base" American press that he had come to the United States to marry—as had more than a few impoverished European aristocrats at this time. The audiences of "amiable and hospitable Americans" turned out to be pro-Boer, and he found himself having to wager that the maligned British Empire would survive. No wonder Churchill came to hate the journey and to long for British territory again.⁵

Although he worked during World War I with Americans, notably Bernard Baruch, Churchill did not revisit the United States for nearly three decades. Then in the late 1920s and early 1930s he made a pair of extended visits, semiofficial and private. Many of his experiences and impressions he promptly converted into the lucrative journalism which he turned out in a steady stream during those years "in the political wilderness." The most interesting of these, a series of articles, "What I Saw and Heard in America," appearing in the *Daily Telegraph* between 18 November 1929 and 3 February 1930, was based on a three-month, fifteen thousand-mile voyage through Canada, California, the Grand Canyon, Chicago, and the East. World War II saw, of course, the climax of Churchill's relations with the United States, as he made numerous Atlantic crossings and dealt in London with American officers and diplomats on a daily basis. After these six years of heavy dependence on, and close contact with, the wartime ally, Churchill-American relations never returned to casual prewar tempo, and the United States took on an unprecedent importance in his thinking. He continued to make various visits, official and private, and near the end of his life, he journeyed to America one last time, "because of his mother."[6]

How then did he see the New World? Are there any leitmotifs running through so many decades of contacts and observations? His initial impressions of American civilization, while interesting, hardly differ from those of countless other visitors. The size of the country, he discovered on his extended tours, is overwhelming; long trips come to seem trifling and are not really fatiguing. American trains are superb, with very good beds and food and with "the darky attendants" always providing comfort and amusement. Because the cities are so large—and not alike, as is often asserted—Churchill hastened to the top of the biggest building to survey the scene and obtain a memorable bird's eye view. New York City, with its vivid contrasts, has perhaps the most magnificent panorama in the world, and though individual buildings may be unattractive, the aggregate is full of grandeur.

If Lincoln Steffens discovered the future working well in Soviet Russia, Churchill, during the same decade, found his kind of future in the opposite direction, in California, a vast and blessed state settled, he believed, by the finest Anglo-Saxon stock in America. Blithely oblivious, like everyone else, to all that we have since learned about the second-class status of blacks, Chicanos, Orientals, Indians, and migrant laborers, he waxes lyrical about the absence of poverty in California, about the size and the lights of Los Angeles, a city where people drive ten miles to lunch or dinner.[7]

What made this future viable in America was, Churchill believed, an emphasis on the utilitarian and practical, an absence of tradition and pomp. Though horrified by the currency, the vulgar press (he had a stormy interview with the New York World on 15 December 1895), the ill manners, the absence of gardens, the excessive discipline at West Point, he was pleased by the hospitality of the people with their good heart, vulgar strength, and crude, boisterous health. In the interwar visits, he found that after a few days in New York he could think faster and do more, whether because of an electricity in the air or a climatic factor. America was, moreover, the most educated nation in the world and the land where oratory still mattered.

This activism, to be sure, he held responsible for wide pendulum swings between optimism and pessimism, boom and bust. Americans seem more fragile emotionally; they can soar and then crash more than most people do. They have the defects as well as the strengths of newness and modernity. They resort to the platitudinous, especially on the melting pot process, and exhibit too great a craving to have everyone living uniformly. But Churchill, accepting the modern assumption that a little more material comfort makes for a fuller life, concluded that Americans are basically happy, as well as being hearty and affable. He found their earnestness a refreshing contrast with European cynicism and levity, and the best promise for the future lies, he believed, in combining this with British reserve, sanity, and plodding determination.[8]

Collaborating with Americans in World War II, he noted as never before their strengths and weaknesses in action. They are the "most resourceful and ingenious technicians in the world," whether quickly reopening captured ports, putting to use someone else's invention (like the British tank), or developing various ideas he had given them. Daredevil American pilots, periodically achieving hazardous voyages, form vivid images in the war memoirs of a race of brilliant adventurers. Americans also respond in kind to fair play; "prepared to take the rough with the smooth," they are "very good to work with" and are hardy warriors who will fight to the last inch. They are uniquely generous, as is seen in the way the nation, after either world war, gave money to Europe—and even to, in lieu of exacting reparations, Germany. Self-criticism and self-correction are more actively at work in the United States than elsewhere, and the American imagination is characterized by bigness and boldness.[9]

These skills, virtues, and charms are, of course, allied with faults. The basic flaw is that the American mind, as he saw it at work in World War II, seeks sweeping logical conclusions, a "mass-production style of thought," on which are built its practical actions. This contrasts with the British preference for improvisation and opportunism rather than abstract logic and clearcut principles. The American way, by concentrating on essentials—on what they called "Overall Strategic Objective"—is the first step out of confusion, but in war a second step of subtle harmonizing and balancing of needs is necessary, and it is hard to change an American's plan. "Their national psychology is such that the bigger the Idea, the more wholeheartedly and obstinately do they throw themselves into making it a success. It is an admirable characteristic, provided the Idea is good."[10]

A prewar example of devotion to an Idea without regard to consequences and practicalities was Prohibition. This tragicomic interlude was an index to moral and psychological realities: "No folly is more costly than the folly of intolerant idealism." Follies tending to vice are easily checked, but those sustained by ideals spread easily and cause "sinister reactions." The results, observed by Churchill at first hand in 1929 and 1932, were hypocrisy and a lower, not higher, standard of behavior. America tried to drive away nature and found instead that terrible consequences ensued: temperance was disgraced, racketeering prospered, and money flowed to the underworld, which had become huge, wealthy, and influential in politics, business, and the judiciary.[11]

That a lofty idea could sometimes turn out to have lamentable results is also the burden of his portraits of a pair of eminent Americans. Too egocentric a memoirist to be proficient at character portrayal, Churchill nevertheless devoted an uncharacteristic amount of attention to the American presidents at the time of each world war. In Woodrow Wilson and Franklin Roosevelt he found a typical moral idealism which, with a naive internationalism, operated to the detriment of European wisdom and order. His World War I memoirs, *The World Crisis*, depict Wilson as an intense, impractical innocent, a man with a striking mixture of nobility and vanity, idealism and folly. A concomitant of Wilson's much vaunted idealism was his "autocratic temper and airs." His partisanship undermined his own postwar solutions and projects. He would discipline the Allies no less than punish the Germans. He would preside alone over the Peace Conference, after having, Churchill believes, vainly wished to rule the world at war's end without even bothering to enter the fray. His deferring of the holding of closed meetings at the Conference, his pressing for the formation of the League before the writing of peace treaties, his articulating the idea of "open covenants of peace openly arrived at"—all seem naive to Churchill. He had the temerity to assert that only the American delegation represented the wishes of its own people, whereas in fact, Churchill asserts, the reverse was true: the Allied leaders only too well represented their people in making nationalistic, vindictive demands, while Wilson himself, it soon became clear, had the backing of neither the Senate nor the people of America.

Churchill had had virtually no dealings with Wilson, and his observations—shared by many Britons of all political persuasion and in good part based on the facts[12]—were those of an observer-commentator. A different situation obtains in the case of Franklin Roosevelt. Their many personal conferences, their lengthy correspondence, and their presiding over a uniquely cohesive alliance made for a special relation. Working now not just with an American official (like Baruch in World War I) but with a shaper of history, Churchill influenced another great power's policy as no Briton ever did. Yet, despite their intimacy and despite lavish praise of the president, the *Second World War* consistently suggests that Roosevelt was rather untutored and naive. He is exhibited committing gaucheries like trying to dispose of the vexed Polish question with platitudes, championing the ineffectual Chiang and China, misinterpreting to Stalin, in Churchill's absence, one of Churchill's statements, opposing any postwar "spheres of influence" policy in the face of current American policy south of the border, neglecting to take his vice president into his confidence shortly before his death, and comparing India to the American colonies. On the India question, an angered Churchill writes, "The President's mind," with its innocent idealism reminiscent, we note, of Wilson's in the *World Crisis,* "was back in the American War of Independence." Here was a clash between Roosevelt's quest for American-style democratic forces in Asia and Churchill's fear of the effects such new currents would have on Britain's hold on India. At Teheran, Roosevelt, bypassing Churchill, spoke informally with Stalin about the education of the Asian people in the art of self-government, the two agreeing not to raise the "sore subject" of India with the prime minister. The latter shrewdly intimates Roosevelt's folly in dealing with the sly bolshevik without the presence of a wiser head: "Roosevelt said that reform in India should begin from the bottom, and Stalin said that reform from the bottom would mean revolution. I passed the morning peacefully in bed nursing my cold."[13]

To side with Russia on a potentially revolutionary situation in India was one major sin; to do so against Britain's imperial holdings compounded it. Just as Wilson had apparently sacrificed Allied interests, traditional European diplomacy, and the emergent Anglo-American alliance on the altar of American internationalism, so did Roosevelt seem to make short shrift of the European empires, the realities of communism, and the now (as Churchill thought) vital Anglo-American concord for the sake of a nebulous democratization of the world and vain appeasement of Russia. Both presidents ignored the realities of power and the special Anglo-American destiny because they were blinded, Churchill suggests, by the American tendency to be carried away by a lofty Idea.

II

Moral idealism is only one big Idea Americans pursue. Another is quite the opposite. What notably characterizes American society, Churchill found, is its devotion to making money. Everything is judged by the dollar. At the time of his 1929 visit, moreover, all Americans were speculating on the stock market on margin, as the nation believed it had nowhere to go but up. Ultimately, however, the goal is not money in itself but a thriving business. Churchill observes, as many others have, that social life in America is built around business rather than, as in Europe, around the military services, diplomatic corps, law, the church. Businessmen work, play, and live together, and important matters are settled at the golf or country club. Like the military in Prussia or the imperial civil service in Britain, business is the great challenge to, and lure of, American youth. Hence, while politics and the military services have been left the poorer, commerce has grown to unique levels of development, and the interest in money helped produce an economic system for which Churchill has great praise.[14]

The sheer bulk of American industry and its mass production of consumer articles is incredible. Entire industries spring up overnight. Despite having, as a young man reading H. D. Lloyd, been angered by the oil trust, Churchill in the 1930s offered a reverent study of the typically American career of Rockefeller, who introduced such American innovations as industrial planning, stabilization of prices, creative selling through the arousal of new wants, systematized efficiency, the exploitation of talent, and the institution of boards of directors.[15] Though it exacts its price—the quality of goods is often inferior, the costs are high, taste is decided by leaders of industry—the American system results in social stability and calm. Management is an exact science, and employee relations are good. Men use machines rather than, as in Europe, the reverse. The industrialists see that prosperity does not rest on long hours and low wages. The masses in turn trust the wealthy class and do not tax it heavily.

The gap between producer and consumer is bridged as nowhere else, with a resulting gospel of higher wages, more leisure, and good times for all. Thus the largest economic theater ever opened to man's enterprise is like an army going forward, and no limits to progress are in sight.[16]

Much of Churchill's optimistic description of American capitalism was, ironically, written in the wake of the stock market crash which, generating the Great Depression, social conflicts, and the growth of unionism, would make all these assertions look fatuous. Nor did his patrician and Americophiliac outlook notice or deign to dwell on the seamier side that struck other Britons, significantly H. G. Wells, that is, the plight of the negro, the horrors of child labor, the rampant moral prudery and ethnic intolerance, the tyranny of the majority, the smug national bragging, the unsettling flood of immigrants, the ineffectual Congress, the sheer disorder, the ubiquitous violence, the possibility that America might go under. Even when writing three years later, in the trough of the depression, Churchill still believed that in 1928, America was closer to a "harmonious circle of human transactions than any other community" in history and to reconciling the interests of Capital and Labor. Through excess and error, she stumbled and fell, but the laws of supply and demand are, America has shown, within man's control. The view from a skyscraper reassured him that America would survive and continue hewing new paths for man, showing much that is to be attempted and much to be avoided.[17]

These observations bring Churchill to another central conclusion about American civilization: it is a great experiment, a trail blazer, in so many ways the leading nation of the world and the carrier of the hopes of mankind. If to the Founding Fathers the new American society was to be a model and a moral example to the world, Churchill is even more impressed by American industrial and commercial than political achievements. The theme of America the vanguard in these matters pervades his early and middle writings. In the American presidential election of 1904, for instance, he saw dramatized as nowhere else the major problem of the new century, that of the confrontation of the individual and the big trusts. In a 1906 review of Upton Sinclair's *The Jungle*, he expressed his belief that America is a pioneering society, where Capital and Labor are more clearly at odds than anywhere else. Arousing America's characteristically deep moral fervor, Sinclair's novel would therefore elicit political answers which might be as applicable to the economic and social questions plaguing Britain as to the New World.[18]

American proficiency in commerce is, according to Churchill, in a symbiotic relationship with the American proficiency in politics. With respect he declares, "There is no country in the world where democratic equality is more frequently proclaimed than in America," and he proudly attributes this to the American roots in old English ideas of justice and liberty, as well as in Christian ethics. Only Britain and America have "massive common sense," "long-trained democracy," and a "spacious and predominant middle zone" in which "class adjustments can be fought out." There are, to be sure, differences between the two; nascent America established a novel set of traditions. It produced "something unheard of in the existing world—a written constitution." Its presidency was accessible to all classes of men. Although standing out by its political idealism, it was, because of its intense local political life, the first country to "show that great national decisions must depend upon the matching and mating of small, local causes."[19] (This anticipates Tip O'Neill's "all politics is local.")

Young Churchill even thought that the differences were not always in the New World's favor, that the American system of government is for gods, while the British one is for men. The American elections cost too much in money and business disruption, and the republic's demeanor is inferior to that of the dignified English monarchy and its orderly elections. Though it is better organized for politics than the mother country, the United States has, like France and Germany, a more rigid and conservative constitution than does Britain. Wartime Britain was run by a coalition government, and its monarchy proved more flexible than the American republic. In World War II, the alliance with Britain was put under strain during a presidential election, when popularity was achieved "in that vast community by demonstrating Americanism in its highest forms" by carping at Britain. Such are the harmless, though sometimes repulsive, side effects of the cultivation of free speech greater even than in Britain and of "great big newspapers about one inch thick." Moreover, the controversies do not make for brilliance. Since they represent compromise, American politicians are platitudinous; Ramsay MacDonald would have made an excellent candidate in America because he did not startle but, reflecting the placid crowd, dwelled in clichés.[20]

Nor is Britain burdened with an elaborate party machinery like America's. In the United States there predominates, in place of the British "national family council" based on public opinion and Parliamentary agreement, the "Rule of the Machine," which is a "limited liability dictatorship," especially in cities and scores of useless state legislatures. The political machines are beyond the reach of public opinion. Prohibition, to which Churchill attributes great political significance as the "most amazing exhibition of the arrogance and impotence of a majority" in history, was caused by "machine-made majorities," by the "rat trap rigidity of the American Constitution," the "spasmodic workings" of the electoral process. Passed in the wake of war hysteria and while two million men were overseas and uncomprehending women were given the suffrage, it produced rampant cynicism about politics; where Englishmen would try to change such an unpopular law, Americans preferred to evade it or to resign themselves to it fatalistically. Churchill noted that Upton Sinclair's *The Jungle* dramatizes the sordid fact that the American Dream is fulfilled only when the protagonist becomes a corrupt (and temporarily successful) politician.[21]

Standing in a curious relationship to the political machine is the American president, who seemed to Churchill not just a politician but a personality, a surrogate monarch above politics. A head of state as well as head of government, he has powers of action in emergencies "far beyond those granted to any other individual in the modern world," and the American system of "periodic autocracies" can better cope with grave emergencies than can the British system. But Churchill wonders whether the democratic forms may not at some time mask an arbitrary rule. Theodore Roosevelt was a "warm hearted autocrat"; Wilson's blind partisanship alienated the Republicans and imperiled the Peace Treaties and the League; and Franklin Roosevelt established, it seemed initially, a dictatorship veiled by constitutional forms.[22]

The latter, of course, came to power amid national paralysis, and neither America's moral idealism, nor her expertise in commerce, her role as pioneer and model, or her presidency's great power proved helpful in the depression of the 1930s which tested them all severely. Churchill conceded that the capitalist United States had fared no better in coping with the Depression than did Communist U.S.S.R. Perhaps she had veered too far from capitalism. At first, Churchill had declared himself an "ardent admirer" of Roosevelt's economic and financial policies, with their "heroic sanity," their "noble effort towards a higher form of social justice." A solitary explorer in the gulf between producer and consumer, the president might not be right in his experiments, but he was at least grappling with the problem. His success would relieve a world in which plenty had become a curse. If he failed, he would still have made a creative assay as only the huge United States could, for his impulse was for a better life, unlike the brutal experiments in Nazi Germany or Soviet Russia. The world watched as the United States once again pioneered in progress.

Churchill nevertheless grew anxious lest in his valiant effort to solve that "riddle of the sphinx," the depression, Roosevelt regulated business too minutely and tried to obtain instant prosperity by passing many laws. Decrying Roosevelt's "ruthless war" on the "great wealth-producing agencies of the capitalist system," Churchill feared that this internecine battle would destroy American financial strength at a critical period and lead the world back to depression. The use of national borrowing power, of "relief, pump-priming and New Deal ideology" would create "fraud, waste and imposture," not to speak of a large bureaucracy.[23] Ambivalence marked his response also to the controversial role of the American Supreme Court in the crisis of the 1930s, as Churchill criticized both liberal and conservative views.[24]

If Churchill found much to praise and blame in America's grappling with the depression, so did he in other aspects of the American social and economic institutions. On the one hand, America is exemplary. Forwarding in 1930 the idea of a "United States of Europe," he cited the United States as a vast land mass in which the free exchange of goods flourishes and as a model not unlike the Roman Empire for the achievement of wealth and rapid growth. During World War II America showed how to "take the profit out of war," and then in the postwar economy, she again led the way. Her demobilization rate was double that of the British; her college students numbered in the tens of millions. Her conversion to a peacetime economy, though "violent, convulsive, passionate," led to an enormous output of goods for domestic use and for export.[25]

On the other hand, the independence and isolation of the United States could be economically stunting. The young Churchill, entering upon a political vocation, asked Cochran, with whom he rejoiced in a common transatlantic free trade cause, to send him American speeches and data about the lobbying and corruption caused by Protection. In this matter, America served as a cautionary example, and in the speeches of the 1900s, he often glanced at unsavory conditions in the United States. He warned Balfour that tariffs would Americanize British policy without neutralizing American speculators. He contrasted Britain's prosperity through Free Trade with the "strangle-hold carrying trade" and the cutthroat competition of "dumping" practiced by the Protectionist United States. Like Germany, America's tariffs did not save her from financial collapse, depression in trade, and unemployment. He feared that Protection, were Britain to adopt it, would produce vast syndicates and tyrannical tycoons, "some Rockefellers and Pierpont Morgans of our own." Even the mighty president of the United States "found himself powerless in dealing with the illicit operations of the great trusts."[26]

America is not only a model for domestic good and evil but also a force with great impact on the international economy. As early as the first decade of this century, Churchill blamed America for the European recession of 1909 and emphasized the importance of her prompt recovery. After World War I, America replaced Britain as the great creditor nation, but Protection made repayment by goods difficult. The crash caused gold to flow to America—where it idled without sustaining the economy—and deflation to the rest of the world. Because she was the least harmed by World War I and because all nations were indebted to her, America, Churchill thought, would for long be the recipient of wealth from Europe. By reinvesting it in Europe, she could gain immense control and cause further social dislocation. Fortunately, since Britain could pay off her war debt to the United States only by means injurious to either country's trade, Roosevelt's de facto cancellation of British debts, which enabled Britain to cancel in turn Allied debts, was a bold and sagacious act in his "historic term of office"—albeit an act first urged by Churchill himself in 1919.[27]

In other ways, as well, pride in his fatherland overcame, or at least clashed with, admiration of his mother's land, and the picture of America as the innovative society had to be qualified by gentle reminders of British anticipations, of British tradition and wisdom. In the 1930s, Churchill noted that the United States had but followed Britain in instituting progressive taxation and in belatedly undergoing the development of trade unionism—albeit in an abrupt and therefore dangerous manner. He was so proud of the Elizabethan poor laws that he would have the United States adopt them. Britain also coped better with the drinking problem; high taxation on and strict regulation of the liquor traffic stole the thunder of the Temperance league and collected large moneys for the Treasury coffers.[28] Churchill was never in fact able to resolve his mixed feelings about the United States, his sense of it as a pioneer society which yet had its dubious moments and which was inferior to Britain in certain important respects. If he admired and revered the one, he loved the other.

III

That the mother country still had much to teach the brash, burly stripling was not without its implications for foreign policy. More even than America's obsession with an Idea or her role as a pioneering society, the most abiding of Churchill's themes in the last third of his life was the concept of an English-speaking community, an Anglo-American "unwritten alliance," a special relationship. The idea evolved with changing political circumstances through the decades. In May 1898, young Churchill privately sounded the first notes of this theme and a prophecy: "As a representative of both countries—the idea of an Anglo-American *rapprochement* is very pleasant [sic]. One of the principles of my politics will always be to promote a good understanding between the English-speaking communities." Transcending any mere alliance—he regarded the popular idea of an Anglo-American alliance as a "wild impossibility"—was the common interest of the two powers.[29]

In 1898 he also wrote an article in the *North American Review* in which he expressed pleasure at being invited by an American journal to speak freely as a citizen of the "Great Empire" to—and here is the initial appearance of a beloved phrase of his—"the Great Republic." He closed the piece by speaking of the "great community with whom we are united by the sympathy of a single language and consciousness of a common aim." Because of the "priceless gift of common language" and the good feeling he discovered on his early visits, even the most delicate topics could be thrashed out with great candor between Americans and Britons, and he was hopeful that the day would soon come when the English-speaking peoples would really understand each other. The sober, pragmatic politician, it is clear, could have had no patience with witty Wildean paradoxes about the two nations divided by a common language. On the contrary, he urged in

1901 the furthering of the linguistic bond through the institution of an English *Academie Française* to regulate usage lest the peoples lose their common tongue and drift apart as a result of its becoming "too common."[30]

Churchill often cited Bismarck's observation that there was a potential alliance secured by an accident of history, namely that the two powers spoke the same language. Having long taken pride in English, with its "priceless literary treasures and worldwide business connections," and in the "glorious classics of our own language," he became interested in the 1940s in developing Basic English as an auxiliary international language and as a supplement to the established literary language. In a fit of linguistic imperialism reminiscent of Tudor times, he wanted the BBC, as part of its World War II propaganda, to teach Basic English every day. This practical step would be a gain "more durable than the annexation of great provinces. It would also fit in with my ideas of closer union with the U.S. by making it even more worth while to belong to the English-speaking club," as large masses of the world's population would thus be able "to participate more easily in our society," even without knowing English in full.[31]

The linguistic accident happily coincided with the political and diplomatic aims of Britain and in turn with her economic policy. In the event of a European war, Churchill said in a 1903 letter, it would be better for Britain if the United States had a vested interest in keeping her English market open rather than, as a result of British Protection, remaining indifferent. In a speech of the same year, he pointed to the obverse: in case of war, the mid-Western American states would be an important source of food for Britain. Hence Britain must "cultivate good relations with the U.S.," and this desideratum shaped his responses to current events. He wanted Britain to be careful not to imperil a growing Anglo-American understanding, even when America was somewhat in the wrong, as in the case of a minor incident in Jamaica. Above all, the granting of Home Rule to Ireland would, he insisted in 1912, gain the sympathy of "the great Republic across the water" with its large Irish population and numerous Irish-American policians, and therefore be of great importance for the Empire's foreign policy in a critical period.[32]

When World War I began and Churchill was at the Admiralty, he eagerly desired to have the United States join the Allies. But the Americans proved, as relatives sometimes will, refractory and unpredictable. While the outburst of sympathy for the Allies in 1914 brought fifty thousand American volunteers, their government seemed "neutral in favor of Germany" in its legalistic attitude on sea traffic. Nor was America's eventual choice so obvious and predetermined. Its national tradition was hostile to Britain and friendly to Prussia and Ireland. Only careful diplomacy and German folly "guarded the English-speaking world and its destiny from measureless injury." Gradually that "great and last reserve of Civilization," the "largest, if not the leading, civilized nation . . . the most numerous democracy in the world," joined the fray.[33] Churchill celebrates in the *World Crisis* the two Atlantic powers carrying on the war in common, dealing with supplies as two friends share a lunch basket—Churchill himself at the Munitions Office working closely with Bernard Baruch.

Alongside the "island race" and the common cause of the Allies, Churchill invoked, in narrating the American advent, a third mystique, that of the English-speaking world. By their numbers and power, this largest group of harmonious people since the days of Rome made English for the first time the second official language at the Peace Conference. Now that Britain and America were together, no one could withstand them; their strength could be applied anywhere, in any form, and to any extent. It would afford the only guarantee of peace, restore world trade, secure a stable world currency, and indeed solve any international problem. After fifty years of strife and hatred and then one hundred years of peace, "the two great branches of the English-speaking world had begun again to write their history in common."[34]

The major fact confronting Churchill on revisiting the United States in 1929 was that the two countries formed, especially in the wake of the World War I cooperation, one civilization. They achieved the greatest "efflorescence of freedom, wealth and power" for so large a population and so long a period. He therefore wanted the wartime "comradeship and sense of reunion" to be kept as a first priority despite differences with the United States at the Peace Conference and elsewhere. The best step, he counseled in 1935, would be an Anglo-American agreement to retain joint forces stronger than any other power and to use them against aggression. Though much could be said against having the English-speaking peoples be the policemen of the world, this measure would prevent war. Churchill even dreamed of a "covenant of the English-speaking Association," with common citizenship and with the inclusion of Canada, Australia, and New

Zealand. The Empire and the United States could become members of one political body, in a healing of the scars, a righting of the wrongs of the American Revolution.[35]

He saw the alliance as especially necessary, at various times, against such specters as Japan, communism, the depression, or, eventually, Hitler. One practical consequence of his dream of a "supreme reconciliation" and of permanent join action would be the transference of responsibility for Palestine to the United States. Another would be the transfer of British responsibility for peace (and for the protection of the white man) in the Pacific and Far East regions, especially in the face of a resurgent Japan, which began to worry him as early as 1921. Indeed after World War II he was happy to see America "looking after" Turkey and taking "over from us the salvation of Greece"; and he hoped that she would do the same with Persia and Egypt. Britain's burdens needed to be lightened.

This new affiliation must not, however, infringe on "existing arrangements," that is, on the Empire. For the survival of the imperial system had also been central to Churchill's thought, and he would obviate any difficulties over this issue by helping to introduce the New World to the old world *modus operandi*. This was an old wish of his. America's size, wealth, political stability, and might naturally sought expression on the world stage, and young Churchill had been quick to grant her admission to the club of big powers. In 1895 he wrote newspaper dispatches and magazine articles which looked at the Cuban war in the context of power politics of the day. He saw that as the war dragged on, attention would turn to "that Great Power of the Western Hemisphere on whom the responsibility of action would then fall." The wanton cruelties of the Spaniards had aroused sympathy in America for the Cubans, and many American adventurers were already fighting on the rebel side. The rebels themselves, he was sure, wanted Cuba to join the American Union and become a resort area for Americans and a hive of commercial interests. Desiring to be just and generous, an interventionist America would therefore solve the Cuban question in a way "equitable to the insurgents, honorable to Spain, and glorious to themselves."

This noble-sounding rhetoric translates into the desire to have an emergent American imperialism replace the decadent Spanish one; the alternative, the establishment of yet another unstable South American republic, would, he thought, be monstrous. Although he came to reprehend the "disgusting" American role in the Cuban war, he insisted on the existence of a basic American probity and nobility,[36] and in the 1930s, when various forces pushed Britain toward dismantling the Empire, Churchill addressed an article, "Defense in the Pacific," to American readers. It urged them to resist the clamor for replacing stable American rule in the Philippines—a by-product of the Cuban war—with local independence. American entry into the sphere of "colonial administration" may have irritated Asians but led to peace in the Pacific, and prosperity and modernization in the Philippines. This was a question of American duty, dignity, honor, and not of money. When he drew a parallel to the British role in India, he made explicit what had been implicit: his complaints about the many slanders perpetrated in the name of anti-imperialism; his accusations against the American Governor Harrison for hastening, like the viceroy in India, the pace to independence and lowered standards; his warning that autonomy would lead to anarchy and a return to the jungle; his fears that Japan would step into the power vacuum—all these merely echoed his concurrent bitter critique of British plans to grant India independence. The article was thus an attempt to rally American support for his dying imperialist position by keeping the United States as an accomplice or at least making her see that she was committing the same error as Britain in the name of progress.[37]

But Churchill went beyond merely talking in political terms of a special relation; he devoted to the subject in the late 1930s a few years of reading and writing, a team of research assistants, and a four-volume tome. This most important expression of his Anglo-American creed, the *History of the English-Speaking Peoples,* was one of the first attempts by anyone to write a joint history of the United States and Britain. Churchill was uniquely qualified for such an approach; from the biological and existential circumstances of his life came his idiosyncratic historiography and philosophy of history, as well as one of the shaping themes of his actions as prime minister. Depicting the glorious spreading of civilization by the British, the ubiquity of the English law and language, the *History* resounds, in its closing pages, with the grand theme of Anglo-American reunion, the vision which is his political testament. His song being about the inevitable convergence of the two titans, he sees himself as a Virgil-like prophet-bard finding in the past the seeds of the future.[38]

The work was hardly uncritical. Too many innovations ascribed to America were, he insisted, in fact British. The Declaration of Independence restated the principles animating the English Revolution of 1688; the Constitution, neither revolutionary nor based on the writings of the French *philosophes,* merely applied to a new situation old English ideas of freedom, "henceforth to be regarded on the other side of the Atlantic," he mischievously adds, "as basically American." The Monroe Doctrine made "resounding claims," whose acceptance by the world depended for a century on the friendly but unacknowledged vigilance of British sea power—which thus made possible America's phenomenal development, her "security and splendor."

Churchill challenges alleged myths about American innocence no less than those about American originality. An incipient New World imperialism, he finds, turned North and South; the War of 1812, fought ostensibly over questions of maritime law and subversion from Canada, was fomented by "War Hawks" with designs on the entire Northern continent. More legends were spawned by the battle of New Orleans, which took place after the signing of peace and was made to seem a decisively victorious end to what was alleged to be "a second War Independence against British tyranny" but was in fact "futile and unnecessary conflict." The Mexican War was, as Churchill quotes Grant, "wicked," and Manifest Destiny produced an explosive expansiveness. By the 1890s, America began to enter upon the world stage in a role commensurate with her strength, and, like the other industrialized powers, sought overseas possession. The result was the Spanish-American War and the acquisition of various territories.

Churchill here is partly like a patriot rescuing his elderly country's reputation from the exorbitant claims made on behalf of the glamorous, young America and partly like a father indulgently reprimanding a loved child's readiness to let its imagination run free. Such criticisms in the book were paralleled by those, public and private, on current foreign policy questions. In 1928, Churchill found the United States arrogant, domineering, hostile to Britain; his "known hostility" to the United States may have even stood in the way of his going to the Foreign Office. He was critical of American insistence that Britain pay her war debts to the United States. In the early 1930s, the French and the pacifists were urged by him to take with a grain of salt the advice liberally proferred by a United States safely ensconced three thousand miles away. Above all, in the *World Crisis* he had at one point peremptorily—and hilariously—punctured American pretensions:

It is difficult to believe that the European emigrants by whom America has been populated took away with them all the virtues and left behind them all the vices of the races from which they had sprung; or that a few generations of residence on the other side of the Atlantic Ocean is sufficient to create an order of beings definitely superior in morals, in culture, and in humanity to their prototypes in Europe. . . . It would seem probable that on both sides of the Atlantic men find it easy to be disinterested upon questions which do not affect them directly; that they are often inclined to prescribe high principles for others to follow; that they can resist other people's temptations.[39]

These reservations and criticisms notwithstanding, Churchill remained optimistic about America and the future. As it turned out, the future approached more quickly than he perhaps expected. If the *History* expresses Churchill's vision of a wise old Britain and a strong young America guiding the world, events transformed, by the time of writing, the old belief in a single community into the practical necessity of forming an alliance against Hitler. The ultimate keeper of the peace was the United States, which alone, in the absence of a European alliance, could save Europe. "How heavily," he wrote in a series of newspaper articles, "do the destinies of this generation hang upon the government and people of the United States!" Would they join the cause of peace, freedom, and law in time? "Under the mask of loquacity, affability, sentimentality, hard business, machine-made politics . . . efficiency and muddle," America still has the "power to pronounce a solemn and formidable word," to become a champion of the world. Here is Churchill, before Henry Luce or World War II, speaking in effect of the "American Century."

In time, the "greatest single power in the world" joined the war on behalf of the "common cause." The English-speaking world, this new supranational entity, was on the move, "the forces of modern progress and of ancient culture" dependent on it. Unlike in World War I, Britain and America enjoyed a protracted and intimate relationship, a unified command, a joint strategy. The Anglo-American cooperation was like nothing "ever seen before . . . unique in all the history of alliances"; it included the "greatest joint operations between two Allies that have ever been planned in history." This is what had been a velleity in 1898— "what I have dreamed of, aimed at and worked for, and now it has come to pass."[40] Indeed, Churchill himself was, poetically enough, its prophet, catalyst, agent, witness, chronicler, and celebrator.

His worship was intense but again not altogether blind. He believed that American isolationism, protectionism, and naively idealistic bias against monarchies and empires had helped prepare the way for World War II. When European hostilities began, the United States had been tardy in responding to British distress signals, perhaps thinking to inherit the Empire and the Royal Navy. Moreover, once she did bestir herself, she had unfortunately to be deferred to on various issues, such as the choice of a supreme commander, the Riviera landing, Chiang (whom she liked), DeGaulle (whom she did not), India, Palestine, and, at war's end, Russia. But America had displaced Britain as leader of the free world, and, on balance, Churchill could live with that fact.

In the postwar years, Churchill still publicly worshipped the United States and harped on the English-speaking mystique. The United States was now to him nothing less than the "greatest state in the world." Possessing the A-bomb on which the world depended for security, she stood "at the summit of the world" in a "sublime moment" in history. Twice in one lifetime had "Europe's children of earlier times"—an America impelled, Churchill insists, by moral sentiment instead of profit and loss calculation—recrossed the ocean to rescue Europe from a "long German night." A source of anxiety now was the resurgent isolationism in America which saw her as the "last remaining haunt of capitalism in a world . . . degenerating into Socialism" and which regarded Britain as only half a big power. Relations with the United States were rendered sometimes problematic by both the Laborites in Britain and the "Hoover-Taft body" of political and military opinion, that is, the American Conservatives "who think that China is more important than Europe." Churchill therefore wrote an article for *Life*, (14 April 1947) on the eve of the inauguration of the Truman Doctrine, which argued that America must set aside her traditional "self-expression in isolation." A Britain exhausted by two world wars had had to end a two-hundred year mission and now welcomed American entry upon the path assigned her by destiny. The two nations could go forward together. He was soon reassured to see America take over from Britain the "first position in world leadership," assume much of the burden Britain had borne hitherto, come round to the anti-Communist position which he had first adopted and been excoriated for, promise to abandon isolation, to maintain her military power for use against aggression, and to join other powers in keeping the peace. Such a declaration by a strong internationalist United

States in the summer of 1914 would have turned the crisis into a parley; in early 1915, might have stopped the war; in 1919, "would have led to a real Treaty of Peace and a real armed League"; between the wars would have prevented the resumption of hostilities.[41]

America's greatness was still mysteriously tied, for Churchill, to her being part of the English-speaking community. He hoped that the "two major groupings of the human family, the British Empire and the United States, who, fortunately for the progress of mankind, happen to speak the same language, and very largely think the same thoughts" and who came together "naturally, without the need of policy or design" or pacts, in a reunion of a family torn asunder long ago, would remain allied this time for "their own safety and the good of all," would avoid the errors of the previous war by no longer assuming that there will never be a war again. The common cultures which might have remained "an interesting historical coincidence" have, on the "anvil of war," been "welded together" to form the force which preserves "Christian civilization" and man's freedom.

Churchill could not but recognize an inequality in the relationship. The once great British Empire was now beholden to the United States, "with whom our fortunes and interests are intertwined": British unemployment was kept down only because of American loans, and British security rested on American nuclear bombs. The war over, the two nations became commercial rivals again, and his fears over a "struggle in the economic sphere" were not soothed by Britain's financial dependence. But he was calmed by the thought that Anglo-American prosperity was interdependent and that Britain still played a "leading part in the modern world." He urged America not to "underrate the strength of Britain," which America needs. The two nations are like "friends and brothers," America being larger and stronger but Britain older and wiser.[42]

Defiantly proud to have American nuclear weapons stored in Britain, he even looked ahead to an "ultimate union," a "free, voluntary, fraternal association," in which, despite the disparity of national power, the two peoples would have common passports, citizenship, voting rights, and virtually a common economy, foreign policy, and military force. He was disappointed, therefore, that the Labor Government had allowed relations with the United States to lapse and that at the close of his own peacetime ministry, Britain found herself no closer to the United States than at the beginning. Though certain that the "increasing association [of Britain and America] will come" not through speeches but through the tides in human affairs and the destiny of the world, he conceded in the 1957 Epilogue to the *Second World War* that such harmony had proved elusive and wondered whether it would take another war to bring it finally about. Still, the American response to his visits kept him buoyant, and he thought that he could make the powerful but clumsy United States sensible. Poignantly, therefore, at eighty-five, "late in the day," he came to America (in 1959) for the last time to tell of what "I have always lived up to, namely: the union of the English-speaking peoples."[43]

The younger, stronger power would not, however, be guided by anyone, and the evanescence of the special relationship was not the only vexation caused by America in his old age. The major turn in his thinking in the years of his peacetime ministry was the readoption of his willingness in the 1930s to be reconciled with Soviet Russia. In this he was opposed by, of all people, the Americans who had been, as he thought, naive about communism in 1944–45. Though he had felt sure before he returned to office that were he prime minister he could make the Americans reasonable, now that he had the power, he found he could not influence the foreign policy of Eisenhower and Dulles, a policy that he feared would lead to conflict. The Americans claimed to have no objection to Churchill's undertaking one last "solitary pilgrimage" to Moscow to see what could be done with the new Soviet leadership in the wake of Stalin's death, but the trip was finally blocked.

It even came to the point when Churchill, visiting the States in 1954, had to reply heatedly to American suggestions that British policy toward Russia was one of appeasement. America behaved in a disappointing fashion because, Churchill thought (according to Lord Moran), the nuclear bomb made her arrogant, Eisenhower and Dulles were blind, and their moralistic rhetoric alienated the Russians and stirred up the satellite states to no purpose. As a result, he could not fulfill his last political ambition, of bringing about detente and climaxing his career of war-making with a great act of peacemaking in a supreme moment of history.[44] While old age, illness, Foreign Office opposition, and Russian suspiciousness played their important roles in frustrating his plan, well might it seem to the old man, with his lifelong fascination with the "Great Republic," that this final apotheosis eluded him as a result of his having taught the now omnipotent Americans the lesson of anticommunism all too well. He had raised a

Coriolanus or Frankenstein monster. For a third time an American president seemed inept in international diplomacy. Once again, the Anglo-American alliance proved inoperative. Once again, and at a fatal juncture in his own career, the Americans had been carried away by an Idea.

IV

The concept of an Anglo-American reunion that Churchill dramatized and literally embodied, is not, of course, his own. It was already in the air when this highly self-conscious and politicized Anglo-American entered the world stage in 1895; he matured at a propitious moment in the history of transatlantic affairs. The tensions of the 1770s, 1810s, and 1860s had been replaced by an uneventful period in Anglo-American relations, toward the close of which, in the 1890s, both sides had begun to take new bearings. The United States became conscious of its role in the outside world at the same time that Britain, growing anxious about hers, was eager to secure her rear.

Changes in national policy were preceded and paralleled by changes in the climate of opinion. There had always been traces of Anglophilia in the literary culture of New England, and theories of American racial and cultural ties to England were propounded by scholars in either country. Transatlantic upperclass marriages, like that of Churchill's parents, proliferated in the last third of the century. But now there appeared proposals which would convert sympathies and affinities based on a shared linguistic and cultural heritage into concrete political measures. One of the earliest of these was an 1893 article in the *North American Review* by Andrew Carnegie, which argued that the eighteenth-century schism was an unfortunate event reprehended by the leaders of the conflict, that modern technology made a reunion feasible, and that mutual needs made it necessary. Such a "Reunited States," or "British-American Union" would, as the biggest world power, secure global peace, engender a less provincial patriotism, and accord with the tendencies of the age toward consolidation.

This essay was followed by others during the next few months, the most important of which was "The Possibilities of an Anglo-American Reunion" by the American who would become the theorist of sea power, Captain A. T. Mahan. Having already in an 1890 *Atlantic Monthly* article spoken in passing of the need for a "cordial understanding" with the one other nation controlled by a "sense of law and justice" and having been lionized in Britain in 1894 amid much talk of one nation, Mahan urged both countries to see their mutual interests as sea powers and as upholders of freedom and civilization. Aware that, although they had a common origin and common destiny, both peoples were not ready for reconciliation, Mahan, like most proponents of reunion, dismissed the idea of an old-fashioned defensive-offensive alliance or written treaty. The convergence could only be brought about by time, patience, and experience.[45]

Experiences came along soon enough. The Venezuelan crisis of 1895 precipitated an Anglo-American confrontation that many (including young Churchill) thought could lead to hostilities—a prospect which delighted Americans and horrified Britons. But it proved to be the last such crisis, and it was followed, surprisingly soon enough, by a wave of interest in Anglo-American cooperation, no less so in the United States, where the Anglo-Saxon ruling elite was estranged from a nation being changed by the immigrant waves from Eastern and Southern Europe, than in a Britain isolated among the world powers. Britain, now feeling family pride in the United States, regarded the rise of the United States as a good thing, and treated relations with her as something beyond normal national rivalry, something "metapolitical." Subsequent Anglo-American disputes were settled to America's advantage, and the mother country in effect resigned to the United States her own place in the world order and her naval supremacy. The policy of a special relationship formulated by Balfour (and, subsequently, Grey) eschewed, remarks Max Beloff, visions of common citizenship but contented itself with not opposing the United States and with soliciting American support for Britain.

During the Spanish-American war and the American repression of the Philippino insurrection, Britain alone encouraged the United States in its emergent imperial venture, while Germany seemed obtrusive in her pro-Spanish stance. There followed, in 1897–99, a flood of articles in British and American journals by men like James Bryce, Joseph Chamberlain, and Charles Dilke, as well as many Americans, which celebrated the affinities and greatness of the Anglo-Saxons, urging common citizenship and currency, free trade, a joint arbitration tribunal, and ruled out defensive-offensive alliances that smacked of traditional power politics. The "Anglo-American League" was formed in July 1898 to promote these ends, and such men as Cecil Rhodes, Lord

Derby, H. G. Wells, Bertrand Russell, Sidney Webb, Rudyard Kipling (and, later, G. B. Shaw, Ian Hamilton, and John Galsworthy) entertained the idea of an English-speaking Union. If in the Venezuelan crisis, Britain came to think that the use of power against America would be tantamount to civil war, the Spanish-American War brought each English-speaking power into the other's system. One enthusiastic English journalist, W. T. Stead, even wrote a febrile book, *The Americanization of the World or the Trend of the Twentieth Century* (1901) that advocated reunion with America at any price. Certain of the primacy of English-speaking civilization and of American hegemony, he would have Britain console herself with the thought that just as Christianity spread the message of Judaism, so Americanization was but Anglicization writ large and universalized. A Britain guilty of the schism of 1776 would either swallow her pride or become an "English-speaking Belgium."[46]

Another dose of experience pushing the two nations together was the Boer War, in which it was Britain's turn to be isolated from Europe and to behold the same Germany that had sided with Spain now encouraging the Boers. Though many Americans were pro-Boer, John R. Dos Passos (father of the novelist) discerned in the two wars an emerging pattern. Writing in 1903 *The Anglo-Saxon Century* (subtitled, *The Unification of the English-Speaking People*), he predicted that the United States and Britain would reunite as a matter of natural sympathy, self-interest, duty, and divine destiny. With power concentrated in the hands of the most worthy, this bloc, replacing the decadent and disunited Spanish-speaking and Portuguese-speaking peoples, could anglicize and predominate over the world, eliminate war, advance civilization and Christianity. Finding the American press, bar, pulpit, and stage favorable to the idea, he believed that a "sudden upheaval or unexpected revolution in international affairs" could forge such an association in a day.[47]

That upheaval turned out to be World War I, and when the United States joined the fray, Henry Adams, who had seen as early as in 1898–1900 the need for an "Atlantic system," rejoiced in the accomplishment of a great objective of his life: "perhaps we can keep it up." That was the faith also of Walter Lippmann and G. L. Beer. The latter, an American historian who had long championed the British Empire and the eighteenth-century colonial system and who regarded the American Revolution as a disaster which might some day be reversed, greeted the redemptive hour. Ceasing his scholarly labors, he wrote a series of articles which became a tract with a significant title, *The English-Speaking Peoples*, and subtitle, *Their Future Relations and Joint International Obligations*. It is actually a compendium of ideas made famous by Churchill's later speeches and writings: a common language is of central importance in securing unity and nationality; British civilization is unique and exemplary; America is a quasi-British society governed by men of Anglo-Saxon stock; the United States by her isolationism, idealism, and unarmed innocence was responsible for the Great War, but her entry into the conflict placed her in a dominant moral position; America had to guarantee world peace through not a League of Nations but an alliance with Britain and a joining of their seapower; the alliance was not to be forced but was part of an evolution, a matter of growing popular sympathy, a new form of political association; because of her empire, Britain had a supranational spirit which could qualify excessive American nationalism; the United States and Britain were now economically interdependent and together they could help the backward and war-harassed lands.[48]

What is surprising, then, is not that Churchill spoke privately in 1898 of his hopes for Anglo-American reconciliation but that, beginning his political career in the late 1890s, he contributed so little to the widespread public discussion of the idea—he whose father had averred prophetically in 1889 that, if Britain ever found herself in a mortal struggle, the United States would come to her aid and whose mother had joined the vogue of Anglo-Saxonism a decade later by naming (over her son's objections) a literary journal she was founding in Britain, the *Anglo-Saxon Review*. Overt commitment by him came only with World War I, and his wishes for a common citizenship were first expressed in the late 1930s and 1940s, nearly a half-century after the idea had been seriously considered. His remarks hardly received a response now, for, far from being a prophet ahead of his time on this matter, Churchill, we can see, was in fact retrogressive and antiquated. Even in 1898 the young man had shrewdly seen that, modern alliances resting on that most fragile and transitory of political entities, common interests, America would not want to pick the imperial chestnuts out of the fire for Britain. Decades later, as Max Beloff observes, it would be the object of Churchill's diplomacy to persuade America to do just that, and his youthful skepticism would prove justified. But now the old statesman, cleaving nostalgically to late Victorian certitudes and intoxicated by his rich World War II experiences as forger of the Grand

Alliance and as friend of Roosevelt, was possessed by reveries of Anglo-American solidarity. He borrowed certain archaic commonplaces, made them the core of his public policy and writings, and gave them a vital if brief life in the realm of politics and diplomacy.[49]

His sense of the special destiny of the English-speaking peoples was, moreover, but the extension, under the impress of events, of his slightly older and equally Victorian belief in the mission of Britain and her Empire. It rests, G. K. Lewis points out, on such dubious assumptions as the existence of a "collection of racial virtues," of an English character that was exported to the United States with the language, and of one age and locale which is the climax of the human experience. Nor does a language necessarily unify people, as Churchill supposed, or else there would never be civil war. Words seemed so central to him, adds Peter de Mendelssohn, that he came to believe that a common language is a stronger bond than are common experiences, institutions, interests.

The interest in the 1890s in a reunion proved to be only a minor flurry. The Anglo-American cooperation of 1917–18, 1941–44, 1947–48, and 1950, temporary expedients in the face of common dangers, were followed by periods of divisiveness. Blind faith in the "special relation" prevented a grasp of the political realities. There were, Beloff notes, insufficient personal, business, and labor contacts to make reunion feasible. The divergence of national goals, like the concurrent British decline and American rise—World War I certified the displacement— made the "special relation" an irritant to America.[50]

If before World War I America's coming of age was viewed with enthusiasm by Britons, the 1920s saw a mutual disillusionment. The United States, turning its back on Europe and on the idealism of its venture, now seemed, as the world's biggest power and an island of prosperity amid worldwide economic dislocation, a land given over to materialism, selfish isolation, commercial rivalry with Europe, braggadoccio over its wartime role, obduracy in collecting debts, and the source of the vulgar changes in Europe known as Americanization. In the 1930s, there was, according to A. J. P. Taylor, no great "lost opportunity," as Churchill complained, to obtain American support, for the United States, enmeshed now in its own depression, was not interested in underwriting any British guarantees of French or European security. Furthermore, in the 1940s, which saw a resurgence of the old dream, Churchill had to invent, or depend on, the Bolshevik peril in order to maintain the Anglo-American concord.

Believing that American would restore British greatness after the war, Churchill chose to regard signs of American awakening (like Lend Lease) as feats of generosity. Even while he projected in 1943 an eventual Anglo-American citizenship, the Americans, lacking the English-speaking mystique, were becoming worried more about British imperialism (in India, the Mediterranean, and the Balkans) than Russian expansionism. Just as in 1917–18 they spoke of the "Associated Powers" rather than "Allies" and did not believe that Britain stood for the general welfare, so now the Americans, perceiving Britain as more dangerous for the postwar world than Russia (which was not a colonial power and with which they shared a disbelief in Churchill's argument that penetration of the Mediterranean was necessary for the Second Front), pushed Britain out of the innermost council. What Churchill took to be the long talked-of permanent English-speaking peoples' reunion, the Americans regarded as only a temporary alliance, soon displaced by the need for an understanding with Russia. America proved, in short, to be neither so idealistic nor so pioneering as he had thought.[51]

The great difficulty, it seemed to Anthony Eden in July 1944, was that the semi-American Churchill regarded with religious awe an American president who was but an astute politician of great vanity and obstinacy. But Max Beloff believes that after the war, Churchill, realizing the physical superiority of America, merely played on the sentiments of a "special relation" and, despite gestures of defiance, did not rely on it. At any rate, scholars, noting that Churchill little explores or understands in the *Second World War* the American suspicions about British intentions, remind us that the last word in the title of the last volume, *Triumph and Tragedy*, refers to the dissolution not of the wartime Western-Russian Grand Alliance but of the special relationship of the English-speaking peoples. (It probably also refers to the death of Roosevelt and the election defeat of Churchill and the decline of the British Empire.)

So, despite his long romance with American civilization, Churchill found himself defeated by what he considered American naivete and perhaps by a residual distrust of the British Empire which had been burned into the American soul at its birth. Admiration for Britain in 1940 could not overcome scorn for the Empire as a relic of the past. For all of the suspicion of socialism and fear of communism that Churchill had through the years discerned in the American psyche, at a critical juncture the American Revolution, the realities of power, and three kinds of American Anglophobia—ethnic, left anticolonialist, right nationalist[52]—temporarily helped America find greater community of interests with another, albeit remote and enigmatic, revolutionary society than with the fellow English-speaking but once oppressive and still imperialist mother country. In the postwar world, furthermore, America's interests were different from Britain's, a fact which Churchill could not either comprehend or confront. Churchill's wish to have the United States replace Britain as the world's policeman, with an avuncular Britain providing guidance, was only partly in accord with American aims. Churchill's rhetoric notwithstanding, America had no need of Britain as counselor, uncle, or ally; in the nuclear age its only de facto ally was the H-bomb.

That one world power replaces another is hardly unusual in history, but doubly unusual is that the emergent power has the same language and similar civilization as the declining one and that the head of government of the latter at this crucial juncture is someone with roots in both societies. Beginning as a detached though interested private observer of America, Churchill was caught up in the rush of history, both in his own career, which led him to the prime ministership, and in the European scene, which led to war and to rescue by the United States. Events turned his interest into an inspired, relevant, and rational idea. The wartime alliance was probably inevitable, no matter who the prime minister, but only Churchill, semi-American historian-prophet of English-speaking civilization, because of his lineage, character, vision, personal contacts, charm, sense of the superiority of Anglo-Saxon culture, and eloquence could endow it with an almost metaphysical quality.

Churchill lived through a tragic phase in British history, from his entry upon the scene, when the Empire was still in its primacy and the United States was emerging from her cocoon, through the period when the United States twice came to the rescue of Britain and finished wars the old World had begun, to the post-World War II period when the United States, as one of the two superpowers, became the protector of the "free world" and Britain a second-rank power shorn of empire. In prominent positions during the crucial period of displacement, he naturally hoped that the ascendent America and descendent Britain would become "more and more mixed up together." What had been at first a matter of curiosity—a personal biological *donnée*—became a velleity, then an aesthetic consideration with reference to two large nations, and finally a political necessity for sheer survival. What others had dreamed of when he was young, Churchill, in old age, with the requisite opportunity, zeal—and naivete—would try to realize. What had been a model among nations, a pioneer society, despite its scabrous character, its socioeconomic storms, its erratic domestic and foreign policy, its naive diplomacy, became a deus ex machina which would miraculously revive and continue the British mission. Rather as some people hope for vicarious immortality through their children, so did Churchill, unconsciously influenced by the reconciliation of the two civilizations in his own family, think to endow Britain with renewed life at the summit of power by this undoing of the American Revolution, this reversion to an older community.

Churchill seized the brief period of equilibrium and harmony between the two nations and projected it into the future as a permanent state of being. He became the epic poet of an imaginary special relationship which he thought to be the climax of an evolutionary process and the call of destiny but which was only a *reductio ad absurdum* of certain temporary assumptions. All his other views and comments on America ran like tributaries into the river of this putative alliance which grew to be the central theme of his life, his last will, his final illusion. Treating a now mature America as a scion of Britain, he was frustrated to discover that America, like most children, developed a will and style of her own, that her aiding Britain in the two world wars were only incidents in a phase and had a significance other than what he attributed to it. History transformed Dos Passos's dream of the "Anglo-Saxon Century" into (at least for a while) Henry Luce's of the "American Century."

Two major themes of Churchill's writing on the New World—America predisposed to possession by a lofty Idea, America as a great experiment—seemed to lead naturally to, but in fact proved inconsistent with, the culminating theme of an Anglo-American union. He had approached an America on the eve of greatness and imagined her, like Britain, better than she, or any nation, ever could be. He had also misunderstood her nature. America was to him a pioneering society because she was a British export or outpost, a flower of English civilization given new vitality by transplantation, and not because of the contribution made by later arrivals. Guided by the supremacy of English in the United States, all that he saw was the Anglo-Saxon stock assimilating the other nationalities and governing the land benignly. Hence he overlooked, as someone like his friend Birkenhead did not, the contribution of non-British immigrants and the shift of power away from the Eastern pro-British establishment. So obsessed was he in fact with the original English settlement of America, with the American roots in the British past, that he did not see in the New World what everyone else in nineteenth-century Europe saw—the golden land of refuge, of individual opportunity, of a fresh start, especially of freedom from the past. He could not understand that this radically new society—with some rather old-fashioned passions—had a trajectory of its own.

As the transitory Anglo-American concord waned, it left in its wake a huge body of writings which are the record of this now quaint dream. Churchill's background interlocking for a while with the course of history to produce a clarifying vision, the result is a prose poem to the idea of supranational groupings based on language and culture rather than on crass local interests, to the idea of an undivided altruistic transatlantic community in whose past the American Revolution was a charming family quarrel patched up rather than a painful permanent wrench. A political doctrine, a foreign policy, a vision of history based on a mystique of language are among Churchill's greatest—and sometimes ephemeral—contributions as writer and statesman. They constitute his supreme tribute to the language he celebrated and adored, the Britain he loved and represented, and the America he admired and wooed.

6
The "Great Man"?

I

THAT Churchill played a prominent role in forging the Anglo-American special relationship is the belief of many historians and is certainly implicit in his own World War II memoirs. Because of his American roots, his maturing in a period of Anglo-Americanism, and his accession to leadership at a critical juncture and during the period of a "Grand Alliance," the man and the hour met. Such a belief commits him rather strenuously to the theory that history is shaped by the deeds of important personages. This was not a lifelong conviction of his. If he is inconsistent here, however, so are many other students of history.

For most thinkers nowadays the Great Man theory of history, the hero-in-history approach, is a relic of the past. Whatever the Bible and writers like Plutarch, Machiavelli, Burke, or Carlyle may have said about the role of outstanding individuals, the modern awareness of historical processes has rendered their analysis of events limited. Hegel helped usher in the new view when he spoke of Reason cunningly realizing itself by using the passions of World Historical persons; or of the World Historical man who, pursuing his selfish goals and overriding the existing morality, is unconscious of the general Idea he unfolds.[1] Another early locus classicus is Tolstoy's reduction of Napoleon in *War and Peace* to what he thought was a properly minute scale. Since then, the studies of economic, geographic, technological, political, intellectual, psychological, and sociological forces have swamped those who would still assign the individual autonomy.

Postwar events would seem to give renewed validity to the modern approach. That men with vaguely liberal commitments like John Kennedy and Lyndon Johnson should push the nation into a Dullesian anti-Communist crusade in Southeast Asia whereas an arch-cold warrior like Richard Nixon should toast Mao and Brezhnev in Peking and Moscow strongly suggests that, election-time oratory notwithstanding, it hardly matters who presides in the White House; for all the talk about the voters' "critical choice" in a "crucial time," presidents seem to bob helplessly in historical currents. The man in the street, to be sure, still evinces belief in the impact of the individual when he blames rising prices and other social ills on the current occupant of the White House or the Town Hall. He likes his politics personalized because that approach simplifies matters by providing both easy scapegoats and leaders who comport with adolescent notions of heroism. His representatives in Congress agree with him: the constitutional amendment limiting presidential tenure to two terms reflects this belief as well as a diffidence about human nature.

Wisdom, or at least prudence, would suggest, however, that such a philosophical question will never be resolved. We have no way of ascertaining whether a Hitler or Stalin determined modern European history or whether an Ernst Roehm or Leon Trotsky would have accomplished nearly the same, give or take a million corpses. Still, neither prudence nor detachment is evident in the way the world's leaders see the question, or at least write about it. Attitudes to the Great Man theory are themselves shaped by circumstances. A scholar, a disinterested observer coming to grips with history through the medium of books, through the filter of theory and intellectual reconstruction, is likely to stress forces rather than individuals. To a prominent politician, on the other hand, unfolding history is more a matter of living memoranda than learned footnotes, of consulting with or ordering about individuals rather than analyzing philosophical principles, of shaking hands and dividing spheres of power with other men loftily situated, of improvising a philosophical patchwork out of unexamined assumptions and meeting socioeconomic problems on an ad hoc basis rather than worrying about ultimate causes or logical conclusions.[2] He is likely to persuade himself, even if he has had the scholar's reflectiveness and especially if, in a democracy, he has had to first persuade the electorate, that he does make a difference. He becomes like the fabled donkey which thinks that it and not the icon on its back is the object of men's genuflection.

What happens when the historian and the man of action coexist in one person? There have been few enough such examples. H. R. Trevor Roper has cited the emphasis in Clarendon's writings on character as the mark of a practical rather than academic historian; the latter, that is, thinks a revolution is caused by God or the Dialectic, and the former thinks it is caused by someone missing a meeting or delaying a message. In the case of Winston Churchill, confronting the problem frequently in his voluminous writings on modern history, we discover an ambivalence, an oscillation, and sometimes even a self-contradiction.[3] His penultimate major work, the *Second World War*, which is a paean to the impact of one great man—himself—should not be regarded as typical of all his books. A historian who preferred to define history in an archaic fashion as past politics and past wars, Churchill was severely hampered by his obliviousness to socioeconomic processes and intellectual currents, but he had a degree of intellectual sophistication, and certain modern puzzles, like the initiation of World War I, periodically drove him, willy nilly, into the modern Tolstoyan position. This is, in short, a theoretical question which all who write history must, if they will not wrestle with it in full public view, dispose of between the lines, sweep under their assumptions; Churchill dealt with it tentatively at first, then grappled with it midway in his career, finally resolved it one way, but never cleared it of difficulties. The long road to the apparent certitudes of the *Second World War* was rarely smooth.

II

Churchill, curiously enough, began his sixty-year writing career espousing, under the influence of diluted Darwinian ideas, the modern, Tolstoyan view. In one of his first books, his only novel, *Savrola* (1900), the hero, a young leader of the liberal democratic faction in a country in political turmoil, thinks that leaders "are but the political waves of a social tide flowing we know not whither"; he can but for a while restrain his followers. When an assistant makes the simpleminded comment of most unphilosophic people, "You have created the agitation, and it is in your hands to stimulate or allay it. There are no unknown forces; you are the motive power," Savrola contrasts the size and "latent potentialities" of the city with the small room in which they converse: "Do you think I am what I am because I have changed all those minds, or because I best express their views? Am I their master or their slave? Believe me, I have no illusions." Most of the other major characters—the tyrant he opposes, the women he loves, the radicals temporarily allied with him—agree that "there are powers behind and beneath him of which he knows little, which he cannot control, but which he has invoked." And when, at the climax of the tale, the revolution succeeds, its leader, Savrola, is in fact eased out by these powers.[4]

Churchill's expressed viewpoint carries over into his contemporary nonfiction books. In the *Malakand Field Force* (1898), he reflects that the Frontier War, coinciding with a famine in India, "vividly displays how little an individual [Viceroy]," with the best of motives and with great power, "can really direct or control the course of public affairs." Or in adopting the "Forward Policy" of imperial expansion, "the rulers of India, ten or a hundred years ago, were as much the sport of circumstances" as their successors are today.[5] Though he continues in this determinist fashion—as when he speaks of General Gordon's being (rather like Churchill himself, it will turn out) "sustained by that belief in personality which too often misleads great men and beautiful women"—Churchill, in his next book, *The River War* (1899), inclines somewhat to the libertarian view. He depicts Kitchener's early career as shaped by a series of acts of will; the Mahdi of the Sudan as a religious fanatic and leader who was the necessary catalyst for transforming the miseries of his people into rebellion; a British officer whose patience, in the "Fashoda incident . . . from which far-reaching consequences have arisen,"[6] prevented a major European war; the British empire as successful because heroic leaders arose in times of trouble.

One would, of course, be ill-advised to extract much philosophic significance from the sketchy remarks in these two nonfiction books or from the fact that three of the Frontier War books are dedicated to the prominent men connected with the expeditions: the *Malakand* to General Blood, the *River War* to Prime Minister Salisbury, the *Ian Hamilton's March* to General Hamilton. Nor is the question directly confronted in Churchill's next major work, *Lord Randolph Churchill* (1906), a biography of his father. Still, implicit philosophical commitments are inescapable in such a book. Churchill observes (as he did in the *River War* of Gordon) that a political leader tends to believe that the "forces he had directed in the past were resident in himself, whereas to some extent they were outside himself and independent." And periodically, the narrator, continuing in the Tolstoyan vein of the *Savrola* and the *Malakand*, is forced by the unfulfilled, premature end of the protagonist's career to the melancholy conclusion that in fact much is outside man's scope. "Men may for a time prosper continually, whatever they do, and then for a time fail continually, whatever they do." Hence because of all the myths about design and plotting, "few people will believe how much is settled by the accident or caprice of the hour." For that reason, the skepticism Churchill had directed at military experts in his first books is now complemented by a skepticism about political man's power to comprehend, predict, and control his destiny. "What a mockery of statesman's leadership and foresight the future was to unveil!"

So also in his analysis of the Irish troubles, Churchill sees something larger than the individual at work. The error of the British government lay precisely in its believing that the agitation sprang from a small number of local leaders, "village ruffians" who, even in the absence of legal evidence, should be incarcerated. "In dealing with a movement which was formidable only because of its almost universal character, [Britain] struck at individuals of minor prominence. [She] encountered profound communistic stirrings, bitter racial hatred and intense national aspirations by methods which might have been effective against the rowdy larrikins of a slum." The places of the several hundred "ruffians" rounded up were "eagerly filled by others. The land agitation increased" and the measure proved futile.

Yet, Tolstoyan though he may be when dealing with general or lesser matters, Churchill changes his philosophical dress whenever he focuses on his protagonist-father. Randolph is portrayed as a heroic pioneer and rebel who, by helping push the Conservative party into the field of welfare legislation, changed the long-run course of English politics and who, had he lived to maturity and old age, would have made an even greater impact. He revitalized the parties and gave the masses renewed faith in the political system. Most of the proposals of his important 1886 Dartford speech became law, as did the Irish policy he delineated in 1889. Churchill presents a prescient Randolph declaring at the time of his "inflicting on the old gang" the "final blow" of his resignation, "I have mortally wounded myself. But the work is practically done; the Tory Party will be turned into a Liberal Party and produce a governing force." The narrator also cites a single incident in young Randolph's life, an altercation with a "great personage" (the Prince of Wales), which led to nearly a decade of ostracism from London society. The exile, he postulates, embittered Randolph and disposed him to iconoclasm and, ultimately, radicalism.[7] Thus, we are to understand, one incident in the life of one politician inaugurated the age of welfare legislation, while the rise of the trade union movement and of the Labor Party is barely mentioned.

Many scholars have pointed out that Randolph was not by any means the only one to discover that the Tories had to woo the new voters, and J. H. Plumb, in particular, has shown to what an extent the author's hero-worship is expressed at the expense of any understanding of social forces. Churchill, according to Plumb, grasps the key to Randolph's success—the curious rallying of the working class to the Tories and Randolph's genius in seeing here an opportunity for "Tory Democracy," in entering into a dialogue with the electorate and affecting thereby the Tory leadership. Churchill does not, however, ask the question which a professionally trained historian would ask: What lay behind this paradox of the proletariat moved by the aristocratic sense of the past? Without conceptual powers or knowledge of social processes, Churchill would have us believe that the workers responded solely because of Randolph's efforts and the rightness of his ideas, and that the individual determined the course of events.[8] Thus the Great Man theory is at the core of the book despite the many contrary suggestions in the text.

Between the *Randolph Churchill* and the next major work, *The World Crisis* (1923–31), lay a busy quarter of a century for Churchill, the politician-administrator, as well as a traumatic event, World War I. Historians are still trying, eighty years later, to ascertain who, if anyone is, responsible for that conflict, and Churchill makes his uncertain contribution to the controversy. Study of prewar developments can easily make it seem to him to have been inevitable and leaves him with a sense of the "defective control of individuals upon world fortunes.... 'There is always more error than design in human affairs.'... Events got on to certain lines, and no one could get them off again." The inheritance of the imperial throne had exercised a sobering effect on the "hitherto careless" crown prince of Germany, but beneath the frantic last-minute diplomatic maneuvers, "the sinister machines of war began to develop their own momentum." The German military plans, requiring that Liege be stormed before the major invasion, made it certain that with mobilization the irrevocable steps of war and violation of neutrality take place. Thus the Austrian ultimatum led to a chain reaction, and military reasons superseded diplomatic ones. "A situation had been created where hundreds of officials had only to do their prescribed duty to their respective countries to wreck the world.

They did their duty." At the very time that Germany declared war on Russia, an agreement had been reached for direct negotiation between Austria and Russia. "The cause of quarrel had disappeared on paper at the same time as the fighting all over Europe began."[9]

This analysis sketches a limited determinism, that is, it deals with the exigencies of a military strategy encompassing months and years, not the unfolding of centuries-old socioeconomic forces. Unsettled is the question of whether the latter made Armageddon inevitable or whether mankind merely stumbled upon it through a lack of civilian leadership. Churchill himself felt helpless both at the time hostilities began and long after he had finished his war memoirs. In July 1914 he wondered, in a letter to his wife, why the "stupid Kings and Emperors" could not "revivify kingship" by jointly preventing war; "but we all drift on in a kind of dull cataleptic trance. As if it was somebody else's operation!" Writing in 1924 on the subject of "If We Could Look into the Future!" and on the role of chance, he said that a glimpse of things to come would only have fortified the Kaiser's decisions; militancy and war-making would have been regarded by Wilhelm as the means of forcing his way through, or averting, his doom rather than as the causes of it. The pressure on men of prominence, in other words, was so great that events extorted actions from them even if they were blessed with clairvoyance. And years later Churchill disagreed with Lloyd George's contention that had Britain committed herself to Belgium, Germany would have stood back; the war's beginning, he concluded, was simply an avalanche.[10]

In the same way, during the war there existed a causal chain from which it was hard to break out. Much as he criticized the Somme offensive, Churchill was aware in retrospect of the "compulsion to an offensive exercised by the blind movement of events." The failure of Gallipoli and the French ordeal at Verdun so "compelled a British relieving counter-attack" that Haig "could not have remained idle. Inexorable forces carried rulers and ruled along together as the wheels of Fate revolved." Haig was not alone in ths predicament. The German chancellor reluctantly bowed to the military's desire for a U-boat war—in vain, as it turned out. In France, Painlevé disliked the offensive that General Nivelle was planning but foolishly yielded to the "logic of circumstances, the sullen drift of events."

If this be the Tolstoyan vision of the *Savrola* full blown, Churchill, aware of the other side of the question, concurrently develops the theme which implicitly informs the *Randolph Churchill*. He refuses, obdurately or inconsistently, to accept historical determinism. Aggression is, to him, a clear sign of someone's guilt; mobilization by itself can only justify counter-mobilization and parley, not invasion. Individual responsibility rather than spontaneous combustion is at issue: Princip's assassination of the Archduke; Berchtold's desire to use violence on Serbia; above all, the Kaiser's encouragement of Austria's stiff demands and his readiness to play with fire. "No one except the doers of these particular deeds bears direct concrete responsibility."

Much action and the play of huge forces may count for little in the final result, yet even small events reveal the "profound significance of human choice and the sublime responsibility of men. No one can tell that he may not some day set a stone rolling or take or neglect some ordinary step which in its consequences will alter the history of the world." The narrative takes account of a sea maneuver by a German admiral as "one of these astounding events utterly outside the bounds of reasonable expectation, which have often been the turning points of history." Or the death in 1920 of King Alexander of Greece by a monkey bite: "It is perhaps no exaggeration to remark that a quarter of a million persons died of this monkey's bite."[11] The powerful President Wilson "played a part in the fate of nations incomparably more direct and personal than any other man," and because Count Berchtold, the Austrian Foreign Minister during the crucial pre-war years, was superficial and weak, "We are appalled that from such lips should have issued commands more fateful to the material fortunes of mankind than any spoken by the greatest sovereigns, warriors, jurists, philosophers and statesmen of the past."[12]

Churchill had stated in a 1916 article that at the summit of power the interplay of personal forces and relationships is fierce and important and insisted in two 1917 articles upon the need to place the supreme war direction in as few hands as possible. His war memoirs celebrated Lloyd George for finally achieving this. No wonder the *Times Literary Supplement* found Churchill the writer a master of highlighting the importance of key men and events. But alongside Berchtold, the Kaiser, Princip, and Lloyd George there lurks in the *World Crisis* another would-be historical hero: the narrator himself. Churchill's frustrating experience in connection with the Dardanelles, his sense that he himself offered a strategic alternative to the military obsession with Western Front offensives, that a way of ending the war much earlier existed; his sense of what he could have achieved, given half a chance in office, leads him paradoxically to celebrate the potential role of the individual will and event in history. Quoting approvingly Admiral Fisher, "You want ONE man. . . . In the history of the world—a Junta has never won! You want *one* man," Churchill presents himself as having been ready to sanction the running of risks, to take responsibilities, provided that his decision was "the one that ruled." We see here an adumbration of the fusion in the *Second World War* of Great Man theory and Churchillian egoism, and Samuel J. Hurwitz concludes not without justice that the *World Crisis* passes as history only if one accepts the premise of Churchill's own importance.[13] From the uncertain vision exhibited in the *Randolph Churchill*, Churchill has been brought by World War I to self-contradiction and confusion; he leaves us with ambiguous statements on the role of the individual in the overwhelming events. In trying in subsequent years to grapple with the problem more directly, he would only render the polarities keener.

III

For Churchill, the 1930s, his decade in "the political widerness," when for the first time since the beginning of the century he was remote from the seat of power for a protracted period, were years of belletristic writing. He produced essays—on history, fate, modern life—with a philosophic cast, such as had not hitherto appeared in his thirty-five year writing career. In one of them, he finally dealt directly with this problem in the theory of history.

The *World Crisis* had been suffused with the sense that the belief in progress was an illusion, that what remained of this Victorian belief had been shattered by the war. The industrialization and the other "mass effects" of the twentieth century, it was becoming clear, had brought many changes in values and relations which were for the worse. In an essay on these mass effects, Churchill now studied one social result: "Is the march of events ordered and guided by eminent men; or do our leaders merely fall into their places at the heads of moving columns? Is human progress the result of resolves and deeds of individuals, or are these resolves and deeds only the outcome of time and circumstance, . . . of their responses to the tides, tendencies and opportunities of their age?" On the one hand, Churchill propounded the Great Man theory as never before: If in the lives of individual and of nation, "accident and chance" are decisive at every moment, if meeting a woman or missing a train changes our lives and affects ultimately the movement of the world, "how much more potent must to be deflection which the Master Teachers—Thinkers, Discoverers, Commanders—have imparted at every stage." Hence history is mainly the story of exceptional men, "whose thoughts, actions, qualities, virtues, triumphs, weaknesses and crimes have dominated the fortunes of the race." The survival of the monarchy in the face of the currents of the age is inseparable from the personality of the "good and wise" George V; the love of Parnell and Kitty O'Shea condemned Ireland to a melancholy fate and the Empire to "curtailment of its harmony"; and personal diplomacy and his own charm, Churchill implies, helped pacify Michael Collins and so end the Irish crisis.[14]

At the same time, Churchill believes that the changes wrought by modern life are placing the human race beyond the influence of outstanding personalities in any field. Mass production, compulsory education, the press, and universal suffrage—all contributors to comfort and progress in their way—vitiate quality and independence of character. In the West, "the decline in personal preeminence is much more plainly visible" than elsewhere; "the great emancipated nations seem to have become largely independent of famous guides and guardians." The more advanced the country, the less it needs to rely on "the Hero, the Commander, or the Teacher," and it wends its way "ponderously, unthinkingly, blindly." Can it do so for long? Can it "dispense with hero-worship," with ceremony and pomp? Can affairs go well when led by men who do not feel special and uplifted above the mass? The leadership of the privileged has passed away without being succeeded by that of the eminent. "Can nations remain healthy . . . in a world whose brightest stars are film stars?" Prophetically, he asks on the eve of Hitler's accession, "Or will there be some big hitch in the forward march of mankind, . . . some vain wandering into the wilderness; and will not then the need for a personal chief become the mass desire?" Many of the parliaments "so hopefully" created in nineteenth-century Europe had already in the first quarter of the twentieth century been replaced by military chiefs or "dictatorships in various forms."[15]

When Churchill asks if nations can survive without men prepared for leadership by "training, situation, abilities," he is, to be sure, speaking not so much of Great Men as of aristocrats; he seems to imply that only the latter can become the former. But this is not the only uncertainty. Does Churchill intimate that the modern rootless tyrant is a surrogate, if illegitimate, monarch who can mold history, or that he is what the masses improvise in the absence of a monarch, a product rather than producer of history? Is Churchill, moreover, lamenting the absence of the history-shaping individual or only of those individuals—kings, religious leaders, noblemen—whom it is the tendency of tradition-oriented societies to surround with ceremony, ritual, and gold, irrespective of whether these individuals play any significant historical role? If, as seems likely, he does mean the history-shaping individual, he has arrived at a compromise between the traditional "Great Man" school and the modern "historical forces" school. His theory would seem to be that the individual did affect history in the past but, as a result of those "mass effects of modern life," no longer does—a hardly original view which has become popular (not through Churchill) among cracker-barrel philosophers, editorial writers, counterculture rhetoricians, and others not overly famous for their knowledge of history or philosophy.

The same degeneration is found by Churchill in the military field. Parallel to the Great Man philosophy is his belief that wars matter. Modern opinion on socioeconomic forces notwithstanding, Churchill insists that battles are "the principal milestones," changing the course of events, creating new standards and conditions in every way; the victory of Blenheim, for instance, settled the destiny of Europe for a century. And if battles matter, the decisions and the personalities of generals matter. World War I left Churchill with the sense that modern generalship was no less petty than modern political leadership. The principles of war, though simple on paper, were once worked out by genius, which cannot be acquired by reading or experience. Since such talent is rare, "most wars are mainly tales of muddle." The great general of the past was at least present at the battlefield and helped determine the course of the battle; the modern general, on the other hand, "working in calm surroundings, often beyond the sound even of the cannonade," without danger or hurry, leads "armies ten times as large and a hundred times as powerful as any that Napoleon led, . . . but it is hard to feel that he is the hero. No, he is not the hero. He is the manager of a stock market, or a stock yard." Ludendorff's March 1918 offensive was a prime example of "how low the art of war had sunk." It had become in "this melancholy and degraded epoch . . . the slaughter of men by machinery." The decline of the general as hero, moreover, continues: "Some spectacled 'brass-hat' of a future world agony" may extinguish entire cities "by pressing a button or putting his initials neatly at the bottom of a piece of foolscap." As the scale of battle has been made gigantic, the "sublime function of military genius has been destroyed forever."[16]

In such passages, Churchill appears to be confusing the tenable idea that modern generals lack genius, courage, and glamor with the arguable one that, as victims of mass effects, they do not influence history. A general wiping out a city by pushing a button may be craven and stupid but could be said, by the Great Man proponents, to be influencing history. In any case, Churchill is faithful to his distinction—between the dashing individualism of the past and the "spectacled" impersonality of the present—in the *Marlborough*, the major work that preoccupied him during the decade in the wilderness. For here is a protagonist set in a premodern world, when, apparently, the individual still mattered, when genius could flourish on the battlefield, and when battles clearly affected the course of history. If Churchill had been continent, sketchy, or inconsistent on the Great Man theory in his other narratives, he now proclaimed it boldly. What his contemporary essays analyzed, the *Marlborough* dramatized.

The hero is presented as nothing less than the fulcrum of history. In the 1702 resumption of the war between France and the Grand Alliance, France had gained to her side Spain, the Indies, South America, Italy, Belgium, Luxembourg, Portugal, Bavaria, Cologne, the Papacy, and nearly all the coasts and seas. Louis XIV was, in short, twice as strong as had been in 1688. But the "scale of the new war was turned by the genius of one man," whose will "outweighed all these fearful inequalities" and built a "structure of surpassing success under the leadership of England." Accepting William III's bequest, Marlborough made the treaties and, as the hub of the wheel of the Alliance, forced or tricked the "foolish-frantic Parliaments, jealous princes, hungry generals, and bitter politicians" in his care along the path he alone knew. But for his efforts, the alliance would have collapsed; in fact, "it had become his war." By 1708, "one man and three battles had transformed all," beating Louis XIV to his knees and raising England to the summit of the world. And in turn Marlborough's deeds were canceled, the Alliance was jolted, and the peace lost by something as trivial as a "bedchamber intrigue"; Abigail Masham was "the smallest person who ever consciously decided the history of Europe." Amid Louis XIV's *Te*

Deums for his first victory in eleven years, he "might have found a place for the trinity of serviceable agents through whom the wonders of the Almighty had been performed—Abigail, Harley, and St. John."[17] It is as if Churchill, in reaction to the horrors of the shapeless Great War and the melancholy postwar world, were, in undertaking the work on *Marlborough*, fleeing to the past in order to contemplate individuals controlling history in an epoch when that was still possible.

Churchill, moreover, exempts Great Men from many frailties of the flesh. Insisting—as he would again about his own ascendancy in 1940—that "the pursuit of power with the capacity and in the desire to exercise it worthily is among the noblest of human occupations," he segregates Great Men from those who happen to be at the top. Though pettiness may accompany the climb to power and unworthy men of eminence may pay off minor scores, he rejects the supposition that "the great minds of the world in their supreme activities are twisted or swayed by sordid or even personal aims."[18]

Upon finishing the *Marlborough* in the late 1930s, Churchill immediately began work on the *History of the English-Speaking Peoples* (revised and first published in 1956–58). In this book, again focusing on the past, the role of the prominent individual becomes part of a recurring pattern, a pervasive historical-philosophical theme: "Almost every critical turn of historic fortune has been due to the sudden apparition in an era of confusion and decay of one of the great figures in history." Bold ideas either are expressed through "a man and a leader"—a Simon de Montfort, Edward I, Strafford, Pym—or remain only ideas. Even individual blunders by, say, George I, Lord North, or the Kaiser had incalculable impact on European history. The role of the fortuitous, in proferring or removing an individual, may enrich or impoverish the life of a nation. The "assassin's bullet," by silencing Lincoln, the only man able to solve the problem of reconstruction, was more baneful "than all the Confederate cannonade." In one operation, Lee and Jackson had within reach the destruction of the main Federal army, but before the battle began Jackson was shot: "no one knew Jackson's plan, and he was now unconscious. Thus on small agate points do the balances of the world turn."[19]

In sum, the "fortunes of mankind are largely the result of the impact upon events of superior beings," men like Alfred, Canute, Cromwell. The elder Pitt, rekindling the spirit which had fired the nation under Marlborough, designed and won a global war; his hour having come, he said with Churchillian gusto, "I know that I can save this country and that no one else can." Churchill's eulogy on Pitt quotes Burke's formulation of the idea: "The means by which Providence raises a nation to greatness are the virtues infused into great men."[20] England suffered during the years of the American Revolution because such men were rare in the days of Lord North, while France's parallel greatness was due to her often "in the great crises of her history" producing such a man. Indeed the Great Men usually appear in England in periods which alternate with eras of sloth, quiescence, apathy, and stagnation: the English Civil War, the Age of Anne, the mid-eighteenth century "first world war," the Napoleonic era, the reform and reconstruction years of Gladstone and Disraeli—as against the Restoration, the first Hanovers, the late eighteenth century, the middle nineteenth century.[21]

In embracing the Great Man theory, however, Churchill has not freed himself of problems and inconsistencies. The *History* contains, as the *Marlborough* does not, an undercurrent which conflicts with these bold assertions. A major theme of the book is that many historical milestones are actually mere by-products of selfishness, the results of the interplay of men with eyes only on the moment. We are ignorant puppets of the historical process, often obtaining the reverse of what we want. As a result of the discrepancy between intent and result, it often happens that "capable rulers by their very virtue sow the seeds of future evil and weak or degenerate princes open the pathway for progress." In the amoral perspective of history, for example, more is owed "to the vices of [King] John than to the labors of virtuous sovereigns."[22] Churchill posits an overall progression, an evolution of British liberty, which is apparently inevitable but which takes place by means of the interplay of conflicting individual wills, by means of detours and digressions in a typically British "muddling through." This view bespeaks a conservative diffidence as to mankind's ability to master its destiny; his judgment being terribly frail, man little knows where he is going, what he really wants, or what will be the consequences of his actions. Such a philosophical surrender by Churchill to the drift of things veers dangerously close to antirationalism and leaves the Great Man little room in which to operate. Also, Churchill's sympathetic identification with others in high position, his readiness to justify them, to show their plight as unavoidable, conveys a fatalistic sense that the individual is not in control of things. Finally, if King John's vices contribute to progress, is that because the prominent individual—be he good or evil, strong or weak—

influences history or rather because progress will take place whether the King aids or hinders it? We are not told.

IV

These were men of the past, when, according to Churchill's distinction, the individual could still influence events. What of modern times? On this Churchill either forgot his distinction or contradicted himself. His *Great Contemporaries* (1937), a series of portraits of prominent late Victorians and moderns, often betrays an unspoken commitment to the Great Man theory. In an article, "Will Lloyd George Come Back?" Churchill, while praising the "salutary reaction against according proprietary credit of world-changing events to the personages who happened to have been in high positions when those great events took place," insisted that Lloyd George must take credit for correct decisions—on Russia, the munitions shortage, the convoy system, the unity of Allied military command—made in the face of expert opinion and political opposition. "In those days and in that sphere megalomania was the highest virtue." He in fact presents Lloyd George as shaping British life in peace and war in the first quarter of the century, and soon he wanted to cope with the economic tumult of the 1930s as he would have had the Allies cope with the military problems in World War I (and again in World War II)—with summit meetings. In "The Way Out of the Crisis," he suggested that the three ex-prime ministers—MacDonald, Baldwin, and Lloyd George, men in a class by themselves—confer together and decide on solutions, by which everyone, he is sure, would abide. For, believing that a politician must have as Lloyd George and even Asquith in the crunch had, "that ruthless side without which great matters cannot be handled," he went so far as to argue that "something may be said for" dictatorship in critical periods, even if such strong-man rule can only be a temporary solution.[23]

It is perhaps no accident, therefore, that he was in those very 1930s a not unambiguous prophet against the dictators. Some he even admired. Franco was a "Republican general" who warned the government of anarchy and now had the "opportunity of becoming a great" man by uniting his country; if he reconciled past with present, helped the working class, and "preserved the faith and structure" of Spain, he would rank with Ferdinand and Isabella, and Charles V. Chiang was a national hero, who could well become a world hero, and "who, amid a thousand difficulties and wants, does not despair of saving China." Ataturk was the hero, champion, and father of modern Turkey who established relations with Russia and Greece, who with "his far-seeing steady vision" and "astonishing and revolutionary reforms modernized" and strengthened Turkish civilization. Even Mussolini and Hitler were—as is little remembered now—at first lauded by Churchill. In the Italian, whom he long admired, he saw a masterly individual, an "extra-ordinary man who embodies and expresses all that Italy means," who, as the "spirited and successful" chief of his "highly vulnerable country," brought Italy out of "incipient anarchy into a position of dignity and order." As he put it in a World War II address in which, by attempting to separate the Italian people from their leader, he found the Great Man Theory indispensable: Italy was in trouble "all because of one man. One man and one man alone has ranged" the people against Britain; "there is where one man, and one man only, has led you."[24] Mussolini, Churchill conceded in early 1941, "is a great man."

In the case of Hitler, not only one nation but all of Europe was in the grip of one man. That the German people might not want war with Britain was irrelevant; "our anxieties and hopes center upon the extra-ordinary man at the summit of Germany," who can with a fatal act cast away all that he has done for Germany. Whether the signal is given depends "on the mood, temperament and decision of a single man, who has raised himself from an obscure position to a grisly summit from which he can perhaps let loose upon the greater part of mankind, immeasurable catastrophe and tribulation." Churchill willingly overlooks moral issues and national concerns to make an objective, pragmatic judgment of the dictator qua political animal, patriot, man of action. "One may dislike Hitler's system and yet admire his patriotic achievement. If our country were defeated I hope we should find a champion as indomitable to restore our courage and lead us back to our place among the nations." Churchill would like to animate British leadership with "something of the spirit of that Austrian corporal who," with ruins all about him and Germany in chaos, "did not hesitate to march forth against the vast array of victorious nations" and turn the tables on them. The Germans must be grateful to him for "leading them back from the trough of defeat to the uplands of power."[25]

Strange and even repulsive as some of these judgments may now seem, they grow naturally out of Churchill's outlook. He had always regarded the constitutional monarchy as providing a framework above politics, as though democracy would be vulnerable without a revered individual formally at the helm. His continuing fear of Bolshevism and his growing domestic conservatism caused him initially to see the strong men of the right who replaced the monarchs as bulwarks against the left, as strong individuals mastering the forces unleashed by the impersonal, shortsighted masses. His hero worship of men like Caesar, Marlborough, and Napoleon (and, for a time, Lloyd George), like his various sarcastic remarks on Asquith, Marlborough, or Neville Chamberlain as being, in certain critical junctures, only chairman of discordant committees, made inevitable Churchill's political weakness for the strong man and, despite his views on modern mass effects, his philosophical weakness for the Great Man theory.

Yet Churchill distinguished the two Axis tyrants. He asserted that Hitler, although a man of destiny like Cromwell, Washington, and Robespierre, rode on the tide of the German revolution, whereas Mussolini was not the instrument of any forces and could thrive in any circumstances. If World War I had not taken place, Mussolini would still be preeminent; Germany under any other government than Hitler's would still be a power. In a world careening to the left and to internationalism, Mussolini had launched the epoch of dictators turning to the right and to nationalism. Mussolini made modern Italy, which was nothing less than the expression of his will, while Hitler was a leader only because he embodied the strong will of Germany; the Weimar Republic had begun, for instance, to rearm even before the advent of the führer, and the nation had been ready for the rise of a Hitler.[26] This differentiation, besides negating or at the least cutting across his earlier separation of the pre-modern world shaped by individuals from the modern world in which the individual is helpless, is especially curious in the light of events, which were to reveal the Italian to be almost a figure from comic opera and the German a diabolical creature.

Churchill's readiness to praise the deeds of the strong man, the general, and the dictator, as well as his laments over the displacement of monarchs and aristocrats by faceless modern democratic politicians, must not cause us to think that he had ruled out the possibility that popularly elected leaders could also be Great Men. During World War II Franklin Roosevelt became to him a classic case of someone who, "by involving the New World irrevocably in the fortunes of the Old, . . . not only anticipated history but altered its course ... for generations to come, ... altered decisively the social [and] moral axis of mankind"; his life must "therefore be regarded as one of the commanding events in human destiny." During the war, Churchill declared that "the fortunes of mankind are principally decided for good or ill by its greatest men and its greatest episodes," and after the war he cited, among the guidelines for measuring the greatness of men serving high causes, the "favorable influence [they] exerted upon the fortunes of mankind." By such criteria, Roosevelt seemed to Churchill greater even than Washington and Lincoln: Independence and abolition being part of the "evolution of events," would have come anyway, whereas had Roosevelt not acted as generously when he did, mankind would have been overwhelmed. This strange distinction between a Washington and Lincoln expressing history and a Roosevelt shaping history is similar to the one between a Hitler expressing his nation and a Mussolini mastering it. It differs only in being more obviously based on shallow reasoning, and it is the more interesting in that Churchill, by representing presidents of earlier times as dependent on, or part of, historical forces and a modern president as controlling them, has once again flouted one of his own theories. Carried away by the emotions and needs of the moment, he has actually stood it on its head![27]

V

Hitler's blitzkrieg of 10 May 1940 helped make Churchill, as A. J. P. Taylor points out, the virtual dictator of Britain. Now the chronicler of men and events, the critic of decisions made by men at the top, was himself plunged into the center of the whirlwind. Did the wartime prime minister feel himself overwhelmed by the mass effect and impersonality of modern life? Certainly he had said a decade earlier that, once war begins, a statesman ceases to be a master of policy and becomes "the slave of unforeseeable and uncontrollable events." In the *Second World War*, to be sure, he cited cases of human limitations. Although he had "as much direct control over the conduct of the war as any public man had in any country at this time," he was unable, depsite much hectoring of his generals, to get Suda Bay fortified, to increase the shipment of tanks to the Middle East, and to improve repair procedures. When the tanks arrived improperly packed, he wanted to pinpoint the responsibility but was too busy and "no one else will do anything"; the story shows, he concluded, "how difficult it is to get things done even with much power, realized need, and willing helpers."

He often deprecates his own climactic role. His wartime speeches merely expressed the will of the nation. Of his actions, signally in the dark days after Dunkirk, he says, "It fell to me in these coming days and months to express their [the people's] sentiments on suitable occasions." He was, in other words, merely the spokesman for the firmness already there, merely the roar of the lion; he only gave good reasons for their resolve. If he had not articulated the people's courage and resolute will, his colleagues "would have pulled me to pieces." We are back in the world of *Savrola:* individuals cannot take credit which belongs to an entire people; the leader is only the instrument of some greater force.

In the later part of the war, his autonomy was encroached upon in another way. Soon after Pearl Harbor, he noted that he now had to defer somewhat to the United States as to a spouse. And with the mass of American troops and supplies becoming preponderant, his influence diminished. He had championed various projected operations in the Mediterranean for their strategic importance against Germany, but not even when they took on political significance vis-à-vis a renascent Russian power could he convince Roosevelt or Eisenhower. "It is not so easy as it used to be for me to get things done."[28]

Yet, if there is any overall impression that the World War II memoirs make, it is that Churchill almost single-handedly shaped and won the war. Like the elder Pitt he was sure he alone could achieve victory; although he came to power amidst the worst possible military conditions, "I knew a good deal about it all, and I was sure I should not fail," for "at the top there are great simplifications. An accepted leader has only to be sure what it is best to do." When he saw a family dispossessed during the Blitz, he—such is the privilege of power—decided at once to initiate a system of state insurance and compensation for victims of bombing. His personal experience, not the momentum caused by welfarist ideas, communal decency, or the necessities of the wartime situation, generated this innovation.

The profile of himself that Churchill draws mingles proficiency in the political sphere with two personal endowments, or even idiosyncracies, which are important catalysts of action—gregariousness and love of travel. These two traits combined to forge his philosophy of diplomacy and to play no small role—the book implies—in maintaining the Grand Alliance. Having stated in the *Marlborough* that great projects often need a personal touch to get them going, he emphasizes in his war memoirs the role of personal diplomacy. Foreign policy is, he believed, best conducted by such means. The leaders of nations cannot come to a true understanding through intermediaries or impersonal dispatches which place days between the joining of question and answer. Problems insoluble at the second level can be settled quickly by direct contact at the top. Although Churchill sent Stalin messages warning of the impending German invasion, he believed that "if I had had any direct contact with Stalin I might perhaps have prevented him from having so much of his air force destroyed on the ground." So too conferring experts and officers have continually to refer back to their capitals: "Only the heads of states face to face could settle the fearful questions that were open.... How difficult everything becomes once one cannot talk together!" His first visit to Moscow in 1942 and his visit to Greece in December 1944 are given as occasions of settlements that could not have been achieved without his own presence, and when losing a telegram debate with the Americans over whether to invade the Riviera or Istria, he asserts, "I was sure that if we could have met, as I so frequently proposed, we should have reached a happy agreement."[29]

The theme of personal diplomacy, so central to this work, naturally grows out of Churchill's varied preoccupations and values, as the Great Man theory becomes fused with his overweening egotism and his love of travel. Finding himself at last in the highest office, confident of his charm, eager to take to the road, he easily persuades himself that all his gadding about and chattering on mattered, that these two peculiar traits of his have, through the medium of power, changed history and won the war.

At crucial junctures, moreover, Churchill finds that the presence in government of certain men and the absence of others (mainly himself) spell the difference between war and peace, defeat and victory. In the early 1930s, the "locust years," the weak governments of MacDonald and Baldwin were responsive to the wave of pacifism which swept Britain at the very time of Hitler's rise and Germany's rearming. The only reason he can find for the appeasement of Germany is poor leadership. The appeasement of Russia at the close of the war is treated in the same way. Roosevelt fell ill in 1945 just at the moment of emergent Russian expansionism and of Churchill's countermoves in Greece. Hopkins, the intermediary, was ailing and out of favor; the state department, hitherto reluctant to heed Churchill's anti-Communist statements, became inert in the absence of leadership. These were "costly weeks for all," weeks of mounting crisis among the victorious allies. Then Roosevelt died "at the supreme climax of the war," and an unprepared Truman took over. Dependent on his military advisers, the new president only slowly grasped the political realities. In that very "deadly hiatus" the Russians thrived—as they would apparently not have otherwise.

A bare few months later a similar unfortunate coincidence again aided the Russians. Churchill expected to have it out with Stalin at Potsdam, but electoral defeat unexpectedly intervened, and his place was taken by Labor leaders as unprepared, he thinks, for their task (albeit for different reasons) as Truman had been for his. "My removal from the scene at the time when I still had much influence and power rendered it impossible for satisfactory solutions to be reached." As he had declared at the very beginning of the huge *Second World War*: "In the fear, anger, and disarray of the French people, the rugged, dominating figure of Clemenceau, with his world famed authority, and his special British and American contacts, was incontinently discarded. 'Ingratitude towards their great men,' says Plutarch, 'is the mark of strong peoples.' It was imprudent for France to indulge this trait when she was so grievously weakened." History now repeated itself. If Brecht said, woe to the nation that has need of heroes, Churchill did not agree. Did he not exclaim in the 1930s of the same Clemenceau—the man who in a burst of Great Man exuberance had said in World War I, "I will fight in the front of Paris; I will fight in Paris; I will fight behind Paris"—"Happy the nation which when its fate quivers in the balance can find such a tyrant and such a champion?"[30]

What Churchill had said of his father, Randolph—that if he had continued to lead the House and the party and had lived the normal span of life, domestic policy in social questions would have been more radical, reform would have come earlier, and Ireland would have fared better—and then of his ancestor, Marlborough—that if endowed with the freedom of a Frederick or Napoleon he "would have made a more ordered and a more tolerant civilization for his own time"—and then of himself in World War I—that if he had been heeded on the Dardanelles, the war would have been over early and Europe would have had a lasting peace, he now said of himself again: If his party had won in 1945, he would have forced a showdown and therefore "in the moment of victory was our best, and what might prove to have been our last, chance of durable world peace allowed composedly to fade away." This abiding faith that the presence of a Churchill at the critical junctures of history would have made a difference in the course of events is the Great Man theory personalized. Churchill's realism about the human condition and the course of history is qualified by a bit of hero worship and self-love. He writes as though politics as we know it would suddenly have ceased at war's end by dint of the sheer presence of himself or Marlborough at peace conferences. But then Churchill always had a propensity to confuse himself with history. What Muggeridge says of the *Contemporaries*, H. G. Wells of the *World Crisis*, and S. R. Graubard of the *History* applies to all of Churchill's writings: They are so many mirrors from which the author smiles at us. What Samuel Hoare said about Churchill's World War I memoirs—that Winston had written an autobiography and called it the *World Crisis*—and Reed Whittemore about the *Second World War*—that it is impersonal biography and personal history—recalls for us Churchill's own remarks in an essay on Alfonso XIII, "Are we dealing with the annals of a nation or with the biography of an individual?"[31]

The point has been best made by Whittemore in an excellent analysis of the *Second World War*. The book presents this as a Churchillian war and the war as an episode in his long life. Churchill himself was the shining hero with the virtues of olden times and the power to do something with them. His book depicts him mapping the grand strategy, pushing his subordinates into action, keeping up the people's morale, forging the Grand Alliance, and even making an important tactical innovation, the small landing craft. He usually presents himself as interchangeable with his nation; he disliked the Burma campaign because "I hate jungles." Just as the only reason he can find for appeasement is poor leadership, so does his excellent leadership, we are to understand, contribute greatly to Germany's surrender. He is, in Whittemore's words, "like a sovereign in a Shakespeare play who personally triumphs over the enemy," a democratic despot who treats the war as his private affair. And when he is dismissed, the democracies resume their normal course of folly. As Whittemore says, "How can poor forked Churchill, as he pulls on his trousers in the morning, say that he secured North Africa?"[32] This outlook comes dangerously close to turning the *Second World War* into a romance.

In his peacetime ministry of 1951–55, Churchill claimed that he clung to office because he alone could make the Russians respond to reason and enlightened self-interest. The spheres of influence that he arrived at with Stalin during World War II had been a matter of a few minutes' conversation; people at the top can do such things simply. The best way of achieving reconciliation is therefore by more summit meetings. Modern locomotion makes frequent conferences of leaders easy. Had it existed in 1914, World War I might have been prevented amid "cryptic and platitudinous" communiqués from gathered world leaders. Signally important was his own presence. Little men were tied to their text, but he alone could break the wall of suspicion between Russia and the West. Great things were within grasp. If only he could confer alone with Eisenhower (who was distrustful of a resumption of the Roosevelt-Churchill type of relationship), he could make the Americans more sensible. Or he could perhaps change the world's bias with only a "solitary pilgrimage" to Moscow.[33] Had he been able to visit Moscow in the early 1950s, Malenkov's own position of power would have been strengthened. If he insisted in 1945 as in 1940 that "we have the future in our own hands" and that we are still "the masters of our fate, captains of our soul," he went on to say in one of his very last speeches, when urging a summit conference with Soviet leaders of post-Stalinist Russia, that, however complex and strange the world had become, "the right people in the right place at the right time" may yet do much for peace.[34]

* * *

Subdued in these postwar years were the vacillations on this philosophic problem—the questions based on post-Darwinian pessimism in the *Savrola*, the muted self-contradictions in the *Randolph Churchill*, the bewilderment over the origin of the Great War, the musings on the impact of mass effects on modern life and individual autonomy, the supposition that a churning Germany merely produced a replaceable, representative man, or the periodic moralizing on the "vanity of human calculation," on the uncertain results of one's intentions and actions. That recurring belief in the preeminent individual was now given full and climactic expression, even in a modern setting. Churchill was his own Marlborough against two modern incarnations of Louis XIV.

This resolution of the lifelong oscillation between the Great Man and the determinist theories is due in part to the archaic qualities of Churchill's mind. Scholars have noted that Churchill's historiography, such as it is, is dependent mainly on Victorian rather than modern writers and values; that he dwelled in a quaint, pre-Marxist and pre-Freudian world; that he flaunted a boyish love of the drama of war and a precocious child's view of history and kings; that his view of history as "past politics" and wars was hopelessly narrow and antique; that he wrote as a court memorialist or Plutarchian soul, or as an aristocrat interested in dashing personalities and leaders rather than in class or economic groups.[35] The longer Churchill lived in the twentieth century and participated in—and shaped?—its history, the deeper, oddly enough, became his commitment to premodern viewpoints.

If, on the one hand, his books bring to this philosophical question ambiguities and ambivalences, reversals and self-contradictions, it is because, when he pauses to reflect amid his adventures or narratives of his adventures, Churchill tends toward the determinist view, while as a politician and a man of action he leans to the Great Man theory. He rarely thinks the question through, and many of his statements on it are ad hoc, inadvertent commitments, practical responses to the sentiments and needs of the moment or part of a political strategy—as when elevating his recent colleague, Roosevelt, over the remote Washington and Lincoln, or when trying to seduce the Italian and German peoples from their leaders by making the latter responsible for all the evils reaped.

If, on the other hand, Churchill seems, despite evidence to the contrary, in his last three major works (the *Marlborough*, *History*, *Second World War*) to radiate a faith in the capacities of the hero, the cause is not only the quasi-philosophical conversion of the 1930s, but also the vast experience of World War II. Had he, instead of becoming prime minister, remained a frustrated onlooker, as in long stretches of World War I, he might perhaps have relapsed to his determinist outlook. But Churchill's experiences on the stage of history have gone to his head—and to his theorizing. Having, after many defeats and detours reached and held supreme power in old age, Churchill abandoned his halfhearted determinism and committed himself to the Great Man theory. Having become a leader at a critical juncture in history and having emerged victorious, the dispassionate philosopher (never too strong) was overcome by the triumphant man of action. Having credited Hitler and Roosevelt with great influence on history, he arrogated a like power to himself, who became, as he liked to think, the arch rival of the one and the great friend and ally of the other. His venerable egoism was inflated to vast proportions by his achievement of the highest power, and the narcissism and solipsism which was budding in the *World Crisis* and which prompted him to write mainly about Churchills—self, father, ancestor—was now full blown. The Great Man theory first suggested in the *River War;* hovering over the *Randolph Churchill;* forwarded in inconsistent and perplexed fashion in the *World Crisis;* by turns analyzed, accepted, qualified, dismissed in the essays of the 1930s; embraced in the *Marlborough,* the *History,* and the great speeches from circa 1936 on was thus given a unique personal interpretation, not without discordant notes, in the memoirs based on his World War II role.

Was Churchill right? While one can make a good case for the notion that without Churchill in 1940 the world would be a vastly different—and mostly nastier—place and that Great Men *do* make a difference, one may still complain that Churchill, suffering for once from a conflict rather than a harmony of interests, overdoes the case. Had his party won the election and had he then remained at Potsdam, he would have made a public break with Stalin over Poland and other issues. But such an action could not have materially altered the course of events.

One's surmise is that if the presence of a Great Man mattered in 1940, the presence of the same Great Man, in greatly altered circumstances in 1945, no longer mattered. Perhaps one has hit here upon a compromise between the two theories: at certain junctures, the Great Man shapes the historical forces, and at other junctures he is shaped by those forces. As to when, where, and whether man or force is definitely in charge, only the Goddess Fortuna knows, and she speaks in no language intelligible to human beings. Or, to complicate the question even more, had Churchill, the Great Man of 1940, been replaced not by historical forces but by the Great Men of 1945, Roosevelt and Stalin?

In Churchill we see writ large—and eloquently expressed—the illusions and premises of many men of action, statesmen, leaders, most of whom do not write history or theorize about it. As Whittemore concludes, "Few of us have the grand opportunity for self-delusion that fate has afforded Churchill, and his delusion here . . . is surely understandable." The belief that the individual makes a difference had given him impetus in his rise, provided momentum for his career, brought him through adversity, endowed his writings with a thrust and relevance, and finally ennobled the office of prime minister, the man, the actions, and the historical memoirs. To have denied that belief would, it seemed to him at the end of his life, be neither humble nor philosophical but an error with reference to the facts.

Notes

Chapter 1. The Polemist.

1. Churchill, *Great Contemporaries* (New York: Putnam's, 1937), p. 35; *News of the World* (13 January 1935); Richard Ellmann, *James Joyce* (New York: Oxford University Press, 1959), pp. 521–22. The chances of his having read the greatest British novel of the century are slim.

2. Some minor but interesting contacts between Churchill and the literary world occurred periodically. In 1928 he defeated G. K. Chesterton, who stood for Edinburgh University as an Independent Liberal (Maisie Ward, *G. K. Chesterton* [New York: Sheed and Ward, 1943], p. 554). In extreme old age, Churchill met T. S. Eliot at Tangier, but the name meant nothing to him (Lord Moran, *Churchill* [Boston: Houghton Mifflin, 1966], p. 816). Robert Graves sent all his books, as soon as they came out, to Churchill, who read them (Moran, p. 319).

3. Churchill, *Step by Step* (New York: Putnam's, 1939), pp. 30, 202; Churchill, *Europe Unite* (Boston: Houghton Mifflin, 1950), pp. 389, 468; Martin Gilbert, *Winston S. Churchill*, vol. V (Boston: Houghton Mifflin, 1977), p. 768.

4. Speech of 3 January 1920; *The Strand* (January 1936): 276 ff.; *The Listener* (17 January 1934): 126.

5. *Europe Unite*, pp. 49, 72, 36, 153; Churchill, *The Sinews of Peace* (Boston: Houghton Mifflin, 1949), pp. 47, 211–13; Churchill, *The Unwritten Alliance* (London: Cassell, 1961), p. 61; Churchill, *While England Slept* (New York: Putnam, 1938), p. 72; Churchill, *The Dawn of Liberation* (London: Cassell, 1945), p. 83.

6. Churchill read *1984* twice and found it "very remarkable" (Moran, p. 426). Orwell, as we shall see, also implicitly agreed with Catskill's (i.e., Churchill's) critique of utopianism in H. G. Wells's *Men Like Gods*, a critique derided by Wells (Mark Hillegas, *The Future as Nightmare* [New York: Oxford University Press, 1967], p. 126).

7. Cf. his outburst in private that cultured people are the scum on the river of production (Gilbert, V, 343). In his worship of science and manufacturing and money (as expressed often in his little-known but revealing *African Journey* of 1908), there was more than a little of the philistine in Churchill.

8. Churchill, *Liberalism and the Social Problem* (London: Hodder and Stoughton, 1909), p. 156; Churchill, *A History of the English Speaking Peoples*, 4 vols. (1956–58; reprint, New York: Bantam, 1963), III, 257; IV, 40.

9. H. G. Wells, *Experiment in Autobiography* (New York: Macmillan, 1934), p. 542.

10. Leon Edel, *Henry James*, vol. V (Philadelphia: Lippincott, 1972), pp. 61, 519, 524–26.

11. Churchill, *My Early Life: A Roving Commission* (New York: Scribner's, 1930), p. 360.

12. The material in the preceding four paragraphs is based on H. V. Marrot, *Life and Letters of John Galsworthy* (New York: Scribner's, 1936), pp. 241, 261, 266, 283, 309, 675–85; Randolph Churchill, *Winston S. Churchill*, vol. II (Boston: Houghton Mifflin, 1967), p. 374. Galsworthy was not the only literary figure to obtain a response from the young minister. When Arthur Conan Doyle sent copies of the book *Crime of the Congo* to various notables, among the more interesting replies he received was one from Churchill at the Board of Trade (in October 1909), expressing a readiness to help and suggesting that change might be imminent (Pierre Nordon, *Conan Doyle* [New York: Holt, Rinehart & Winston, 1967], p. 76).

13. A decade later, Churchill worked much more closely with a part-time literary personage, Lawrence of Arabia. Over the course of several years, they cooperated on military and diplomatic affairs. Churchill even offered Lawrence a post in the Colonial Office and carte blanche there. His "valued friend," in turn, praised him and his writings highly. See the essay on Lawrence in Churchill's *Great Contemporaries* (New York: Putnam's, 1937), pp. 129–40. Offering government posts to literati he liked appears to have become a habit of Churchill's in the late 1910s. Reciting at the front Siegfried Sassoon's war poems and often expressing admiration for him as a man, Churchill was determined to look him up and offer him a position in the Ministry of Munitions even though the poems were antiwar. Sassoon, he declared, can think, and only those who cannot think repelled him. See Martin Gilbert, *Winston S. Churchill*, vol. IV (Boston: Houghton Mifflin, 1975), pp. 140, 150.

14. Randolph Churchill, II, 247; Moran, pp. 352, 750–51; *Daily Mail*, 17 November 1932; *Collier's* (27 June, 1935): 12 ff.; *Saturday Evening Post* (15 February 1930): 25 ff.

15. The material in the preceding three paragraphs is based on *Experiment in Autobiography*, pp. 74–76, 583–85; Antonina Vallentin, *H. G. Wells*, trans. D. Woodward (New York: John Day, 1950), pp. 190–91. Wells was not alone. Visiting France in 1916, Arthur Conan Doyle approached Lloyd George and Churchill with ideas for protecting the troops. Churchill, citing an earlier fiasco, replied that plenty of good ideas were available but what was needed was the power to implement them. Churchill and Doyle, who particularly enjoyed the company of men of American birth or descent and men favoring Anglo-America cooperation, were friends, exact contemporaries and, as late as 1949, nearly equally famous as writers. They also thought alike, both being diehard advocates of reprisal air raids against German cities in 1916. Both wrote military histories of World War I. Churchill even conceded to Doyle superiority in certain judgments. They shared a love of battle scenes, and their narrative styles were in some ways alike. See Nordon, pp. 49, 76, 80, 83, 94–97, 106, 232–33.

16. Vallentin, pp. 191–92; H. G. Wells, *Mr. Britling Sees It Through* (New York: Macmillan, 1917), p. 324; E. Warner in E. M. Earle, *Makers of Modern Strategy* (Princeton: Princeton University Press, 1943), p. 486; Herbert Howarth, "Behind Churchill's Grand Style," *Commentary*, XL (1951): 550. Though outsiders like the scientist-novelist C. P. Snow believe that Churchill may have picked up the idea for the tank from Wells's writings (*Variety of Men* [New York: Scribner's, 1966], p. 163), and though in a magazine article during World War I Churchill at least raised the question of whether Wells, the Germans, Russians, or Americans invented the tank (*London Magazine* (December 1916): 395–404), in his definitive version of the war, *The World Crisis*, Churchill does give Wells credit in connection with the tank.

17. *Sunday Express*, 5 December 1920; Gilbert, IV, 441–42; *Winston S. Churchill: His Complete Speeches*, ed. R. R. James, 8 vols. (New York: R. R. Bowker, 1974), III, 3025; Vallentin, pp. 7–8. Wells's intermittent praise was not insincere. In his novel, *Mr. Britling Sees It Through*, he presents Churchill (in the background of the story) as being made a scapegoat by gossipy Tory ladies and a vicious Tory press filled with personal spite against any real, imaginative leader (pp. 324, 353–54).

18. The material in the preceding three paragraphs is based on *The Empire Review* (November 1923): 217–23; George Orwell, *Dickens, Dali and Others* (New York: Harcourt Brace, 1946), p. 120; *Sunday Pictorial*, 23 August 1931: 8.

19. The material in the preceding two paragraphs is based on L. S. Amery, *My Political Life*, 3 vols. (London: Hutchinson, 1953–55), II, 253; S. J. Hurwitz in *Some Modern Historians of Britain*, ed. H. Ausubel et al. (New York: Dryden Press, 1951), p. 313; P. Guedella, *Mr. Churchill* (New York: Reynal & Hitchcock, 1942), 225; Vallentin, p. 316; Brian Gardner, *Churchill in His Time* (London: Methuen, 1968), p. 266; Lovat Dickson, *H. G. Wells* (New York: Atheneum, 1969), p. 315.

20. Archibald Henderson, *Bernard Shaw* (New York: Appleton, 1932), pp. 714, 729, 875. A curious parallel: Each man had warned during a world war that Britain must win in a big way lest the Russian menace should spread—Shaw pointing to the Czarist government in World War I and Churchill to the Soviet in World War II. See Julian Kaye, *Bernard Shaw and the Nineteenth Century Tradition* (Norman, Okla.: Oklahoma University Press, 1958), p. 180. For some of Shaw's teasing, see Stephen Winston, *Days With Bernard Shaw* (New York: Vanguard, 1949), p. 90: "Churchill smokes, drinks, and eats meat and has managed to survive." In 1950, when Shaw fell and broke a limb, Churchill, who was visiting America, sent some peaches from Florida (R. J. Minney, *Recollections of G. B. Shaw* [Englewood Cliffs, N.J.: Prentice-Hall, 1969], p. 184). In short, beneath the public mask, Shaw, who got on well with the ebullient Jennie, also liked her son (Blanche Patch, *Thirty Years with G. B. Shaw* [New York: Dodd, Mead, 1951], p. 52).

21. *Great Contemporaries*, pp. 39-44.

22. Peter de Mendelssohn *The Age of Churchill* (New York: Knopf, 1961), pp. 550–51; *Great Contemporaries*, p. 35; *Complete Speeches*, I, 687; on Shaw's intellectual style, see Richard Ohmann in Edward Corbett, *Rhetorical Analysis of Literary Works* (New York: Oxford, 1969), p. 211, 213.

23. The material in these two paragraphs is based on "Common Sense about the War," *The New Statesman* (14 November 1914), Supplement, reprinted in *What I Really Wrote about the War* (New York: Brentano, 1932), p. 22, 32; "Socialism and the Labour Party" (lecture of 29 January 1920), in Lloyd J. Hubenka, *Bernard Shaw: Practical Politics* (Lincoln: University of Nebraska Press, 1976), pp. 158–61; Minney, p. 131; Henderson, p. 319; Hesketh Pearson, *Bernard Shaw* (London: The Reprint Society, 1942), p. 385; *Sunday Pictorial*, 16 August 1931.

24. The material in these five paragraphs is based on *Nash's (Pall Mall) Magazine* (August 1929): 16–18; *Great Contemporaries*, pp. 39–44; William Irvine, *The Universe of George Bernard Shaw* (New York: McGraw, 1949), p. 300. De Mendelssohn (pp. 550–51) finds the essay on Shaw to be one of Churchill's best character portraits. Despising the Irishman's deliberate irresponsibility, Churchill yet understood Shaw. In a manner touching, generous, and memorable, he presented the saint and the sage as well as the clown. He praised Shaw in the final analysis because the "word" is definitive: say what

you like, Churchill implies, but say it well.

25. "Biographers' Blunders Corrected," in G. B. Shaw, *Sixteen Self Sketches* (New York: Dodd Mead, 1949), pp. 129–34.

26. The material in these five paragraphs is based on *Sunday Pictorial*, 9 and 16 August 1931, p. 8; *Great Contemporaries*, p. 42; "What Indeed?" (lecture of 26 November 1931) in Hubenka, pp. 211, 222; Maurice Collis, *Nancy Astor* (London: Faber and Faber, 1960), pp. 168–72.

27. *Sixteen Self Sketches*, pp. 134–37; Collis, p. 168; Churchill, *The Second World War*, 6 vols. (Boston: Houghton Mifflin, 1948–53), IV, 493.

28. *The Complete Prefaces of Bernard Shaw* (London: Paul Hamlyn, 1965), pp. 872, 878; Martin Gilbert, *Winston S. Churchill*, vol. VI (Boston: Houghton Mifflin, 1983), p. 190.

29. The material in these three paragraphs is based on Charles Eade, *Churchill by His Contemporaries* (London: Hutchinson, 1953), pp. 417, 463–64; Henderson, pp. 316, 350; Kaye, p. 199; Patch, p. 295.

30. C. R. Coote, *A Churchill Reader* (Boston: Houghton Mifflin, 1954), p. 66.

31. One of the earliest literary attacks was a poem by Osbert Sitwell at the time of the British intervention in the Russian Revolution, *The Winstonburg Line* (London; Hendersons, 1919). It is a monologue by a thinly disguised Churchill: "My new war / Is one of the nicest we've had." Nor is it "war really" but "only a training for the next one", "merely restoring order— / As the Germans did in Belgium" and as he hopes to do in Ireland. The persona, fearing that the "nation's heroic mood / Is over," looks with nostalgia back to the heroics of Sidney St. and Antwerp and, above all, to the time when he was allowed to waste a million lives at Gallipoli. Getting killed should be the normal occupation of other people, and the persona regrets that the world war stopped before he could go out again. Preferring a system of compulsory-voluntary-compulsory military service, "I shall be free to create / A really fine war elsewhere." Those who like war, like him; the rest are Bolsheviks. He needs to be sent to Russia to save the people there. A query: Is T. S. Eliot's "Coriolan" (1931–32) based, however indirectly, on less than favorable impressions of Churchill, impressions similar to Sitwell's?

32. Arnold Bennett, *Journals* (New York: Literary Guild, 1933), pp. 640, 669, 718, 937. On another occasion, dining out, Bennett was seated next to Churchill, who, noting that Bennett looked dour, hoped that it was not because he disliked Churchill. See Reginald Pound, *Arnold Bennett* (New York: Harcourt Brace, 1953), p. 10.

33. *Journals*, pp. 804, 806, 824, 844; Dudley Barker, *Writer by Trade* (New York: Atheneum, 1966), pp. 190, 224–25; Pound, p. 313.

34. Bennett, *Lord Raingo* (London: Cassell, 1926), pp. 37, 56–67, 145, 154–58, 247–48, 263, 267, 341–43, 356–57.

35. *Journals*, p. 917; Barker, pp. 224–25; Pound, pp. 9–10, 313, 320.

36. H. G. Wells, *Meanwhile* (New York: Doran, 1927), pp. 135, 199–203, 214–18, 223, 241, 257.

37. Unlike Bennett's assertion in print that Lord Raingo was not the portrait of any living person, Wells acknowledged that "*Men Like Gods* frankly caricatures some prominent contemporaries" (*Experiment*, p. 421).

38. Aldous Huxley said years later that *Brave New World* began as a parody of *Men Like Gods* but grew into something quite different. It remains indebted heavily to Wells—being an anti-Wells vision in the form of Wellsian science fiction. See Hillegas, pp. 111, 118. For the negative reactions to *Men Like Gods*

of other utopia or dystopia writers, see Zamyatin and Orwell in Hillegas, pp. 104, 126.

39. The material in the preceding four paragraphs is based on H. G. Wells, *Men Like Gods* (New York: Macmillan, 1923), pp. 22, 102–3, 106–9, 125, 173, 180, 185–87, 204–7, 219–21, 229, 243, 300. It is interesting to note that in May 1923 Bennett wrote to Wells's wife that *Men Like Gods* was very fine, but to someone else he noted that he had his doubts about the book. See *Arnold Bennett and H. G. Wells*, ed. Harris Wilson (Urbana, Ill.: University of Illinois Press, 1960), p. 223.

Chapter 2. The Conservative

1. Randolph Churchill, *Winston S. Churchill: Companion Volume One* (Boston: Houghton Mifflin, 1967), part 2, 836–39.
2. Ronald Hyam, *Elgin and Churchill at the Colonial Office 1905–1908* (London: Macmillan, 1968), pp. 116, 141, 208–18, 225–28, 494; Randolph Churchill, *Winston S. Churchill: Companion Volume Two* (Boston: Houghton Mifflin, 1969), part 1, 328, 337.
3. W. S. Blunt, *My Diaries 1888–1914*, 2 vols. (New York: Knopf, 1921), II, 276–77, 284–88.
4. *The Empire Review* (July 1923): 691–98; A. J. P. Taylor, *English History 1914–1945* (New York: Oxford University Press, 1965), pp. 277–78, 319, 356.
5. *Scribner's Magazine* (December 1930): 587–97.
6. Vladimir Dedijer, "Historians as Participants," *TLS* (30 May 1968): 555–56.
7. Churchill, *Step by Step* (New York: Putnam's, 1939), pp. 53–54, 214.
8. *Companion Volume Two*, part 2, 1045, 1114–16, 1207; Blunt, II, 276–77, 284–88; Lucy Masterman, *C. G. F. Masterman* (London: Frank Cass, 1968), pp. 97, 109, 172–73, 205.
9. Martin Gilbert, *Winston S. Churchill*, Volume III (Boston: Houghton Mifflin, 1971), pp. 284–85, 492; *Living Age* (13 September 1919): 641; *Weekly Dispatch* (13 July 1924): 8.
10. Winston Churchill, *Great Contemporaries* (1937–38; reprint Chicago: Chicago University Press, 1973), pp. 375–78; *Collier's* (25 February 1933): 10; (20 January 1934): 11; (29 December 1934): 24; (24 September 1938): 13.
11. Winston Churchill, *Victory* (Boston: Little Brown, 1946), pp. 242, 251, 260, 305.
12. Winston Churchill, *Europe Unite* (Boston: Houghton Mifflin, 1950), pp. 67, 100, 368.
13. *Companion Volume One*, part 2, 765–68; *Companion Volume Two*, part 3, 1441–47, 1466, 1483; *Daily Mail* (23 March 1932).
14. *Companion Volume One*, part 2, 765–68; Churchill, *The Unwritten Alliance* (London: Cassell, 1961), pp. 150, 298.
15. *Daily Mail* (30 June 1932); Churchill, *The Unrelenting Struggle* (London: Cassell, 1942), p. 265; *Unwritten Alliance*, pp. 70, 150, 298; Churchill, *Amid These Storms* (New York: Scribner's, 1932), p. 230; Churchill, *A Roving Commission: My Early Life* (New York: Scribner's, 1930), p. 357.
16. *Amid These Storms*, pp. 232–39; *Companion Volume Two*, part 1, 210; part 2, 968–70, 1092; *Collier's* (16 February 1935): 95; (22 August 1936): 22; *The Listener* (17 January 1934): 85; *Daily Mail* (3 July 1931): 10.

17. *Companion Volume Two*, part 2, 1092; *Step by Step*, p. 296; *Second World War*, I, 10–11.
18. *Unwritten Alliance*, p. 41.
19. *Companion Volume Two*, part 3, 1543; *News of the World* (13 January and 24 March 1935); *Daily Mail* (1 December 1931); *Companion Volume One*, part 2, 774; *Collier's* (22 August 1936): 22.
20. *Collier's* (5 August 1933): 16; (13 August 1932): 20; *Daily Mail* (23 March 1932): 10; *News of the World* (25 September and 23 October 1938): 12.
21. Churchill, *Liberalism and the Social Problem* (London: Hodder and Stoughton, 1909), p. 37; *Step by Step*, p. 161.
22. Randolph Churchill, *Winston S. Churchill*, Volume I (Boston: Houghton Mifflin, 1966), pp. 223, 270; *PTO* (16 June 1960): 25–27; Hyam, p. 171.
23. Churchill, *Stemming the Tide* (Boston: Houghton Mifflin, 1954), p. 332.
24. *Collier's* (16 February 1935): 14; *Stemming*, p. 10; Churchill, *Onwards to Victory* (Boston: Little Brown, 1944), p. 56; *Unrelenting*, pp. 74, 90; *Companion Volume One*, part 2, 712–3.
25. Hyam, p. 341; Churchill, *Europe Unite* (Boston: Houghton Mifflin, 1950), p. 99; *News of the World* (13 January 1935): 5.
26. Churchill, *A History of the English-Speaking Peoples*, 4 vols. (1956–58; reprint New York: Bantam, 1963), I, 156; II, 207, 151.
27. For intelligent observations on Churchill's conservatism, see Isaiah Berlin, *Mr. Churchill in 1940* (London: John Murray, 1949), pp. 31–38; G. K. Lewis, "Mr. Churchill as Historian," *The Historian* 20 (August 1958): 394–98, 404–05, 412–14; J. H. Plumb, "The Historian," in *Churchill Revised*, ed. anon. (New York: Dial, 1969), pp. 133–38; R. R. James, *Churchill: A Study in Failure 1900–1939* (London: Weidenfeld and Nicolson, 1970), pp. 32–40, 150–51, 198–201, and, esp. 299–305; also R. R. James, A. J. P. Taylor, and B. H. Liddell Hart in *Churchill Revised*, pp. 58, 114, 202.

Chapter 3. The Warhorse

1. Brian Gardner, *Churchill in His Time* (London: Methuen, 1968), p. 115; Martin Gilbert, *Winston S. Churchill. Companion Volume III* (Boston: Houghton Mifflin, 1973), part 2, 1541n.; Harold Nicolson, *Diaries and Letters*, ed. Nigel Nicolson, 3 vols. (New York: Atheneum, 1966–68), II, 244. Cf. Stalin on Churchill as the "old war-horse": Churchill, *The Second World War*, 6 vols. (Boston: Houghton Mifflin, 1948–53), IV, 493.
2. Randolph Churchill, *Winston S. Churchill. Companion Volume I* (Boston: Houghton Mifflin, 1967), part 1, 147, 163, 181, 522; B. H. Liddell Hart, "The Military Strategist" in *Churchill Revised*, ed. anon. (New York: Dial, 1969), p. 173; Virginia Cowles, *Churchill* (New York: Harper, 1953) p. 36.
3. *Cosmopolitan* (October 1924): 4; W. G. Stevens and A. G. Gardiner, in Martin Gilbert, *Churchill* (Englewood Cliffs, N.J.: Prentice Hall, 1967), pp. 76–77, 84; Gordon K. Lewis, "Mr. Churchill as Historian," *The Historian* (August 1958): 389. As a young man, Churchill was eager to win and wear medals. See *Companion Volume I*, ii, 1191, and Randolph Churchill, *Winston S. Churchill, Companion Volume II* (Boston, Houghton Mifflin, 1969), part 3, 1984.
4. Churchill, *The Sinews of Peace* (Boston: Houghton Mifflin, 1949), p. 113; Cowles, p. 96.
5. *Illustrated Sunday Herald*, 30 November 1919, p. 5; *Sinews of Peace*, p. 120; Martin Gilbert, *Winston S. Churchill, Volume III* (Boston: Houghton

Mifflin, 1971), p. 141; R. R. James, "The Politician" in *Churchill Revised*, p. 80; Lord Riddel, *War Diary 1914–1918* (London: Nicolson and Watson, 1933), p. 352; *Companion Volume III*, 2, 1401.

6. Churchill, *London to Ladysmith via Pretoria* (London: Longmans, Green, 1900), p. 339; *The Malakand Field Force* (London: Longmans, Green, 1898), pp. 72, 246–47, 172, 253, 268; *The River War*, 2 vols. (London: Longmans, Green, 1899), II, 73; *Savrola* (1900; reprint, New York: Random House, 1956), p. 74.

7. Trumbull Higgins, *Winston Churchill and the Second Front* (New York: Oxford, 1957), p. 136; *Companion Volume I*, ii, 794; Churchill, *A Roving Commission: My Early Life* (New York: Scribner's, 1930), pp. 65–67; *The Second World War*, III, 200, 611; IV, 67; *The Unwritten Alliance* (London: Cassell, 1961), p. 141.

8. Gilbert, *Winston S. Churchill*, pp. 10, 111, 115, 586–68, 651, 672; *Companion Volume II*, ii, 850, 1419, 1432, 1467; Cowles, pp. 211, 229; Liddell Hart, p. 175; Gilbert, *Churchill*, p. 93.

9. Churchill, *A History of the English-Speaking Peoples*, 4 vols. (New York: Bantam, 1963), IV, 132.

10. *The Second World War*, II 279, 345, 699; VI, 19; *Companion Volume III*, i, 650; ii, 1288, 1429; Nicolson, II, 103, 186; Cowles, p. 324; Martin Gilbert, *Winston S. Churchill*, vol. V (Boston: Houghton Mifflin, 1983), pp. 165, 580, 828.

11. Lord Moran, *Churchill* (Boston: Houghton Mifflin, 1966), p. 348; *Malakand*, p. 281; Gardner, pp. 190, 254; Aneurin Bevan in *Churchill by His Contemporaries*, ed. Observer (London: Hodder and Stoughton, 1965), p. 60. Cf. Angus Calder, *The People's War* (London: Cape, 1969), p. 90; London *Times Literary Supplement*, (3 August 1951): 477–78; Lewis, p. 387.

12. *Companion Volume II*, ii, 893; Gilbert, *Winston S. Churchill*, pp. 121, 223, 449, 475; *Companion Volume III*, ii, 898, 1171n., 1361–62; Lord Riddel, *More Pages From My Diary* (London: Country Life, 1934), p. 139; H. H. Asquith, *Memories and Reflections*, 2 vols. (Boston: Little, Brown, 1928), II, 50–55.

13. Gilbert, *Winston S. Churchill*, pp. 31, 58, 111, 565; *Companion Volume III*, i, 32, 79, 143, 150, 163, 166, 177, 189, 296, 313–14, 524.

14. Gilbert, *Winston S. Churchill*, pp. 58, 475; *Companion Volume II*, iii, 1491–99; *Companion Volume III*, i, 163n.; ii, 1193–99, 1303–8, 1354, 1413, 1582; Moran, p. 347; Gardner, pp. 150, 214, 218, 221, A.J.P. Taylor, *English History 1914–45* (New York: Oxford, 1965), pp. 480–82; Arthur Byrant, *The Turn of the Tide* (Garden City, N.Y.: Doubleday, 1957), pp. 202, 210, 241.

15. *Stemming the Tide*, pp. 288.

16. *Companion Volume III*, i, 326, 641, 211, 99.

17. Gilbert, *Winston S. Churchill*, pp. 588, 781; *Companion Volume III*, i, 211, 781; Byrant, pp. 334, 368, 386–87; Correlli Barnett, *The Desert Generals* (New York: Viking, 1961), p. 222.

18. *Roving Commission*, p. 212; Anthony Storr, "The Man," in *Churchill Revised*, pp. 263, 267; Churchill, *In the Balance* (Boston: Houghton Mifflin, 1952), p. 304; Gardiner, quoted in Peter Stansky, ed. *Churchill* (New York: Hill and Wang, 1973), p. 50.

19. *History*, I, 256; *Windsor Magazine* (July 1901): 124.

20. *Companion Volume II*, i, 104; *Unwritten Alliance*, p. 51; Cowles, p. 8.

21. *Sinews of Peace*, p. 28; *Collier's* (3 June 1939): 9ff.; Epilogue to *The Second World War*, abridged ed. Denis Kelly (Boston: Houghton Mifflin, 1959), p. 1013.

22. *Collier's*, (15 May 1937): 12ff.; *News of the World*, (13 January 1935): 5;

Foreword to D. S. Daniell, *Fourth Hussar* (Aldershot: Gale and Polden, 1959); *Companion Volume III*, i, 148; ii, 1533.

23. Bryan Magee, "Churchill's Novel," *Encounter* (25 October 1965): 45–49; *Companion Volume III*, 1435; *Anglo-Saxon Review* (March 1901): 245; Churchill, *Onwards to Victory* (Boston: Little Brown, 1944), p. 285; *Step by Step* (New York: Putnam's, 1939), p. 162; *The Dawn of Liberation* (London: Cassell, 1945), p. 154; *Victory* (Boston: Little, Brown, 1946), p. 263.

24. *Savrola*, p. 81; *Malakand*, pp. 41, 230.

25. *Unwritten Alliance*, pp. 147, 306. Cf. *Companion Volume II*, ii, 896–98.

26. *River Wall*, II, 48; *Daily Mail*, 7 September 1933, p. 8; *Step by Step*, p. 294.

27. *Onwards to Victory*, pp. 56, 312; *Unwritten Alliance*, pp. 78, 100, 141; *The Listener* (21 November 1934): 841; *Collier's* (29 June 1934): 49.

28. Nicolson, III, 45; Gilbert, *Winston S. Churchill*, p. 478; *Companion Volume II*, ii, 708; A.J.P. Taylor, "The Statesman," in *Churchill Revised*, pp. 58–59; Asquith, II, 11, 26, 32–36.

29. Gilbert, *Winston S. Churchill*, pp. 23–4, 440, 480; Gilbert, *Churchill*, pp. 99, 136; Nicolson, I, 211; Cowles, p. 201; *Companion Volume III*, i, 40, 99, 211, 326, 641.

30. *Companion Volume III*, i, 99, 108, 140, 590.

31. *Europe Unite*, pp. 56–7.

32. *River War*, I, 178; *London to Ladysmith*, p. 24; *Sinews of Peace*, p. 104.

33. Harold Nicolson, "A Portrait," *Life* (15 March 1948): 104; A. MacCallum Scott, *Winston Spencer Churchill* (London: Methuen, 1905), p. 67; *Strand* (January 1936): 276–86; *Companion Volume I*, ii, 938.

34. *Second World War*, VI, 254; *Dawn of Liberation*, p. 257; Jones in *The New York Review of Books* (23 May 1968): 34; Lewis, p. 387.

35. Bevan, pp. 62–63; Herbert Howarth, "Behind Churchill's Grand Style," *Commentary*, 11 (1951): 551; Violet Barbour in *American Historical Review*, 41 (1936): 332; 43 (1938): 377; 44 (1939): 887; R. R. James, *Churchill* (London: Weidenfeld and Nicolson, 1970), pp. 38–39, 48, 61, 130, 132, 333–34; Nicolson, *Diaries*, III, 224; Gilbert, *Churchill*, p. 16; Lewis, pp. 392–96, 407, 412–43; *Companion Volume III*, ii, 1347n.; *Weekly Dispatch*, 25 May 1924, p. 8. On rare occasions, Churchill confessed to a killing. See *London to Ladysmith*, p. 223; *Companion Volume I*, ii, 963.

36. Gilbert, *Winston S. Churchill*, 680, 816, 823; *Companion Volume III*, ii, 1402, 1416, 1531; Nicolson, II, 59, 93–94; Moran, p. 772.

37. Moran, p. 475; James, *Churchill*, pp. 46, 175; Taylor in *Churchill Revised*, pp. 17–19.

38. Goronwy Rees, "After the Ball," *Encounter*, (25 November 1965): 7–9.

Chapter 4. The Dreamer

1. All quotations from Churchill's writings in this chapter will indicate volume and page number of the following editions: *Lord Randolph Churchill* (hereafter RC), 2 vols. (New York: Macmillan, 1906); *The World Crisis* (hereafter WC), 6 vols. (New York: Scribner's, 1923–31); *A Roving Commission: My Early Life* (hereafter MEL), (New York: Scribner's 1930); *Great Contemporaries* (hereafter GC) (New York: Putnam's, 1937); *Marlborough* (hereafter M), 4 vols. (1933–38; reprint. 2 vols. London: Harrap, 1947); *The Second World War* (hereafter SWW), 6 vols. (Boston: Houghton Mifflin, 1948–53); *A History of the English-*

Speaking Peoples (hereafter HESP), 4 vols. (1956–58; reprint, New York: Bantam, 1963).

2. He would thereby, says S. R. Graubard, Burke, Disraeli and Churchill (Cambridge, Mass.: Harvard University Press, 1961), pp. 199–200, see his own disappointment in perspective, find new sources of energy, and remind his slothful generation of British greatness.

3. A modern student, Admiral Percy Gretton (Winston Churchill and the Royal Navy [New York: Coward, McCann, 1968], p. 146), ventures the hypothesis that the study of Marlborough confirmed Churchill in his Dardanelles strategy and may well have been the genesis of his "soft underbelly" policy and of the 1940 Middle Eastern campaign. Both in Marlborough's and Churchill's day, the admirals lamented the diversion to the Mediterranean of ships from home waters.

4. Marlborough's military victories, his agile diplomacy, and his masterly amphibious Mediterranean strategy, say historians like Gretton (p. 246) and G. M. Trevelyan, (England Under Queen Anne, 3 vols. [London: Longmans, Green, 1931–34), II, 248–259) wrought a revolution at sea, for he saw the naval war as part of the larger strategy.

5. Although Churchill wrote later in the History, "No closer parallel exists in the history than that presented by the Tory conduct in the years 1696 to 1699 with their similar conduct in the years 1932 to 1937" (III,20), questions have been raised whether the Tories of the early 1700s may be compared at all to the Conservatives of the 1930s. See R. R. James, Churchill (London: Weidenfeld and Nicolson, 1970), p. 313; Gordon K. Lewis, "Mr. Churchill as Historian," The Historian XX (August 1958): 389.

6. Martin Gilbert, Winston S. Churchill, Vol. III (Boston: Houghton Mifflin, 1971) pp. 321, 332.

7. Virginia Cowles, Churchill (New York: Harper, 1953), p. 68.

8. Charles Eade, ed. Churchill by His Contemporaries (London: Hutchinson's 1953), p. 463; Randolph Churchill, Winston S. Churchill Vol. I (Boston: Houghton Mifflin, 1966), p. 367; A. MacCallum Scott, Winston Spencer Churchill (London: Methuen, 1905), pp. 254–55.

9. Gilbert, III, 573, 578, 588, 727; James, p. 38; G. M. Thomson, Vote of Censure (New York: Stein & Day, 1968), p. 92; Shane Leslie in Review of Reviews LXVII (May 1923): 477; Martin Gilbert, Winston S. Churchill, Companion Volume III (Boston: Houghton Mifflin, 1973), part 2, 1283.

10. Harold Nicolson, Diaries and Letters, ed. Nigel Nicolson, 3 vols. (New York: Atheneum, 1966–68), I, 258; L. S. Amery, My Political Life, 3 vols. (London: Hutchinson, 1953–55), III, 400; Thomson, pp. 131, 150, 187; Arthur Byrant, The Turn of the Tide (Garden City, N.Y.: Doubleday, 1957), p. 334; Brian Gardner, Churchill in His Time (London: Methuen, 1968), pp. 176–79, 186n., 285; Correlli Barnett, The Desert Generals (New York: Viking, 1961), pp. 222, 255; Lewis, p. 395; Cowles, p. 325.

11. Gilbert, III, 744.

12. The years 1689–97, notes A. L. Rowse (The Churchills, 2 vols. [New York: Harper, 1958], I, 178; II, 318), were like 1914–18, each a period that saw bad generalship. Both Churchills were thus provided with the necessary apprenticeship and the dress rehearsal for the heroic ardors of the second phase of either war, a phase that saw superior generalship and results, as a consequence, in part, of their roles.

13. Both were, observes Rowse (II, 284), men of the sensible center—Marlborough, a Trimmer, Churchill, a Coalitionist. Neither was a "good party man"

and Harley was too obviously a Baldwin.

14. V. Barbour, review of M, *American Historical Review* XLI (1936): 332; H. S. Commager, "Preface," M. (New York: Scribner, 1968), p. xxiii.

15. Eade, p. 20; Trumbull Higgins, *Winston Churchill and the Second Front* (New York: Oxford University Press, 1957), pp. 52, 143, 196; Arthur Byrant, *Triumph in the West* (Garden City, N.Y.: Doubleday, 1959), p. 124; *Turn*, pp. 12, 25, 160, 271, 592, 500; Rowse, II, 350. Denis Brogan ("Great House" in *Spectator*, 4 July 1958, p. 27) believes that Churchill was heroic but ultimately less like Marlborough than like Chatham.

16. Rowse, I, 228; D. C. Somervell, "Winston Churchill," *Nobel Prize Winners*, ed. E. J. Ludovici (London: Arco, 1956), p. 17. For these various dissenting views, see my *Sword and Pen: A Survey of the Writings of Sir Winston Churchill* (Albuquerque, N.M.: University of New Mexico Press, 1974), pp. 116–19, 252 n. 49–54.

17. Rowse, I, 121, 210.

18. Martin Gilbert, *Winston S. Churchill*, Vol. V (Boston, Mass.: Houghton Mifflin, 1977), 47, 318.

19. Rarely, concludes Peter de Mendelssohn (*The Age of Churchill* [New York: Knopf, 1961], p. 303), has a man been able to read his own character in the mirror and, especially, discern "in advance and in detail, over decades yet unlived, the situation into which his character must lead him." Churchill's way back to prominence began, adds V. Cowles (p. 285), with his telling this story so strangely parallel to the unknown story that lay ahead. It has been noted that the *Marlborough* has a special role in Churchill's development. Identifying with the subject of his biography, seeing himself in Marlborough, Churchill, by vindicating his ancestor, was in a sense vindicating himself. Subject and author throw light on each other, as Churchill, regarding the world wars in the perspectives of history, was unwittingly using his book as preparation for the future. He would relive many of Marlborough's adventures. He would mature, draw inspiration from his hero worship, and find a fusion of political and military ideas. Turning to the past helped him to become—to whatever degree depends on the observer—the Marlborough of the Grand Alliance of his own epoch. For a more detailed analysis and a listing of secondary sources, see my *Sword and Pen*, pp. 127–29, 253 n. 77.

Chapter 5. The Semi-American

1. Leo Maxse quoted in Earl Winterton, "Sir Winston Churchill in Parliament," in *The Illustrated London News Eightieth Birthday Tribute to Churchill*, ed. Bruce Ingram (London, 1954): p. 3.

2. Randolph Churchill, *Winston S. Churchill* (Boston, Mass.: Houghton Mifflin, 1966), I, 15, 369; *North American Review*, 167 (December 1898): p. 736; A. L. Rowse, *The Churchills* (New York: Harper, 1958), p. 196. Kay Halle's *Winston Churchill: An English-Speaking Union* [*Churchill on America*](New York: Walker, 1970) is a useful compendium of most of Churchill's utterances on the United States, but the essays in it by the editor and by Averall Harriman offer anecdotal material in lieu of historical background or analysis. See also Robert H. Pilpel, *Churchill in America* (New York: Harcourt Brace, 1976).

3. Randolph Churchill, *Winston S. Churchill, Companion Volume I* (Boston, Mass.: Houghton Mifflin, 1967) part 2, 817; *Companion Volume II*

(Boston: Houghton Mifflin, 1969), part 2, p. 894; Randolph Churchill, I, 272, 369.

4. *A Roving Commission [My Early Life]* (New York: Scribner's, 1930), p. 360; Randolph Churchill, I, 525.

5. Randolph Churchill, I, 525–26; *Companion Volume I*, 2, 1220–28; II, 2, 1082.

6. Lady Spencer Churchill quoted in Lord Moran, *Churchill* (Boston, Mass.: Houghton Mifflin, 1966), p. 800.

7. *Daily Telegraph*, 18 November 1929, weekly, through 3 February 1930; *Collier's* (20 June 1936): 11ff.

8. Randolph Churchill, I, 258–61; *Companion Volume I*, 1,590,620–21; *Strand Magazine* (August 1931): 141–50; Moran, pp. 443, 567, 599. On the sensationalist parochial press, see Gustav Ohlinger, "Winston S. Churchill: A Midnight Interview," *Michigan Quarterly Review*, 5 (Spring 1966): 75–79.

9. Winston Churchill, *The Second World War*, 6 vols. (Boston, Mass.: Houghton Mifflin, 1948–53), II, 565; V, 489; *The Unwritten Alliance* (London: Cassell, 1961), p. 138; *Collier's* (27 August 1932): 10ff.; Moran, pp. 565, 595.

10. *Second World War*, V, 561. But Trumbull Higgins (*Winston Churchill and the Second Front* [New York: Oxford, 1957], p. 205) believes that Churchill is here merely elevating his own opportunism into a philosophy of war, not shedding any light on the American or British character.

11. *Daily Telegraph*, 2 December 1929; *Collier's* (13 August 1932): 20ff. Churchill cites the Fifteenth Amendment, which gave the vote to the Negro, as another example of a noble American idea soured by implementation.

12. Winston Churchill, *The World Crisis*, 6 vols. (New York: Scribner's, 1923–31), III, 233–39; V, 98–100, 112–24, 147, 208. Cf. on the evils of Wilsonian idealism, Churchill's friend, the Earl of Birkenhead, *America Revisited* (Boston: Little, Brown, 1924), pp. viii–ix, 108–10; A. S. Link, *President Wilson and His English Critics* (Oxford: Clarendon, 1959), pp. 6–12, 16, 19–20; Cushing Strout, *The American Image of the Old World* (New York: Harper, 1963), pp. 162–63, 170–71.

13. *Second World War*, IV, 219; V, 347. Cf. Strout, p. 226.

14. *Strand* (August 1931): 141–50. Cf. T. W. Stead, *The Americanization of the World* (New York: Markley, 1901), pp. 382–83. In a fragment of a short story Churchill wrote at the turn of the century, we meet a type dear to the imagination of that period, that is, a senator who is the richest man in the world. Churchill depicts him as having gone into business because he found no other outlet for his energies in America. See *Companion Volume I*, 2, 916–21.

15. *Collier's* (11 July 1936): 21ff. Cf. Winston Churchill, *The River War*, 2 vols. (London: Longmans, 1899), I, 298–99; Birkenhead, p. 1.

16. Americans are, he found, so wedded to the status quo as to regard "socialism" as a dirty word, as to be shocked by the spectacle of the British king negotiating with the Socialists, and as to be commendably quick (after World War I) to expel foreign bolsheviks. See Winston Churchill, *Great Contemporaries* (New York: Putnam's, 1937), p. 279; *Daily Telegraph* (3 February 1930); *Illustrated Sunday Herald* (25 January 1920): 5. Churchill did not see what W. T. Stead (pp. 368, 389) saw in 1901: that American prosperity and progress were the results of planned obsolescence in her manufactured products.

17. *Collier's* (17 August 1932): 10ff.; *Daily Telegraph* (3 February 1930); (9 December 1929); H. G. Wells, *The Future of America* (New York: Harper, 1906), pp. 111–15, 169–202, 206, 244. Cf. Birkenhead, pp. xvii, 13, 31, 138; G. K.

Chesterton, *What I Saw in America* (London, 1922; reprint, New York: DaCapo, 1968), pp. 173–80; *American Social History as Recorded by British Travellers*, ed. Allan Nevins (New York: Holt, 1931), pp. 289, 513–17; George Harmon Knoles, *The Jazz Age Revisitd* (Stanford, 1955; reprint, AMS, 1968), pp. 73, 92.

18. *Companion Volume I*, 2, 1082–83; *PTO*, 1 (16 and 23 June 1906): 25–27, 65–66; *Collier's* (13 August 1932): 20ff. Britain, he would declare in after years, has no antitrust legislation of the American kind because "the same issues have not arisen in a sharp form. Many things in this island are not pushed to extremes" (*Europe Unite* [Boston: Houghton Mifflin, 1950], p. 453). Others remarked in like fashion on America as a daring social and economic experiment, and Churchill was not alone in being more interested in economic than in political matters. In the 1920s, observes Knoles (pp. 38, 57, 81–83, 87, 134) American prosperity and European depression made all visiting Britons curious as never before as to the secret of American success. Cf. Nevins, pp. 453, 502, 513.

19. "British Cavalry," *Anglo-Saxon Review* (March 1901): 243, *Step by Step* (New York: Putnam, 1939), p. 122; *A History of the English-Speaking Peoples*, 4 vols. (1956–57; reprint, New York: Bantam, 1963), II, 138; III, 210; IV, 251.

20. Winston Churchill, *The Dawn of Liberation* (London: Cassell, 1945), pp. 20, 172; *Companion Volume I*, 2, 678, 699–700; *Illustrated Sunday Herald* (30 November 1919); *Sunday Pictorial* (26 July 1930). Churchill's observation accords with Wells's (pp. 72–74) that, America lacking upper and lower classes, Tory and Labor parties, its two political parties are basically middle class and liberal; or J. A. Spender's that American parties are not wedded to any principles and that most American politicians (unlike Woodrow Wilson) are cautious souls who follow rather than lead public opinion. See Nevins, pp. 559–61; Knoles, pp. 91, 137.

21. See *PTO*, 1 (16 and 23 June 1906): 25–27, 65–66; *For Free Trade* (London: Humphreys, 1906), p. 52; *Weekly Dispatch*, (5 October 1924): 8; Introduction to *Dictatorships on Trial*, ed. O. F. deBattaglia (New York: Harcourt, 1931), pp. 7–10; *Collier's* (13 August 1932): 20ff. The fatalism and pessimism in the face of universal commercial and, especially, political corruption was noted by many, who attributed it to the American's concerning himself exclusively with making money. See, e.g., Wells, pp. 129–32; Bertrand Russell, *Autobiography*, 3 vols. (New York: Bantam, 1967) I, 182; Nevins, pp. 452, 491–93, 521–22, 565–67; Knoles, pp. 91–92. But contrast Lord Bryce, quoted in Nevins, p. 435.

22. Moran, p. 698; *Unwritten Alliance*, p. 245; *PTO*, 1 (16 June 1906): 25–27; *Illustrated Sunday Herald*, (30 November 1919); *Collier's* (29 December 1934): 24ff. *The World Crisis*, III, 232. Bryce and Wells (p. 206) also worried over possible "Caesarism"; cf. Nevins, p. 576.

23. The material in these two paragraphs is based on *Daily Telegraph* (27 January 1930); *Daily Mail* (11 November 1932); *Collier's* (4 November 1933): 12ff.; (29 December 1934): 24ff; *News of the World* (20 June 1937); *Step by Step*, p. 235.

24. *Collier's* (16 February 1935): 14; (22 August 1936): 22ff. Cf. on the Constitution, Stead, p. 25, 408, and Birkenhead, pp. 139–41, 156.

25. *Saturday Evening Post* (15 February 1930): 25ff.; Winston Churchill, *Blood, Sweat, and Tears* (New York: Putnam's, 1941), p. 89. The phrase, "United States of Europe," like the idea of the United States as a model for the concept, goes back at least as far as William Archer in 1899. See Nevins, p. 445.

26. Randolph Churchill, II, 57, 73, 96; *Companion Volume II*, 1, 183–84, 210; *Free Trade*, pp. 57, 94, 96. Cf. Wells, pp. 84, 244; Birkenhead, p. 7.

27. *Companion Volume II*, 2, 834, 903, 922; *Collier's* (27 August 1932): 10ff. (4 November 1932):12ff.; *Weekly Dispatch* (29 January 1919): 6.
28. *Collier's* (12 August 1932): 20ff.; (25 February 1933):10ff.; (29 December 1934): 24ff.; (16 October 1937): 18ff.; (24 September 1938): 13ff.
29. *Companion Volume I*, 2, 937–38, 947, 1012.
30. *North American Review* (December 1898): 736, 743; *The Inlander* (5 February 1901): 169.
31. Winston Churchill, *Liberalism and the Social Problem* 2d ed. (London: Hodder and Stoughton, 1909), p. 37; *Companion Volume I*, 2, 858; *Onwards to Victory* (Boston, Mass.: Little, Brown 1944), pp. 237, 342; *Second World War*, V, 651.
32. Ronald Hyam, *Elgin and Churchill at the Colonial Office 1905–1908* (London: Macmillan, 1968), pp. 289, 295, 303, 479–80; Randolph Churchill, II, 56, 160, 439; *Free Trade*, p. 10; Martin Gilbert, *Winston S. Churchill*, Vol. III (Boston, Mass.: Houghton Mifflin, 1972), pp. 77, 79.
33. Gilbert, p. 688; *World Crisis*, II, 306; *News of the World* (6 June 1937).
34. *Sunday Pictorial*, 20 May 1917; *Illustrated Sunday Herald*, 30 November 1919; *World Crisis*, V, 2; IV, 195, 266; *Strand* (August 1931): 141–50; *Collier's* (27 August 1932): 10ff.; *Step by Step*, p. 113.
35. *English Life* (January 1924): 74–75; *Weekly Dispatch* (22 June 1919): 6; *Daily Telegraph* (18 November 1929); *Collier's* (4 November 1933):12ff.; (29 January 1935):12ff.; (15 February 1935):14ff.; *Scribner's Magazine* (December 1930): 587–97.
36. *Daily Graphic*, 13 December 1895; *Saturday Review* (London, 29 August 1896): 214; (7 March 1896): 244; Randolph Churchill, I, 268–70; *Companion Volume I*, 1, 665; 2, 937–38.
37. *Collier's* (17 December 1932): 12ff. In a private letter, young Churchill noted that since Britain had given America moral support against Spain, the United States should return the favor over the issue of South Africa (*Companion Volume I*, 2, 1082–83). See also his strictures on the attempt to graft "white democratic institutions" on the "simple, docile, gifted" but undeveloped blacks in the wake of the Civil War, on the "idiotic assertion of racial equality" (*Scribner's* [December 1930]: 587–97).
38. At the time of composition, the *History* antedates the publication of the *History of the English-Speaking Peoples* by R. B. Mowat and Preston Slosson (1943), which one of its authors calls "an experiment and an adventure," and *The English-Speaking Peoples* by E. McInnis and J. H. S. Reid (1949).
39. *History*, III, 210, 297; *World Crisis*, IV, 184.
40. *Step by Step*, p. 233; *The Unrelenting Struggle* (London: Cassell, 1942), p. 221; *The Sinews of peace* (Boston: Houghton Mifflin, 1949), p. 42; *Onwards to Victory*, pp. 149, 237; *The Dawn of Liberation*, pp. 11, 20; *The End of the Beginning* (Boston, Mass.: Little, Brown, 1943), p. 66. Many have indeed called it a unique alliance. See, e.g., H. C. Allen, *Great Britain and the United States* (New York: St. Martin's, 1955), pp. 201–2, 781, 880–81. But for a demurrer, see Bruce Russett, *Community and Contention* (Cambridge: MIT, 1963), p. 185.
41. Winston Churchill, *Victory* (Boston, Mass.: Little, Brown, 1946), p. 295; *Sinews of Peace*, pp. 29, 42, 82, 94, 120; *Stemming the Tide* (Boston, Mass.: Houghton Mifflin, 1954), pp. 22, 314; *Life* (14 April 1947): 106ff.; *European Unite*, p. 355.
42. The material in these two paragraphs is based on *The Unrelenting Struggle*, pp. 230, 340; *In the Balance* (Boston, Mass.: Houghton Mifflin, 1952), p. 442; *Europe Unite*, p. 174.

43. *The Sinews of Peace*, pp. 98, 115–16, 119; *History*, IV, 299; *The Unwritten Alliance*, p. 317. Few had made such pilgrimages before him. See Max Beloff, "The Special Relationship: An Anglo-American Myth" in *The Intellectual in Politics* (New York: Library, 1971), p. 221.

44. Moran, pp. 436, 440, 459, 536, 540, 575, 580, 608, 611; Harold Macmillan, *The Tides of Fortune* (New York: Harper and Row, 1969), pp. 511, 523–35; A. J. P. Taylor, "The Statesman" in *Churchill Revised*, ed. anon. (New York: Dial, 1969), p. 58.

45. Andrew Carnegie, "A Look Ahead," *North American Review* (June 1983): 685–710; Capt. A. T. Mahan, "The U.S. Looking Outward," *Atlantic Monthly* (August 1890): 27; "The Possibilities of an Anglo-American Reunion," *North American Review* (July 1894): 107–34; Strout, pp. 140, 146; Allen, pp. 518, 549, 563; Coral Bell, *The Debatable Alliance* (London: Oxford University Press, 1964), p. 11.

46. Allen, pp. 20, 126, 176, 199–202, 518–609; Strout, pp. 134–38, 145–46; Bell, pp. 10–14; Beloff, pp. 211n. 213, 221; *Imperial Sunset* (New York: Knopf, 1970), p. 44; Knoles, pp. 7–10; John R. Dos Passos, *The Anglo-Saxon Century*, 2d ed. (New York: Putnam's 1903), pp. 61, 157, 188, 213–26, 233; W. T. Stead, pp. 1–3, 5–6, 9, 12, 15, 396, 406–7, 421–36.

47. Dos Passos, pp. vii, 2–3, 33–35, 49–52, 151, 210–11, 234; Allen, pp. 127, 590–92. German writers, extending Bismark's obiter dictum, had also become obsessed with the idea of the growth in power and influence of the English-speaking peoples.

48. On Henry Adams, see R. P. Blackmur, "The Atlantic Unites," *Hudson Review* (Summer 1952): 212–32; Strout, p. 160; Grace Cockroft, "George Louis Beer" in *Some Modern Historians of Britain*, ed. Herman Ausubel (New York: Dryden, 1951), pp. 270–79, 285; G. L. Beer, *The English-Speaking Peoples* (New York: Macmillan, 1917), pp. vii–ix, xi, 45, 69–70, 87, 98, 105, 134, 154, 162–69, 187, 193, 246–47, 253–57, 270–71. Link (pp. 3, 18, 21) insists that Wilson was the first great American champion of an English-speaking alliance.

49. Randolph Churchill, quoted in Peter de Mendelssohn, *The Age of Churchill* (New York: Knopf, 1961), p. 75; *Companion Volume I*, 2, 947, 1012–13; Cockroft, p. 285; Beloff, *Sunset*, p. 46.

50. Gordon K. Lewis, "Mr. Churchill as Historian," *The Historian* 20 (August 1958): 402–5; de Mendelssohn, p. 256; A. J. P. Taylor, *English History 1914–45* (New York: Oxford, 1965), p. 315; Beloff, *Sunset*, p. 44; "Anglo-American," pp. 209–10, 219, 221; Russett, p. 24.

51. Knoles, pp. 3–7, 13, 21, 87; Taylor, *History*, pp. 422, 495, 537–39, 557–66, 574, 585–90; in *Churchill Revised*, pp. 46, 52, 55–56; Harold Nicolson, *Diaries and Letters*, ed. Nigel Nicolson, 3 vols. (New York: Atheneum, 1966–68), II, 385. On Churchill's unique and illusory sense of an Anglo-American destiny—not shared by Americans—see Lewis, p. 402; Taylor, in *Churchill Revised*, pp. 34, 46, 52, 55; *History*, pp. 495, 586–90; Moran, pp. 33, 322, 350, 834, 837; Strout, pp. 276–77; Beloff, "Anglo-American," pp. 202, 205, 216–17, 222–23; Allen, pp. 670, 690–91, 705, 723–28, 742–43, 826, 889–91.

52. Bell, p. 5. Cf. Birkenhead, pp. xvii, 27.

Chapter 6. The "Great Man"?

1. See, e.g., Bruce Mazlish, *The Riddle of History* (New York: Minerva, 1966), pp. 152, 157. Seeds of the new outlook can actually be found in Gibbon

and Hume; see Leo Braudy, *Narrative form in History and Fiction* (Princeton: Princeton University Press, 1970), pp. 76, 230, 251–52).

2. Hence Stalin, himself an important participant in history, said that he could not think of another juncture in which the future of the world depended on one man's—Churchill's—courage (quoted in Lord Moran, *Churchill* [Boston: Houghton Mifflin, 1966], p. 244).

3. Trevor Roper quoted in Braudy, p. 42n. To be sure, reputable academic historians, without Churchill's excuse of a dual career, have also been inconsistent on this question. See, e.g., Otis Pease, *Parkman's History* (New Haven, Conn.: Archon, 1968), p. 43; Ronald Steel, in *New York Review of Books* (31 May 1973): 31, on Gabriel Kolko.

4. *Savrola* (1900; reprint, New York: Random House, 1956), pp. 54, 62, 109–10, 117, 227. Yet Byran Magee ("Churchill's Novel," *Encounter* [25 October 1965]: 49–50) finds the tale to have exactly the opposite import: Its theme is the precariousness of authority, which ceases to exist as soon as it is no longer acknowledged by the subjects. All leadership turns out to rest on strength of character, on the force of personality; and the natural leader is shown to be morally different from the people he leads. One might add that, almost inevitably, a novel focusing on one man's adventures leaves one with the impression that that man does matter. Cf. also the young Churchill's remark that the orator is an "independent forum in the world" (Randolph Churchill, *Winston S. Churchill: Companion Volume I*, 2 vols. [Boston: Houghton Mifflin, 1967], part 2, 816).

5. *The Malakand Field Force* (London: Longmans, Green, 1898), pp. 76, 310. Yet he cites India as an example of how, with only a few men, civilization can bring order to the human species. See his letter to the London *Times* (3 May 1898): 15.

6. *The River War*, 2 vols. (London: Longmans, Green, 1899), I, 65; II, 301.

7. The material in these three paragraphs is based on *Lord Randolph Churchill*, 2 vols. (New York: Macmillan, 1906), II, 217, 296; I, 187, 200, 419, 456, 473.

8. *Randolph Churchill*, II, 264; I, 74; J. H. Plumb, "The Historian" in *Churchill Revised*, ed. anon. (New York: Dial, 1969), pp. 145–47. One perceptive remark about leadership seems to commit Churchill to the "Great Man" theory: "Real leaders of men do not come forward offering to lead. They show the way, and when it has been found to lead to victory they accept as a matter of course the allegiance of those who have followed" (II, 128). Cf. A. J. P. Taylor (*The Origins of the Second World War*, 2d ed. [Greenwich, Conn.: Fawcett, 1961], p. 73) on Hitler: "He did not 'seize' power. He waited for it to be thrust upon him by the men who had previously tried to keep him out."

9. *The World Crisis*, 6 vols. (New York: Scribner's, 1923–31), I, 6; II, 213; VI, 102, 109.

10. Martin Gilbert, *Winston S. Churchill*, Vol. III (Boston, Mass.: Houghton Mifflin, 1971), 10; *Weekly Dispatch* (21 September 1924): 8; *Daily Mail*, 7 September 1933. The Kaiser, Churchill said bluntly at another time, had not the brains to plunge the world into World War I (*Illustrated Sunday Herald* [1 February 1920]: 5).

11. David H. Fischer (in *Historians' Fallacies* [New York: Harper and Row, 1970], p. 172–74) uses Churchill's remarks on Alexander and the monkey as a "famous example" of the reductive fallacy.

12. The material in these three paragraphs is based on *World Crisis*, III, 194–96, 285; VI, 75; II, 2; III, 149; V, 409; III, 234; VI, 41–42.

13. *London Magazine* (November 1916): 235; (February 1917): 653–60; *Collier's* (24 March 1917): 7ff.; *TLS* (7 March 1929): 171; *World Crisis*, II, 88, 368; Samuel J. Hurwitz, "Winston S. Churchill," *Some Modern Historians of Britain*, ed. Herman Ausubel (New York: Dryden, 1951), p. 314.

14. *Amid These Storms* (New York: Scribner's, 1932), pp. 222, 225, 255; *Great Contemporaries* (New York: Putnam's, 1937), pp. 279–80; *Strand* (October 1936): 600–10.

15. *Amid These Storms*, pp. 259, 261, 264–66, 230; *Great Contemporaries*, p. 82.

16. *Marlborough* (4 vols., 1933–38; reprint, 2 vols., London: George Harrap, 1947), I, 569; *Amid These Storms*, pp. 155, 262–64. Cf. the German General Schlieffen's remark at the turn of the century that modern generals are no Napoleons on the scene but instead are men sitting in comfortable offices far from the front, reading telegrams (quoted in E. M. Earle, ed., *Makers of Modern Strategy* [Princeton: Princeton University Press, 1943], p. 194).

17. *Marlborough*, I, 483, 741; II, 286, 764, 962. The reference to God in the last quotation—perhaps the only one in the book—is merely figurative and devoid of philosophical import. For criticism of the simple-minded Great Man approach in the *Marlborough*, see Maurice Ashley, *Marlborough* (New York: Macmillan, 1939), pp. 88, 156; Violet Barbour in *AHR*, 44 (1939), 887.

18. *Marlborough*, I, 919; II, 154.

19. *A History of the English-Speaking Peoples*, 4 vols. (1956–57; reprint, New York: Bantam, 1963), I, 76, 202, 266; II, 190: IV, 176, 203, 207, 289. Cf. in his very first book: "Fortune, especially in war, uses tiny fulcrums for her powerful lever" (*Malakand*, p. 203). Cf. also G. M. Trevelyan's (in *England under Queen Anne*, 3 vols. [London: Longmans, Green, 1931–34] II, 317, 395) remark that the history of religion, war, and politics often turns on "straws."

20. *History*, IV, 132; III, 125. In his treatment of these cruxes, Churchill often perpetrates, according to Fischer (pp. 172–4), the reductive fallacy, while the *TLS* complained that in the first volume Churchill presents the various medieval kings of England as seeing, foreseeing, and designing with great craft. The *TLS* nevertheless detected a compromise in the *History*: If the individual influences history, history is also shown to go its own way (see 27 April 1956, pp. 245–46, and 30 November 1956, pp. 705–6). For some of the widespread criticism of the *History*, as marred by Churchill's focusing on prominent and dashing individuals at the expense of ideas, classes, subject peoples, ideological factions, and social forces, see Gordon K. Lewis, "Mr. Churchill as Historian," *The Historian* 20 (August 1958): 392–93, 395–99, 410–11; Plumb, pp. 154–55.

21. Cf. his remarks that, if leaders flourish only in proportion "as they express and meet the public need, bold captains are required for perilous seas," whereas MacDonald and Baldwin were men who specialized in inactivity and seem fitted for a time of necessary "somnolence and tranquility" after the great effort and exhaustion of the war (*Step by Step* [New York: Putnam's, 1939], p. 33).

22. *History*, I, 178, 231.

23. *Daily Mail*, 12 August 1931; 2 October 1931; *Great Contemporaries*, p. 117.

24. *Step by Step*, pp. 185, 215, 284, 287, 295, 321; *Blood, Sweat, and Tears* (New York: Putnam's 1941), pp. 440, 443.

25. *Blood, Sweat, and Tears*, pp. 50, 146, 149, 165, 176; *Step by Step*, pp. 144, 224, 252.

26. *Collier's* (3 September 1938): 16ff.
27. *Europe Unite* (Boston, Mass.: Houghton Mifflin, 1950), p. 290; *Sinews of Peace* (Boston, Mass.: Houghton Mifflin, 1949), p. 217; *Blood, Sweat, and Tears,* p. 447.
28. The material in these three paragraphs is based on *A Roving Commission* (New York: Scribner's, 1930), p. 232; *The Second World War,* 6 vols. (Boston, Mass.: Houghton Mifflin, 1948–53), II, 100, 165, 549; III, 863–64; VI, 267; *Europe Unite,* p. 239; *The Unwritten Alliance* (London: Cassell, 1961), p. 202. For Churchill overruled by the military and diplomatic bureaucracy and by social forces, see Vladimir Dedijer, "Participants as Historians," *TLS* (30 May 1968): 556.
29. The material in these two paragraphs is based on *Marlborough,* I, 75; *Second World War,* I, 667; II, 15; III, 361; VI, 280; IV, 489, 502, 666, 703; VI, 65, 323, 479, 579. Cf. The seventeen-year-old Churchill to his mother: "I hope that you will come down tomorrow as it is so much easier to explain things [in person]" (Randolph Churchill, *Winston S. Churchill,* Vol. I (Boston, Mass.: Houghton Mifflin, 1966), p. 154.
30. *Second World War,* VI, 654, 674; I, 12; *Great Contemporaries,* p. 273. Cf. on Marlborough: "Happy the State or sovereign who finds such a servant in years of danger!" (*Marlborough,* II, 492).
31. *Marlborough,* II, 19, 21, 1040; *Second World War,* VI, 603; Reed Whittemore, "Churchill as a Mythmaker" in *Language and Politics,* ed. T. P. Brockway (Boston, Mass.: Heath, 1965), p. 57; *Great Contemporaries,* p. 183. That such obsession with the self is not necessarily peculiar to Churchill among statesmen-memoirists is Dedijer's (p. 556) point.
32. Whittemore, pp. 63–67; Plumb, p. 166.
33. *Unwritten Alliance,* p. 93; Harold Macmillan, *The Tides of Fortune* (New York: Harper and Row, 1969), pp. 523, 525, 530–35. For remarks by Churchill on how only people at the top can carve out spheres of influence in a few minutes and how only he could tame the Russians, and on the tendency of his optimism and delusions to keep out the facts, see Moran, pp. 436, 440, 481, 529, 623, 742. He was also sure that the death of Dr. Chaim Weizmann and the assassination of the King Abdullah prevented the reconciliation of Arabs and Jews.
34. Moran, p. 673; *Sinews of Peace,* p. 77; *Unwritten Alliance,* p. 245. On the other hand, Churchill could acknowledge that the "increasing association of Britain and America will come" not through the speeches of individuals but through the tides in human affairs and the destiny of the world (*Sinews,* pp. 115–16). A. J. P. Taylor ("The Statesman" in *Churchill Revised,* pp. 34, 58), who also credits him with being the "savior of this country," suggests that Churchill was indeed the one man to achieve a reconciliation with Soviet Russia in what would have been the last touch of his grandiose approach.
35. Lewis, pp. 395, 409; Barbour, p. 887; Plumb, pp. 132–35, 152–57; Isaiah Berlin, *Mr. Churchill in 1940* (London: John Murray, 1949), p. 21; Angus Calder, *The People's War* (London: Cape, 1969), p. 90; H. S. Commager, ed., *Marlborough* (New York: Scribner's, 1968), p. xxvi.

Bibliography

Allen, H. C. *Great Britain and the United States.* New York: St. Martin's, 1955.
Amery, L. S. *My Political Life.* 3 vols. London: Hutchinson, 1953–55.
Ashley, Maurice. *Marlborough.* New York: Macmillan, 1939.
Asquith, H. H. *Memories and Reflections 1857–1927.* 2 vols. Boston: Little Brown, 1928.
Barbour, V. Review of *Marlborough.* In *American Historical Review,* 41 (1936):332; 43 (1938):376; 44 (1939):886.
Barker, Dudley. *Writer by Trade.* New York: Atheneum, 1966.
Barnett, Correlli. *The Desert Generals.* New York: Viking, 1961.
Beer, G. L. *The English-Speaking Peoples.* New York: Macmillan, 1917.
Bell, Coral. *The Debatable Alliance.* New York: Oxford, 1964.
Beloff, Max. *Imperial Sunset.* New York: Knopf, 1970.
———. *The Intellectual in Politics.* New York: Philosophical Library, 1971.
Bennett, Arnold. *Journals.* New York: Literary Guild, 1933.
———. *Lord Raingo.* London: Cassell, 1926.
Berlin, Isaiah. *Mr Churchill in 1940.* London: John Murray, 1949.
Birkenhead, Earl of. *America Revisited.* Boston, Mass.: Little Brown, 1924.
Blackmur, R. P. "The Atlantic Unites." *Hudson Review* 5 (1952): 212–32.
Blunt, W. S. *My Diaries 1888–1914.* 2 vols. New York: Knopf, 1921.
Braudy, Leo. *Narrative Form in History and Fiction.* Princeton, N.J.: Princeton University Press, 1970.
Brogan, Dennis. "Great House." *Spectator* 201 (4 July 1958): 26–7.
Bryant, Arthur. *The Turn of the Tide.* Garden City, N.Y.: Doubleday, 1957.
———. *Triumph in the West.* Garden City, N.Y.: Doubleday, 1959.
Calder, Angus. *The People's War.* London: Cape, 1969.
Carnegie, Andrew. "A Look Ahead." *North American Review* 156 (1893): 685–710.
Chesterton, G. K. *What I Saw in America.* 1922. Reprint. New York: Da Capo, 1968.
Churchill, Randolph. *Winston S. Churchill.* Volume I. Boston, Mass.: Houghton Mifflin, 1966.
———. *Winston S. Churchill.* Companion Volume I, Parts 1, and 2. Boston, Mass.: Houghton Mifflin, 1967.
———. *Winston S. Churchill.* Volume II. Boston, Mass.: Houghton Mifflin, 1967.
———. *Winston S. Churchill.* Companion Volume II, Parts 1, 2, 3. Boston, Mass.: Houghton Mifflin, 1969.

Churchill, Winston S. *Amid These Storms (Thoughts and Adventures)*. New York: Scribner's 1932.
———. *Blood, Sweat, and Tears (Into Battle)*. New York: Putnam's, 1941.
———. *Complete Speeches*. Edited by R. R. James. 8 vols. New York: Bowker, 1974.
———. *The Dawn of Liberation*. London: Cassell, 1945.
———. *The End of the Beginning*. Boston, Mass: Little Brown, 1943.
———. *Europe Unite*. Boston, Mass.: Houghton Mifflin, 1950.
———. *For Free Trade*. London: Humphreys, 1906.
———. *Great Contempories*. 1937–38. Reprint. Chicago: University of Chicago Press, 1973.
———. *A History of the English-Speaking Peoples*. 4 vols. 1956–58. Reprint. New York: Bantam, 1963.
———. *In the Balance*. Boston, Mass.: Houghton Mifflin, 1952.
———. *Liberalism and the Social Problem*. London: Hodder & Stoughton, 1909.
———. *London to Ladysmith Via Pretoria*. London: Longmans, 1900.
———. *Lord Randolph Churchill*. 2 vols. New York: Macmillan, 1906.
———. *Marlborough*. 4 vols. 1933–38. Reprint. 2 vols. London: George Harrap, 1947.
———. *Onwards to Victory*. Boston, Mass.: Little Brown, 1944.
———. *The River War*. 2 vols. London: Longmans, 1899.
———. *A Roving Commission (My Early Life)*. New York: Scribner's, 1930.
———. *Savrola*. 1900. Reprint. New York: Random House, 1956.
———. *The Sinews of Peace*. Boston, Mass.: Houghton Mifflin, 1949.
———. *Step by Step*. New York: Putnam's, 1939.
———. *Stemming the Tide*. Boston, Mass.: Houghton Mifflin, 1954.
———. *The Second World War*. 6 vols. Boston, Mass.: Houghton Mifflin, 1948–53.
———. "New Epilogue." In *The Second World War*. Abridged edition. Edited by Denis Kelly. Boston, Mass.: Houghton Mifflin, 1959. Pp. 995–1016.
———. *The Unrelenting Struggle*. London: Cassell, 1942.
———. *The Unwritten Alliance*. London: Cassell, 1961.
———. *Victory*. Boston, Mass.: Little Brown, 1946.
———. *While England Slept (Arms and the Covenant)*. New York: Putnam's, 1938.
———. *The World Crisis*. 6 vols. New York: Scribner's, 1923–31.
Churchill Revised, ed. anon. New York: Dial, 1969.
Cockcroft, Grace. "George Louis Beer." In *Some Modern Historians of Britain*. Edited by Herman Ausubel. New York: Dryden, 1951. Pp. 270–285.
Collis, Maurice. *Nancy Astor*. London: Faber, 1960.
Commager, H. S. Preface to *Marlborough*. New York: Scribner's, 1968.
Coote, C. R. *A Churchill Reader*. Boston, Mass.: Houghton Mifflin, 1954.
Cowles, Virginia. *Churchill*. New York: Harper, 1953.
Daniell, D. S. *Fourth Hussar*. Aldershot: Gale and Polder, 1959.

deBattaglia, O. F., ed. *Dictatorships on Trial.* New York: Harcourt, 1931.
Dedijer, Vladimir. "Participants As Historians." *TLS* (30 May 1968): 555–56.
Dickson, Lovat. *H. G. Wells.* New York: Atheneum, 1969.
Dos Passos, John R. *The Anglo-Saxon Century.* 2d ed. New York: Putnam's, 1903.
Eade, Charles, ed. *Churchill by His Contemporaries.* London: Hutchinson, 1953.
Earle, E. M. *Makers of Modern Strategy.* Princeton, N.J.: Princeton University Press, 1943.
Edel, Leon. *Henry James.* Volume V. Philadelphia, Pa.: Lippincott, 1972.
Ellmann, Richard. *James Joyce.* New York: Oxford, 1959.
Fischer, David H. *Historians' Fallacies.* New York: Harper & Row, 1970.
Gardner, Brian. *Churchill in His Time.* London: Methuen, 1968.
Gilbert, Martin, ed. *Churchill.* Great Lives Observed Series. Englewood Cliffs, N.J.: Prentice Hall, 1967.
———. *Winston S. Churchill.* Volume III. Boston, Mass.: Houghton Mifflin, 1971.
———. *Winston S. Churchill.* Companion Volume III, Parts 1 and 2. Boston, Mass.: Houghton Mifflin, 1973.
———. *Winston S. Churchill.* Volume IV. Boston, Mass.: Houghton Mifflin, 1975.
———. *Winston S. Churchill.* Volume V. Boston, Mass.: Houghton Mifflin, 1977.
———. *Winston S. Churchill.* Volume VI. Boston, Mass.: Houghton Mifflin, 1983.
———. *Winston S. Churchill.* Volume VII. Boston, Mass.: Houghton Mifflin, 1987.
———. *Winston S. Churchill.* Volume VIII. Boston, Mass.: Houghton Mifflin, 1989.
Graubard, S. R. *Burke, Disraeli, and Churchill.* Cambridge: Harvard University Press, 1961.
Gretton, Peter. *Winston Churchill and the Royal Navy.* New York: Coward McCann, 1968.
Guedella, Phillip. *Mr. Churchill.* New York: Reynal and Hitchcock, 1942.
Halle, Kay. *Winston Churchill: An English-Speaking Union (Churchill on America).* New York: Walker, 1970.
Henderson, Archibald. *Bernard Shaw.* New York: Appleton, 1932.
Higgins, Trumbull. *Winston Churchill and the Second Front.* New York: Oxford, 1957.
Hillegas, Mark. *The Future as Nightmare.* New York: Oxford, 1967.
Howarth, Herbert. "Behind Churchill's Grand Style." *Commentary* 11 (1951): 549–57.
Hubenka, Lloyd J. *Bernard Shaw: Practical Politics.* Lincoln: University of Nebraska Press, 1976.
Hurwitz, Samuel J. "Winston S. Churchill." In *Some Modern Historians of Britain.* Edited by Herman Ausubel. New York: Dryden 1951. Pp. 306–324.

Hyam, Ronald. *Elgin and Churchill at the Colonial Office 1905–1908*. London: Macmillan, 1968.

Ingram, Bruce, ed. *Illustrated London News Eightieth Year Tribute to Winston Churchill*. London, 1954.

Irvine, William. *The Universe of George Bernard Shaw*. New York: McGraw, 1949.

James, R. R. *Churchill: A Study in Failure, 1900–1939*. London: Weidenfeld and Nicolson, 1970.

Jones, D.A.N. In *New York Review of Books* (23 May 1968): 33–37.

Kaye, Julian. *Bernard Shaw and the Nineteenth Century Tradition*. Norman: Oklahoma University Press, 1958.

Knoles, George Harmon. *The Jazz Age Revisited*. 1955. Reprint. New York: AMS, 1968.

Leslie, Shane. "Winston: A Sketch." *Review of Reviews* 67 (May 1923): 470–77.

Lewis, Gordon K. "Mr. Churchill as Historian." *The Historian* 20, (August 1958): 387–414.

Link, A. S. *President Wilson and His English Critics*. Oxford: Clarendon, 1959.

Macmillan, Harold. *The Tides of Fortune*. New York: Harper & Row, 1969.

Magee, Bryan. "Churchill's Novel." *Encounter* 25 (October 1965): 45–51.

Mahan, Captain A. T. "The U.S. Looking Outward." *Atlantic Monthly* 65 (August 1890): 1–27.

———. "The Possibilities of an Anglo-American Reunion." *North American Review* 159 (July 1894): 107–134.

Marrot, H. V. *The Life and Letters of John Galsworthy*. New York: Scribner's, 1936.

Masterman, Lucy. *C.G.F. Masterman*. London: Frank Cass, 1968.

Mazlish, Bruce. *The Riddle of History*. New York: Minerva, 1966.

de Mendelssohn, Peter. *The Age of Churchill*. New York: Knopf, 1961.

Minney, R. J. *Recollections of G. B. Shaw*. Englewood Cliffs, N.J.: Prentice Hall, 1969.

Moran, Lord. *Churchill*. Boston, Mass.: Houghton Mifflin, 1966.

Nevins, Allan, ed. *American Social History as Recorded by British Travelers*. New York: Holt, 1931.

Nicolson, Harold. "A Portrait of Winston Churchill." *Life* 24 (15 March 1948): 94–98.

———. *Diaries and Letters*. Edited by Nigel Nicolson. 3 vols. New York: Atheneum, 1966–68.

Nordon, Pierre. *Conan Doyle*. New York: Holt, Rinehart & Winston, 1967.

Orwell, George. *Dickens, Dali and Others*. New York: Harcourt Brace, 1946.

Ohlinger, Gustav. "A Midnight Interview with Churchill." *Michigan Quarterly Review* 5 (1966): 75–79.

Ohmann, Richard. "George Bernard Shaw." In *Rhetorical Analyses of Literary Works*. Edited by Edward Corbett. New York: Oxford, 1969. Pp. 204–213.

Patch, Blanche. *Thirty Years with George Bernard Shaw*. New York: Dodd, Mead, 1951.

Pearson, Hesketh. *Bernard Shaw*. London: The Reprint Society, 1942.

Pease, Otis. *Parkman's History.* New Haven, Conn.: Archon, 1968.
Pilpel, Robert. *Churchill in America.* New York: Harcourt Brace, 1976.
Pound, Reginald. *Arnold Bennett.* New York: Harcourt Brace, 1953.
Rees, Goronwy. "After the Ball." *Encounter* 16 (1956): 7–9.
Riddell, Lord. *More Pages from My Diary.* London: Country Life, 1934.
———. *War Diary 1914–1918.* London: Nicholson and Watson, 1933.
Rowse, A. L. *The Churchills.* New York: Harper, 1958.
Russell, Bertrand. *Autobiography.* 3 vols. New York: Bantam, 1967.
Russett, Bruce. *Community and Contention.* Cambridge: MIT Press, 1963.
Scott, A. MacCallum. *Winston Spencer Churchill.* London: Methuen, 1905.
Shaw, George Bernard. *Sixteen Self Sketches.* New York: Dodd Mead, 1949.
Sitwell, Osbert. *The Winstonburg Line.* London: Henderson, 1919.
Snow, C. P. *Variety of Men.* New York: Scribner's, 1966.
Somervell, D. C. "Sir Winston Churchill." In *Nobel Prize Winners.* Edited by E. J. Ludovici. London: Arco, 1956. Pp. 1–20.
Stansky, Peter, ed. *Churchill.* New York: Hill and Wang, 1973.
Stead, T. W. *The Americanization of the World.* New York: Markley, 1901.
Steel, Ronald. In *New York Review of Books* (31 May 1973): 31–3.
Strout, Cushing. *The American Image of the Old World.* New York: Harper, 1963.
Taylor, A.J.P. *English History 1914–1945.* New York: Oxford, 1965.
———. *The Origins of the Second World War.* 2d ed. New York: Fawcett, 1961.
Thomson, George Malcolm. *Vote of Censure.* New York: Stein & Day, 1968.
TLS, 27 April 1956: 245–46; and 30 November 1956: 705–06.
Trevelyan, G. M. *England under Queen Anne.* 3 vols. London: Longmans, Green, 1931–34.
Vallentin, Antonina. *H. G. Wells.* Translated by D. Woodward. New York: John Day, 1950.
Ward, Maisie, *G. K. Chesterton.* New York: Sheed and Ward, 1943.
Weidhorn, Manfred. *Sword and Pen: A Survey of the Writings of Sir Winston Churchill.* Albuquerque, N.M.: University of New Mexico Press, 1974.
Wells, H. G. *Experiment in Autobiography.* New York: Macmillan, 1934.
———. *The Future of America.* New York: Harper, 1906.
———. *Meanwhile.* New York: Doran, 1927.
———. *Men Like Gods.* New York: Macmillan, 1923.
———. *Mr. Britling Sees It Through.* New York: Macmillan, 1917.
Whittemore, Reed. "Churchill as Mythmaker." *Language and Politics.* Edited by T. P. Brockway. Boston, Mass.: D. C. Heath, 1965. Pp. 56–68.
Wilson, Harris. *Arnold Bennett and H. G. Wells.* Urbana: University of Illinois Press, 1960.
Winston, Stephen. *Days with Bernard Shaw.* New York: Vanguard, 1949.

Index

A-bomb. See Nuclear weapons
Admiralty, 64–65, 77, 85, 87, 95, 97–98, 101, 106, 124, 130
Africa, 42, 46–47, 66, 93
African-American. See Negro
Air power, 27, 29, 65
Allies, 26–27, 47–48, 53, 90–91, 124, 138, 153, 156
America, 23, 47, 49, 51, 53–55, 57–58, 68, 83, 110–41, 155, 160–61, 168 n. 16, 169 n. 20, 177 nn. 14 and 16, 178 nn. 18 and 20, 179 n. 37, 180 n. 51, 183 n. 34
Anglo-American, 22–23, 27, 57, 89, 111, 116–17, 123–42, 168 n. 15, 180 n. 51
Anglo-Saxon, 50, 113, 134, 136, 139–40
Anglo-Saxon Review, 17, 22, 136
Anne, Queen, 81, 95, 101, 107, 155
Antwerp, 64, 104
Arms and the Man (Shaw), 30
Army, 26–27, 30
Asia, 42, 47, 70, 116
Asquith, H. H., 17–18, 22, 64, 98, 156, 158
Asquith, Margot, 22, 62
Astor, Lady, 34–36
Austria, 81, 147–49, 157

Baldwin, Stanley, 80, 96, 161, 182 n. 21
Balfour, A. J., 41, 122, 134
Balkans, 91, 102, 138
Barbour, Violet, 74
Baruch, Bernard, 112, 116, 125
Battle of Britain, 110
Beaverbrook, Lord, 39, 93
Belgium, 64, 67, 82, 85, 91, 135, 147–48, 153
Beloff, Max, 136–38

Bennett, Arnold, 38–41, 170 nn. 32 and 37, 171 n. 39
Beveridge Report, 51
Birkenhead, Lord, 40, 65, 141
Black. See Negro
Blenheim, 61, 70, 79, 94, 107, 152
Blunt, W. S., 17, 46, 49
Boer War, 23, 77, 135
Boers, 46, 54–55, 112
Bolshevism. See Communism
Brave New World (Huxley), 41
Britain. See Great Britain
British Empire, 20, 28–29, 42, 46–47, 49, 109, 112, 126, 130–31, 138, 151
British Navy, 21
Brooke, Rupert, 18, 23
Burke, Edmund, 35, 56–57, 142, 155
Burma, 47, 85–86, 163

Caesar, Julius, 69, 158
Cairo, 89, 94
Canada, 112, 125, 128
Capitalist, 33, 121
Carnegie, Andrew, 133
Catskill, Rupert, 41–43
Chamberlain, Neville, 48, 80, 87, 90, 97–98, 158
Charles XII, 88, 92
China, 68, 74, 116, 130, 156–57
Christ, 56
Christian, 54, 70–71, 131, 135
Churchill, Jennie, 17, 22–23
Churchill, Lord Randolph, 23, 49, 51, 145–47, 162
Churchill, Randolph, 19
Civil War, American, 60–61, 63, 70, 72, 111, 179 n. 37
Clemenceau, Georges, 101, 162
Cold War, 68
Colonial Office, 46, 66
Commons, House of, 57, 66, 80, 83

189

Communist, 20, 27–29, 33–34, 36, 47–49, 53, 57–59, 65, 68, 120, 126, 130, 132, 138, 158, 177 n. 16
Congo, 66
Congress, 118
Conservative, 23, 29, 31, 42, 45–58, 77, 90, 99, 102, 110, 121, 130, 146–47, 169 n. 17, 175 n. 5
Constitution, 53, 120, 128
Cuba, 60, 111, 126–27
Czar, 47–48, 53, 55

Dardanelles, 27, 47, 64, 77–78, 80, 85–86, 95, 101–2, 104, 110, 148–49, 162
Darwin, Charles, 18, 41, 144
de Mendelssohn, Peter, 31, 137, 169 n. 24, 176 n. 19
Depression. See Great Depression
Disraeli, Benjamin, 39, 49, 155
Doyle, Arthur Conan, 23, 168 nn. 12 and 15
Dutch, 55, 73, 83–87, 90–91, 98–99

East Africa, 65
Eden, Anthony, 138
Edward VIII, 53
Egypt, 46, 55, 88, 126
Eliot, T. S., 18, 167 n. 2, 170 n. 31
Emancipation, 47, 55
England. See Great Britain
English-speaking peoples, 111, 123–42, 180 n. 47
Eugene, Prince, 86, 89, 92, 100, 105
Europe, 42, 47, 53, 57–58, 61, 67, 81, 88, 91–92, 102, 107, 114, 116–17, 121–22, 129, 134, 137, 139, 141, 151–52, 162, 178 n. 18
Exchequer, 77–78

Fascist, 45, 48
Feminist. See Suffraget
Fifteenth Amendment, 55, 177 n. 11
Flanders, 65
Foreign Office, 87, 128
France, 19, 39, 47, 57, 64, 68, 70, 80–82, 84–87, 90, 92, 98, 101, 104, 107, 109, 119, 128, 137, 148, 153, 155
Franco, Francisco, 54, 156
Frederick the Great, 102, 162
Free Trade, 49, 122, 124
Freud, Sigmund, 18, 165

Gallipoli. See Dardanelles
Galsworthy, John, 18, 23–27, 43, 135
Gandhi, 54, 73
Gardiner, A. G., 69, 93
General Strike, 40, 67, 80
Germany, 20, 26, 31, 37, 43, 46–48, 59, 65, 67–70, 73, 76, 79–80, 87–88, 91, 97–98, 100, 114–15, 117, 119, 121–22, 125, 130, 134–35, 147–49, 157–58, 161, 163–65, 168 nn. 15 and 16, 180 n. 47
Gettysburg, 47
Gibbon, Edward, 17, 180 n. 1
Gilbert, Martin, 19
Gladstone, W. E., 17, 155
God, 32, 143, 155, 182 n. 17
Golden Bowl, The (James), 23
Gosse, Edmund, 17–18
Grand Alliance, 81–82, 91, 100, 108, 142, 161, 163, 176 n. 19
Great Britain, 20–23, 29–30, 32–33, 35–37, 40, 43, 47–48, 54–55, 57–61, 66, 68, 73, 75, 78–80, 102, 108, 110–41, 147–48, 178 n. 18, 183 n. 34
Great Contemporaries (Churchill), 34, 36–37, 156, 163
Great Depression, The, 50, 52, 118, 120–21, 126
Great War, The. See World War I
Greece, 29–30, 53, 88–89, 104, 126, 157, 161
Grey, Sir Edward, 31, 73, 134
Gulliver's Travels (Swift), 28, 41

Haig, General, 105, 148
Harrow, 60, 63
H-bomb. See Nuclear weapons
History of the English-Speaking Peoples (Churchill), 57, 63, 127, 129, 154–55, 163, 165–66, 175 n.5
Hitler, Adolf, 20, 26, 37, 44, 48, 54, 58–60, 64, 69, 73, 75, 79–82, 85–86, 90–92, 95, 99, 106, 126, 129, 143, 151, 157–59, 161, 165
Hogarth, Tom, 39–40, 43
Huxley, Aldous, 41, 170 n. 38

Ian Hamilton's March (Churchill), 145
India, 20, 29, 46, 48, 51–52, 55, 60, 62, 72, 83, 116, 127, 130, 138, 145, 181 n. 5

Intelligentsia, 19–21, 44
Ireland, 30, 67–68, 125, 151
Irish, 30, 55, 83, 124, 146
Italy, 48, 53, 70, 81–83, 87, 153, 157–58, 165

Jackson, Stonewall, 63, 154

James, Henry, 18, 22–23
Japan, 60, 82–83, 126, 128
Jews, 83, 183 n. 33
Jungle, The (Sinclair), 23, 56, 118, 120
Justice (Galsworthy), 24

Kaiser. *See* Wilhelm II
Keynes, J. M., 61, 67
Kipling, Rudyard, 18, 23, 38
Kitchener, Lord, 26, 65, 145
Kremlin, 34, 36

Labour, 20, 49–51, 131, 162
Lawrence, T. E., 23, 27, 43, 64, 106, 168 n. 13
League of Nations, 20, 115
Lee, R. E., 47, 63, 154
Left wing, 19–21, 42–43. *See also* Communism, Socialism
Lenin, Nikolay or Vladimir, 32, 47–48, 54
Lewis, G. K., 64, 137
Liberals, 23, 25, 45, 48–51, 53–55, 58, 61, 99, 110, 121
Lincoln, Abraham, 154, 159, 165
Lloyd George, David, 23, 36, 39, 48–49, 62, 80, 98, 148–49, 156, 158, 168 n. 15
Lord Raingo (Bennett), 39–41, 43
Lord Randolph Churchill (Churchill), 145–46, 149–50, 164, 166
Lords, House of, 52–53, 55
Louis XIV, 80–82, 87, 90, 109, 153, 164

MacDonald, Ramsay, 80, 119, 156, 161, 182 n. 21
Machiavelli, Niccolo, 31, 48, 71, 142
Mahan, Captain, 133–34
Mahdi, The, 71, 145
Malakand Field Force, The (Churchill), 145
Marlborough (Churchill), 63, 79–109, 153–55, 161, 165–66, 176 n. 19,
182 n. 17
Marlborough, Duke of, 37, 66, 69, 77–110, 153–54, 158, 162–64, 175 nn. 3, 4, 12, and 13, 176 nn. 15 and 19, 183 n. 30
Marsh, Edward, 17
Marx, Karl, 18, 34, 36, 165
Meanwhile (Wells), 40–41, 43
Mediterranean Sea, 93, 138, 160, 175 n. 3
Meliorist. *See* Left wing
Men Like Gods (Wells), 18, 41–44
Middle East, 27, 64, 88, 159, 175 n. 3
Mr. Britling Sees It Through (Wells), 27
Monarchy, 31, 53, 120
Moscow, 36, 65, 89, 92, 132, 142, 161, 164
Munich, 81
Munitions, 78
Murray, Gilbert, 24, 44
Mussolini, Benito, 54, 64, 97, 103, 157–59

Napoleon, 21, 29, 37, 66, 68, 70, 80–81, 88, 92, 98, 102, 106, 110, 142, 152, 155, 158, 162, 182 n. 16
Navy, British. *See* Admiralty
Nazi, 48, 92, 101, 121
Negro, 47, 54–55, 113, 118, 177 n. 11, 179 n. 37
New Deal, 50, 52, 121
New York, 111–13
Nietzsche, Friedrich, 41, 74
1984 (Orwell), 21
Nobel Prize, 38
North Africa, 85–86, 163
Nuclear weapons, 58, 71–72, 109, 130–31, 139

Orwell, George, 19, 21, 28, 43, 167 n. 6

Palestine, 67, 126, 130
Parliament, 24, 33, 37, 52, 56–57, 80, 92, 94, 99
Pitt, William, 75, 154–55, 160
Poland, 82–83, 91, 116, 166
Potsdam, 102, 162, 166
Poverty (Rowntree), 69
Prohibition, 51, 115, 122
Protection. *See* Free Trade
Prussia. *See* Germany

Punch, 30, 94

River War, The, 63, 145, 166
Rome, 54, 121, 125
Roosevelt, Franklin, 48, 50, 65, 89, 105, 115–16, 120–22, 137–38, 158–62, 164–66
Roosevelt, Theodore, 17, 112, 120
Roving Commission, A, (Churchill), 78–79
Russia, 19, 25, 27–29, 33, 46–48, 68, 82, 88, 91–92, 101, 116–17, 120, 130, 132, 138, 148, 156–57, 161–64, 168 n. 16, 169 n. 20, 183 nn. 33 and 34
Russian Revolution, 19–20, 35

Sassoon, Siegfried, 18, 168 n. 13
Savrola (Churchill), 68, 71, 144–45, 148, 160, 164, 181 n. 4
Second World War (Churchill), 79–109, 132, 138, 142, 144, 150, 159–63, 165
Shakespeare, William, 33, 99, 163
Shaw, George Bernard, 17–18, 21, 23, 25, 28–38, 40, 43, 93, 135, 169 nn. 20 and 24
Socialism, 19–21, 25, 30, 32, 34, 42, 50–52, 130, 138, 177 n. 16
South Africa, 17, 29, 46, 54, 60, 83, 93, 179 n. 37
Soviet, 32, 34–35, 46, 73, 92, 101, 113, 121, 126, 128, 132, 134, 153, 179 n. 37
Spain, 48, 53, 60, 80–81, 83, 111, 135, 156
Spanish Civil War, 55, 72
Stalin, Josef, 34–36, 47–48, 74, 116, 132, 143, 161–63, 166, 181 n. 2
Strife (Galsworthy), 24
Sudan, 60, 93
Suffragets, 34, 51, 54
Supreme Court, American, 50, 53, 121

Tanks, 26–27, 29
Taylor, A. J. P., 137, 159, 181 n. 8, 183 n. 34
Tolstoy, Leo, 142, 144, 146, 148
Tory. *See* Conservative
Tory Democracy, 19, 37, 49, 147
Trotsky, Leon, 54, 143, 145
Turkey, 67–68, 73, 88, 91, 126, 157
Twain, Mark, 23, 93, 112

United States. *See* America
Utopia, 20–21, 40–43, 51

Victorian, 18–19, 46–47, 54–55, 58, 136, 150, 164

Washington, George, 158–59, 165
Waterloo, 70, 102
Wells, H. G., 18, 21–23, 25–30, 32, 34, 36, 40–44, 118,1 35, 163, 167 n. 6, 168 nn. 15 and 16, 169 n. 17, 170 nn. 37 and 38, 171 n. 39, 178 n. 21
Western civilization, 20, 42, 101
Westminster Gazette, 55, 110
Whig, 21, 99
Whittemore, Reed, 99, 163, 166
Wilde, Oscar, 33, 123
Wilhelm II, 32, 67, 81–82, 148–49, 154, 181 n. 10
William III, 82, 95, 97, 100, 106, 153
Wilson, Woodrow, 72, 115, 149, 178 n. 20, 180 n. 48
Wizard War, 86
World Crisis, The (Churchill), 29, 38, 77–109, 115–16, 128, 147–50, 163, 166, 168 n. 16
World War I, 19, 26, 29, 33, 35, 39, 46–47, 49, 51, 53–54, 61, 63–69, 72–73, 75–76, 78–109, 112, 122, 124–25, 129, 135–37, 144, 147, 152, 156, 162–65, 168 nn. 15 and 16, 169 n. 20, 181 n. 10
World War II, 20, 29, 36–38, 43–44, 47–51, 53, 57, 61–63, 65, 68, 70, 76–109, 111, 114, 116, 119, 121, 124, 136, 139, 156, 159–65, 169 n. 20

Yeats, W. B., 18, 23, 78

DATE DUE			
~~OCT 04 1994~~			
~~OCT 21 1994~~			
~~APR 3 1996~~			
			Printed in USA